The Importances of the Past

The Importances of the Past

A MEDITATION ON
THE AUTHORITY OF TRADITION

George Allan

STATE UNIVERSITY OF NEW YORK PRESS

ACKNOWLEDGEMENTS

The Marvell Press, London, England, has given permission to reprint the poem "Church Going" by Philip Larkin from his book *The Less Deceived* (1955).

Anne-Ruth Ediger Baehr has given permission to print her poem "The Bridge" from the not-yet-published *A Glimpse of Dragonflies.*

Published by
State University of New York Press, Albany

© 1986 State of University of New York

For information, address State University of New York
Press, State University Plaza, Albany, N.Y., 12246

Library of Congress Cataloging in Publication Data

Allan, George, 1935-
    The importances of the past.

    (SUNY series in philosophy)
    includes index.
    1. Tradition (Philosophy) 2. Authority.
3. Values. I. Title. II. Series.
B105.T7A44 1985   121'.3   85-2752
ISBN 0-88706-116-8
ISBN 0-88706-117-6 (pbk.)

For my daughter Susan
  whose loyalty to friends and to ideals
  is what this book describes

CONTENTS

PREFACE

According to the ancient legends, Menelaus needed to learn a truth from Proteus that the sea-god was not about to divulge. Every careful argument, each appeal to emotion, even an attempt to evoke the answer by force of arms, was to no avail. Proteus, wily shape-shifter that he was, had a thousand ploys for avoiding the advances of Menelaus. The outcome of the confrontations was therefore always the same. For all his energy and nobility of purpose, Menelaus was in the end no closer to the truth than in the beginning.

But Idothea, the daughter of Proteus, counseled Menelaus to seize hold of her father tightly while he slept, to take him thus by surprise and then to hang on determinedly and patiently no matter what strange shapes Proteus might assume in his efforts to shake loose. And so Proteus is surprised, and he responds by running through his repertoire of shapes, the many masks behind which he hides the truth that Menelaus demands. Proteus becomes a lion, then a dragon, a panther, a giant hog, and in growing desperation becomes first a running brook and next a sturdy oak. At last exhausted, the spectrum of his deceptions having all been tried in vain, Proteus assumes his real form and, his cunning now given way to candor, tells Menelaus the long-sought truth.[1]

Plato was after the same insight in his notion of the divided line.[2] Truth is protean, and if asked directly to reveal itself will offer instead some clever disguise, some beguiling or fearsome surface by means of which it can elude us. But if we grasp hold of the world firmly and allow it to run through its repertoire of possibilities, the truth of things will eventually emerge.

There are basically four shapes, says Plato, in which truth presents itself. One is imagination, another action, a third science, and a fourth dialectic. All four must be experienced by us, each for its own sake and for the totality to which it contributes. But none of these shapes by itself suffices to disclose truth in its totality. Each provides at best a glimpse, a limited perspective, but never the truth whole and complete. Yet if we are patient enough and steadfast enough in our determination, the four shapes will at last collectively yield up their secret.

These four kinds of knowing are usually interpreted as composing for Plato an epistemological ladder by which the pilgrim searching after truth might mount up from ignorance to understanding. Imagination, the lowest level of the ladder, is the furthest from truth, whereas dialectic at the top of the ascent brings one into the pure presence of that truth. The earlier stages are to be set aside as the subsequent ones are each in its turn obtained.

Robert S. Brumbaugh, a cherished colleague and once my graduate professor, taught me long ago the error of this familiar reading of the Platonic texts. Each rung of the ladder, each segment of the divided line, he argued, is a vantage point on truth. Each is in itself partial, but each is nonetheless accurate and in some distinctive way essential to the achievement of knowledge. Truth, which is not reducible to any one perspective on reality, is grasped only through the totality of those perspectives, by holding them all together all at once.

My topic in this book is social value. I would like to know how human beings within a community create and sustain the values they share in common. Collective and individual aims, assumptions, assessments, expectations are at the root of a culture, the source of those beliefs and practices that give it historical presence and power. What these values are for any given society, and how they compare with those of other societies, is an inexhaustible topic for investigation. But I am more interested in how these values emerge and endure, how they manage to gain the authority they exercise over the hearts, minds, and actions of a motley gathering of individuals.

In order to grasp the shifting truth of this vast topic, I must heed the admonitions of Plato and the insight of Menelaus. That is, I must begin my search for truth at the bottom of the ladder, working out of a perspective provided by the human effort to find meaning from within the flux of momentary experience. Memory, feeling, and imagination are the resources available to this primordially fundamental perspective. Its teaching is that tradition is the sole source and best custodian of social value.

The authority of tradition is therefore the object of my inquiry in this book. I will discuss its experiential base, the way by which common sense and need, everyday events and the confusions that surround them, are transformed into beliefs and practices rooted in the importances of the past. I will conclude by assessing the contemporary rejection of these traditional convictions and the cultural decline to which that rejection bears witness. My method is that of a search, a meditation in the Cartesian sense, a personal quest for conceptual and physical security that I think is also a paradigmatic one. The style of this book, its arguments, and its conclusions are all of a piece. They attempt to present the truth of social value when it is remembered imaginatively and shaped historically into traditions which compose the world's meaning and define its purposes.

So Proteus on this occasion is a lion, and within the confines of this book I must handle him in what I hope is an appropriate fashion. He will escape me even while I have him full in hand, however, for the lion is also a dragon and a panther. I will need, accordingly, to take up my task again and still once more. And even then there remain the torrential stream and the mighty oak with which to contend. Yet this god eventually will yield up his truth if I, and others joined in a similar pursuit, can but persist. So I am content to limit myself in this book to merely one of the protean forms in which the truth of social value is disclosed. If I can grasp it tight and true, showing what it means for truth to be a lion of this sort, that will be accomplishment enough. The challenge of the dragon should properly be postponed, after all, until the lion has first been tamed.

- - - - -

I have been helped in my thinking about the past and the importances it harbors by innumerable friends and colleagues. As those who persist to the end of Chapter Eight will discover, David Hall and I are probably as far apart as two speculative philosophers can be, and yet I have learned more from him than from anyone else. My deference to the excellence of his insights and convictions, which have been extensively poured out in red ink over the pages of a draft copy of my manuscript, is gladly acknowledged. I am also grateful to Paul Kuntz and Frederick Ferré, both of them old friends and mentors, whose comments on early drafts of the manuscript have been stimulating because at once kindly and critical. Gunlög Anderson, David Kranz, Lonna Malmsheimer, and Ralph Slotten, all non-philosopher colleagues at Dickinson College, have provided extensive and helpful commentary on my various drafts. Michael Kline, Cyril Dwiggins, and Peggy Garrett have lent their critical eye to specific chapters. They, and other campus friends such as Leon Fitts, Clarke Garrett, and Harry Booth, have responded uncomplainingly to my interminable requests for references or concepts I felt I needed as guides in my labyrinthine wanderings.

A special thank you is reserved for another of my colleagues, Marge Fitzpatrick, whose Irish temperament and French expertise provided a running critique of my chapters that was singularly perceptive and insistently humanistic.

My wife Betsy took time from her own busy hours to proofread the final draft of the manuscript and to add tangy comments about readability and relevance.

I am animated by distrust for all high guesses, and by
sympathy with the old prejudices and workaday opinions of
mankind: they are ill expressed, but they are well grounded.

George Santayana

One

The elucidation of immediate experience is the sole justification for any thought; and the starting point for thought is the analytic observation of components of this experience.

A. N. Whitehead, *Process and Reality*

i

A short drive from home and I am up into the surrounding mountain ridges. Hills march off to the horizon, mantled by trees of varied size and age, fading gradually into mist and cloud cover. The forest is newly cleared at one place in order to make room for a housing development which offers crossed white spires of new lumber against the darker background of pine, oak, and walnut. My drive into the mountains is along a road first laid down to accommodate the wagon wheels of settlers turning south at the gap to begin their long journey down the valley in search of unclaimed land. I stop by a country church, nestled snugly within a quiet grove of ancient oak. Stepping past cracked gravestones that have become obscured by new spring grass, I join for worship in an ancestral liturgy I've never understood but much of which I know by heart. As I leave the church, dusk has come, the new construction is shrouded, blurring with the trees. The road winding back home is a rescue from the impending darkness.

The spatial massiveness of the mountains dominates these experiences. Elongated ridges of green gently circumscribe my horizon as I leave home and then rise ever higher as I move toward them and into them. Soon

1

they fill my whole field of vision, define the lie of the land on which I stand, and shape fundamentally the extent and character of my plans for further movement. At a distance I may well misjudge the sheer volume of these hills, presuming them to be nearer and therefore smaller than they really are. As I approach them I am impressed by the way they seem to swell in size, to outgrow my expectations. Finally they loom above me, around me, escaping the neatly defined space to which they had been originally assigned, instead assigning me my proper insignificance in contrast to their dominating presence.

When I leave my car and attempt to walk from one ridge to the next, the scramble downward and the slow climb upward translate this domination into very practical terms. I am all too quickly breathing hard, strained muscles resisting my effort to press on briskly toward some destination. The fact of the mountain, the way its mere presence gives new meaning to such familiar distances as an hour's walk or a day's journey, makes it a presence to be reckoned with. In redefining the meaning of the world I take for granted, the mountain startles me by its silent but irresistible power.

As I near the churchyard I encounter a grove of stately oak. Any one of these trees is insignificant in comparison to the mountain, but it intrudes massively into my experience when I stand before its wide, roughly contoured trunk and its complex network of spreading branches. It signals its recalcitrance by the way it obscures my view of the valley and forces a detour in my proposed route of progress along the ridge. Yet at the same time it befriends me, offering a distinctive environment of shade and cool in protection from the noonday sun, presenting aesthetic opportunities for my enjoyment.

Were I to seek to climb it or to cut it down, to sketch it or to survey its branches for the songbirds it might harbor, I would discover that the oak not only resists me physically but also has the power to resist my understanding of it. What the oak is remains always partly hidden, a lode of possibilities to be mined only a bit at a time as I interact with it. This oak, like the mountain upon which it grows, is a reality which requires me to acknowledge and to respect it as an independent presence within my experience.

My physical size and my plans for action both have quite a bit to do with these experiences of spatial massiveness, of course. Were I a titan the mountains would be insignificant ripples on the surface of a gently curving planet. Were I a microbe the oak would be my universe. The upward slope of the hills provides no obstacle if I do not choose to hike, nor is the oak an environing coolness if I remain in the comfort of my air-conditioned car. There are contexts within which any specific entity would appear massive, and other contexts in which that massiveness evaporates. But tall trees and ancient mountain ridges are realities the presence of which have been a recurring aspect in my experiences. Given my human form and my all-too-human purposes, that gnarled oak and those dark hills have again and yet again presented themselves to me as awesome achievements capable of dominating the horizons of my experience for better or for ill.

Achievements, did I say? I know that an oak tree is an achievement because I know about acorns and can count the rings of a felled oak to determine the years of its growth into massiveness. And I have learned how the land in this area was lifted up to form rugged snowcapped mountains which have subsequently worn down into the ridges and valley with which I am familiar. Yet even setting this knowledge aside, the tree and the ridge still present themselves to me as achievements of an impressive sort. By their very massiveness they exhibit control over vast regions of space that would otherwise be free and undefined. The space they occupy is not available to me or to my purposes, or at least it is not available until I have taken account of the tree or the terrain in a way properly respectful of the extensive achievement each represents.

Suppose I know nothing of geologic evolution. I stand amid the uplifts and folds of this sedimentary rock and wonder. Have these mountains been here forever, timelessly occupying this portion of reality in just the way they now do? Such a continuity in character, preserving itself through time, lasting until it is everlasting, would be an achievement worthy indeed of my respect. Or did the mountains instantly appear just now, occupying this space for the first time in the moment of my present consciousness, transforming flat lands into hills and valleys in the twinkling of an eye? This would be a miracle, indeed, a spurt of inventiveness unsurpassably exquisite in its capacity to transform so much of the past without encountering resistance.

It is unlikely, however, that mountains and trees are forever or for an instant. The more likely judgment I would make about the duration of these mountains is one that works from the common everyday assumption that whatever presents itself as an actual independent reality will have achieved that reality through some process of development. This is more wondrous than either timeless presence or instantaneous presence. For to develop into something from something else, to grow into an oak from an acorn or to wear down into a hill ridge from a mountain peak, involves two capacities and not just one. It requires at one and the same time both extensive preservation and timely invention. For an entity to be successful, it must invent in each new phase of its development a reformed version of itself able to conserve under changed conditions the essentials of its past reality. What is eternal is exempt from the ravages of time, possessing a treasured status that neither moth nor rust can corrupt. Anything created an instant ago has no history and so by virtue of its very brevity is protected from change. But I know very little about such esoteric realities. My awe of them pales beside the respect I cannot help but have for the familiar things of my familiar world. For these have demonstrated their power to survive amid change and have done so without any prior guarantee of their success.

To be, in the sense of being what must be taken account of, means to be dominant in a region of the world. Whether for ever, for an instant, or for a finite duration, this domination is something achieved. It is an accomplishment. To be a 'there', organizing a volume of space within my perceptual world and continuing to do so throughout the span of my attention, a presence that may be uncaused or spontaneous or emergent but is in any case independent of me, is to be an impressive presence. My implicit recognition of that achievement, and my inchoate respect for it, is something adumbrated in each experience I have of the things that populate the world around me.

My respect is not limited to a specific entity, however, to the single lofty oak within a grove or to the massive mountain on which it grows. My respect extends beyond the achievements they each represent to embrace as well the supporting environment that permits, causes, sustains, or fails to overcome such presences. I am bemused that this particular tree should be an oak rather than a walnut or spruce, since all three are equally abundant in the area. And I am puzzled why this oak should be surrounded by other oaks, a ghetto of one species nested within a wider more variegated forest ecology. Why, indeed, does this oak exist at all? What has permitted its sprouting, caused its victory over competing vegetation, sustained its requirements for water and nutrients, protected it against the wind, disease, and erosion that have ravaged the nearby hillside?

Each spatially massive presence within my experience raises these same haunting questions. These dominating realities: what accounts for their presence? What lies behind the absence of their absence? I cannot explain why there is this rather than that character to the regions that surround me, nor why this character has endured and endures against the manifold possibilities that would entail its not being there at all. The mountain wears down, but reluctantly. The oak bends in the wind, is deformed by disease and malnutrition, yet it hunkers down and survives, its branches grasping toward the sky, its roots reaching downward toward water, and its trunk producing ever-new sheaths of the vitality served by both leaf and root. The things that are cling to their existence tenaciously. What is it about the world that this should be so?

ii
I continue my walk amid the mountains and soon come to a churchyard. The crumbling gravestones carry inscriptions that are barely legible. They bespeak the years that have passed by since those names and dates and pious mottos were first carved and tears shed because of the cruel realities they commemorate. The sounds of a congregation at worship in this mountain church indicate a liturgy in progress that is older than the people buried in the graveyard, a ritual seamed with beliefs and behaviors already ancient when that liturgy was first performed. Beyond the church a road winds through the gap in the mountain ridge and down into the valley. Its meander is responsive to no current purposes but rather echoes older trails formed when streams were forded rather than bridged, when outcroppings were bypassed instead of bulldozed. When the first trail was made through here no one can guess. Before the churchyard and its gravestones, before the liturgy, before the stand of oaks, people came and went along this route, their original comings lost in the forgotten past, a beginning old as the hills themselves.

There are times, it seems, when massiveness is temporal instead of spatial. The striking quality of the grave markers is their age and not their size or number. The chants and songs of the worshippers require an archeology of attitude and of language if I am to comprehend their significance. The woodland trail directs me not only to the place on the map where it ends but to the past time when human feet were first tentatively set down across an unknown terrain toward that distant goal.

In fact, my mountain is more impressive temporally than it is spatially. When eighteenth-century geologists first began to estimate with reasonable accuracy how old a given mountain range had to have been in order subsequently to have eroded into the hills now visible, they reluctantly but firmly decided to reject the erosion hypothesis. Their belief that the origin of the earth was comparatively recent conflicted with the much longer time-spans required for sufficient erosion to take place. For reasons of religion and habit they were not about to abandon their convictions regarding creation simply in order to make room for a new belief regarding geological processes. It took a radically new concept of time's duration and a new respect for forces which display their power slowly rather than dramatically before an evolutionary understanding of mountain-building and erosion could make sense within the accepted framework of general beliefs prevailing in society at that time.[1] Now, to the informed eye, the awesomeness of my mountain ridge is not its spatial enormity but the tremendous temporal spans required to transform seabed into mountains and mountains into the rubble of worn down hills.

The words chiseled on a gravestone wear down over the years in much the same way a mountain does. The process is regular and predictable. The antiquity of the stone markers can be awesome, but the span of time is minuscule compared to that of the mountains. Yet my awe before the gravestones is more poignant, more intense, than my reaction to the wearing away of upthrust rock. Why? Because my understanding of the process by which the letters wear down and my recognition of the length of time this has required do not explain why what has been eroding away got there in the first place. The striking thing about the gravestones is that they were selected from the rock of the mountain, shaped in a distinctive way, chiseled with words, and set in geometric patterns within a bounded rectangle of land. These grave markers are not merely old stones. They are old markers, and their existence as markers resulted from human purposes rather than from natural necessities.

A particular individual died long ago, a young woman in the prime of her life. Other particular individuals were led, as a result of their emotional response to that event and because of the blandishments of custom, to carve a name and dates into the hard rock as an indication to others of what had transpired. The act was designed to overcome the transitory qualities of the mortal flesh involved, to give veracity to fragile memories, to insure the temporal extensiveness that is a sure sign of a thing's significance.

The gravestone is a modest piece of rock, failing in its spatial proportions to command the respect desired for the event it commemorates. But by choosing granite, a rock that does not readily erode, by engraving that rock with marks that signal meanings ensconced in a language of enduring importance, and by locating both the rock and the remains of the person it celebrates in an area set aside from the changing impact of utilitarian needs, these ancestors of mine gave their rock a new kind of massiveness. Its survival through decades and centuries has transformed its modest proportions into immodest ones.

As I look down at this stone, puzzling over the partially obliterated inscription, my wonderment focuses not on the woman it names but on those who thought it important to do the naming and at no small expenditure of effort. The deceased, after all, was merely human. She was born one day, she grew to adulthood, married the husband whose name is also mentioned on her tomb, and bore the child who was the death of her. It happens a thousand times a day, the average tale of any average human being. So the awe I feel is not the sort of awe inspired by visiting the tomb of a king or president, a saint or poet laureate. The question that haunts this gravestone is who these people were that thought this woman worth remembering. I wonder what kind of society it was that encouraged this homage to routine human existence and equipped these rememberers with the instruments for translating their desire for significance into the temporal massiveness that has in fact given it significance.

It takes less than a day to dig a grave and carve a headstone. In running my fingers over the worn lettering, I evoke in imagination that day, that act of homage. All else is silence. I do not know whether the husband stayed in the community or moved on further down the valley, whether he remarried or remained a widower. Did the child survive, and if so what were its attitudes regarding the mother who died that it might live? The gravestone has nothing to say on the matter, although other stones might speak and I certainly have recourse to church and county records, possibly to diaries and any of innumerable other tracings of what followed after the woman's burial day.

The origin of the gravestone lies in wonderment, in an act seeking to be victorious over the ravages of time. Everything else is everyday occurrence, the life lived to that agony of death in childbirth, the slow stealthy weathering of the granite until sharp corners crumble, surfaces erode, markings blend imperceptibly into the background from which they were carved. Someday the inscriptions will be totally gone, the stone no longer its distinctive shape. The origin in an act of homage which gave temporal expanse to the gravestone will be lost. The granite, continuing now to endure merely as all stones do, will no longer have significance except as a portion of the surrounding mountain ridge.

The roadway running out through the mountain gap is linked more solidly to its origins than the woman's crumbling gravestone to her burial day. The trail first blazed by the first human adventurer must have been walked and rewalked by others, year in and year out, grass trampled down into a visible line of progress. Generations of travelers must have pounded the earth so hard that grass could no longer grow. The brush and trees would have been cut back to define a pathway, the path widened into a road and covered with pulverized rock, twists and turns smoothed out and inclines graded, asphalt laid down. From the first to the present, the activities that give significance to this ribbon of compacted earth had to have been deliberately repeated. The solitary wanderer identifies the route as important for his momentary purposes. Those who follow after him on another day reaffirm that decision, with characteristic modifications appropriate to their somewhat different aims. And so it goes, the temporal volume of the trail increasing as each new day brings some kind of reconfirmation regarding the usefulness of that route as the way to get from here to there or from there to here.

Thus the respect I have for this road is not simply that it is very old, that it was first traversed a long, long time ago. My respect comes also, and primarily, from recognizing that the original act has been repeated and repeated, endorsed by countless generations of travelers. If the trail is ten centuries old, then its presence in my experience is massive with the weightiness of a millenium of continued deference.

When a woman died, some grieving friends thought the sad event important enough to show it honor for a day, and their act presents itself to me across the centuries that separate us. When a solitary wanderer trod out his trail, a thousand years of followers confirmed his original judgment by their own independent decisions that the pathway made some sense. Each of them, one after the other, gave it significance for himself as well as for the original traveller, and so helped lift a particular deed into a general one. I find it awesome that so many people for such a very long time should have continued to think the same thing so unquestionably important.

Were the roadway to be abandoned it would survive for a time, and like the gravestone the duration of that survival could be traced by marking the devolution of the road into evidences of a former road and eventually into terrain of no significance except insofar as it is an aspect of the enduring mountains. It takes sustaining homage to keep a road in existence as a special reality not reducible to the natural meanings of the surrounding environment. But the constant repetition of the travelers' activities eventually engraves itself into the slow-changing rocky environment. The road becomes an inscription on the landscape. Like the inscription on the gravestone, it is a mark that has meaning for those who know the language. A pathway through the forest is a treatise in earth and rock for those trained to read the language of a people's conquest over nature. As with all inscriptions, it can endure independently of those who fashioned it if the medium on which it was written is sufficiently slow-changing.

My awe at the capacity of the rock or the terrain to sustain an inscription for centuries is akin to the awe I have for mountain ridges. I am impressed by the way these natural phenomena exhibit control over a spatial region of the universe, and then sustain that control through time, resisting alterations in the character of the space they command. There is an additional dimension to my awe when I direct my attention toward human activities such as carving letters in a stone or beating a path through the forest. I recognize that the originating events are unique. They are not instances of widespread activities capable of being expressed in general laws. So they are not spatially extensive nor temporally secure. Yet they have in fact endured, the one because it transformed its fleeting sorrow into a more enduring medium, the other because its momentary relevance was confirmed again and again across the years. What would have been expected to perish has survived. I need to learn what it is about the agencies of origination and their supporting environment that has led to such unexpected consequences.

The massiveness in temporal massiveness is the power to overcome, to remain in control of a spatial region for a long time despite all expectations to the contrary. I am in awe that there can be mountains or oak trees, that the present is not just a pile of randomly varied shapes and qualities. But I am even more in awe that there can be evidences of human activity that do not perish in the doing, that instead extend their control of a modest region from one present moment into another until the duration of repeated affirmation becomes impressive.

The church liturgy in which I briefly participated is even more transient than the gravemarker and the road, for it never inscribes itself into an enduring material medium. The phrases of the liturgy are repeated from worship service to worship service. If the rites are not performed they will be lost and their passing no longer even remarked. There will be the church buildings, to be sure, and the books with words and hymns. But these are signs pointing to the possibility for worship; they are not the liturgical activities themselves.

The road remains a road, for a while at least, even if no one is walking it. A ritual exists only in its performance. It requires repetition from person to person, week to week, generation to generation, and in each repetition it still remains but one step from oblivion. The ritual activities come after a time to be inscribed into the habits of the participants, but these habits are not automatic and they are not biologically inheritable. The material environment does not objectify the human purposes exhibited in ritual and so does not rescue them from transience. The rescue comes only by the decisions of individuals, constantly renewed, to reiterate the rite rather than not to do so.

My sense of awe is especially poignant in these cases. For in these instances human freedom, that creature of the momentary, has become the instrument for overcoming the momentary. The temporal massiveness of an ancient liturgical rite performed so as to be present to my own lived experience takes its monumental dimensions from the fact that countless people through the years have chosen to conform to its demands, and it has survived solely in virtue of those choices. Why, I wonder, were these people so iterative? I wish to find out why they made those same choices over and over instead of letting that particular activity disappear. Surely boredom or indifference or curiosity about some new possibility for action would have lured them eventually into other behaviors. I wonder why this liturgy has endured instead of some other one, instead of none at all. There must be something about the human environment such that it encourages and supports such behavior. There must be something about the world such that it permits that human environment.

Why, I ask myself, do these things go on and not just silence? Yet if I ever encounter the silence, if I stumble across the remnants of a dead civilization and discover that there were ritual practices its people once performed, practices now vanished without a trace, my question about the silence is inverted. Why, I then ask, aren't these rites still going on? Why have they instead lapsed into silence?

iii

Again I am faced with incessant 'whys'. There is something that impresses me about any reality having the power to determine the character of some extensive region of the universe. The immensity of spatial domination leads to an awareness of the complementing immensity of temporal domination. Bulk and antiquity are interconnected evidences of a special kind of accomplishment, and it is one to which I find myself deferring despite myself. There is an aura of importance that clings to the massive accomplishments of nature, to old tall trees and lofty mountain ranges. A similar aura surrounds cultural antiquities. Indeed the mystery of human domination is more profound than that of nature, for it includes the survival of an order dependent primarily upon the fragile, volatile character of freedom rather than upon the far more resistive force of material continuities.

These dominatings in space and time are the most salient feature of my experience. They pervade my consciousness, all the way out to the very boundaries of its sensible horizon. The world as I encounter it, the content of my everyday experience, has a character that predates me and my purposes. There are orders of things so entrenched that they exclude whole ranges of other possible orders. The world around me is this rather than that, and the 'this' of it sets limits for me whether I want it to or not, opens up possibilities for me whether I recognize them or not.

The sheer givenness of things is no mere collection of facts, a heap of sensations all equal in their significance. My direct experience of things is of them as differentiated. Some are new, their hold on time's duration problematic, a threat or a promise but in either case something unsure as to its future. Some of the things differentiated in experience are old, taken for granted because they have been around time out of mind. They may perish tomorrow or be discovered to be in slow decline, but in either case their having been gives them a settled presence that is different from the tentativeness of new creation, just as the tender green of a new leaf bud is different from the deeper green of late summer's foliage.

This world in which some things are old and others new, some things predominant and others marginal, is a world haunted by the absence of what if present would provide an accounting of them all. I do not simply experience this differentiatedness. I am led willy-nilly to believe in a circumambience that permits such differences, that allows some characteristics to pervade vast expanses of space while resisting the spread of other characteristics, that fosters the endurance through time of some qualities rather than others.

My world is rooted in realities that are its reasons, that are the reasons for why some aspects of the world are more important than others are. For me to survive in this world, to understand it, to anticipate its transformations and utilize them to my benefit, it is crucial that these hidden reasons be revealed.

Two

HOLY GROUND

The present contains all that there is. It is holy ground; for it is the past, and it is the future.

A. N. Whitehead, *The Aims of Education*

i

After the mountain journey, I return to my study, and settle back with a philosophy book and a glass of sherry by my side. I must insist upon a far more rigorous approach than I have so far been providing to this question of what comprises the shape and contours of my experience. As a child of my civilization, I should seek guidance from those great minds who have defined for the West the scope and limits of human experience.

This means Plato and Aristotle, to be sure, but above all it means René Descartes. His seventeenth-century reflections on knowledge and the proper method for acquiring it have defined the issues, and the possible solutions to those issues, that we who are his successors have since struggled to resolve. So if philosophic precision and systematic rigor are needed in order to answer my questions about the reasons for the character of the experienced world, Descartes is a required companion.

I settle back in my chair and page through the volumes penned by Descartes. I turn also to the writings of those who have taken Descartes as their point of departure. All these mentors tell me that my world is in fact far less complex and varied than I have been taking it to be. I discover that I am inhabiting, or perhaps simply am, only a present conscious moment.

Whatever its extent, whatever the characteristics of its landscape, it is a bounded moment, an experience with a perimeter. The inside of that perimeter, the immediacy and vitality of my experiencing, is felt solely as a here and now reality. It excludes the differentiating textures I have been describing as so fundamental to my everyday experience.

In its most radical form, this rigorous Cartesian parsing of my experience threatens to collapse the here and now into a splotch of qualities existing at an instant. Yet even should my philosophizing uncover temporal thickness within immediacy, that region, I am told, remains throughout its domain a reality located here and occurring now. Only in moving beyond this perimeter of immediacy would I be able to experience something which is not here but over there, not happening right now but once or soon. If Descartes' analysis is correct, however, such a movement out of the present is not experientially possible. I can make an inference from my experience to there and then, but my experiencing is exclusively of the intimately present reality that comprises the content of momentary consciousness.

I take another sip of sherry and pull the table lamp nearer to my chair. Clearly it is important for me to look closely at what Descartes has to say about knowing the world. I need to understand why he proposes to lead me away from the commonsense world of distant mountains and ancient liturgies into his confining prison of immediate consciousness. Descartes' purposes, if they can be used to disclose his errors, might then lead me to a kind of understanding that is able to account for the character of things without losing what is important about them. Surely my awe before the oak tree, the respect and sense of mystery triggered by my musings at a gravesite, are not illusions that evaporate like the morning fog under the penetrating rays of philosophic rigor. I must come to terms with this man Descartes, and with those whose discipleship has defined modern European philosophy, if I am ever to find objective value in my world, to find its texture of meaning more than a fancy of consciousness.

René Descartes completed his Latin text of the *Meditations on First Philosophy* in 1640 and published it the next year, followed shortly by a version in French.[1] It describes an intellectual journey leading from a condition of unstable, confusing, and contradictory knowledge to the acquisition of systematic and certain truth. Descartes' itinerary is familiar, but the mood of the traveler has been often neglected. In sojourning with this man, I shall be attempting to discern the ways in which his emotions have shaped the nature of the journey and the character of its endpoint. Perhaps I shall then learn why Descartes sacrificed so much of experience in order to guarantee the securities he sought.

Descartes begins his first meditation by indicating that he has been deeply upset for a long time by the "multitude of errors" infesting both his everyday beliefs and the scientific principles underlying them. He resolves to "make a clean sweep" of all this crumbly intellectual rubble and to build the edifice of knowledge anew, this time on solid foundations and out of trustworthy materials. His strategy involves what might seem merely a genteel form of self-deception. Not a single one of his beliefs is to be exempted from being called into question, even those beliefs which he plainly thinks to be true beyond question.

But this is no casual gesture, a surrender for the moment of what Descartes knows in advance he will not really lose. Were I methodically to doubt everything, absolutely everything, it would surely be an act of desperation on my part, an attempt to solve a problem that has persisted despite all more reasonable, more measured, efforts to eradicate it. Thus Descartes is not simply exasperated. He is at wits' end and is prepared to go to extremes if necessary in order to regain the security of a world in which things can be trusted to be as they seem.

George Santayana, 300 years later, echoes this desperation as he prepares to undertake a similar enterprise:

The brute necessity of believing something so long as life lasts does not justify any belief in particular; nor does it assure me that not to live would not, for this very reason, be far safer and saner. To be dead and have no opinions would certainly not be to discover the truth; but if all opinions are necessarily false, it would at least be not to sin against intellectual honour. Let me then push scepticism as far as I logically can, and endeavour to clear my mind of illusion, even at the price of intellectual suicide.[2]

For Santayana, intellectual suicide is preferable to living under the illusion that I possess the truth when actually it is error in clever disguise. Honor is more valuable than life to the noble-minded soul, to any truly civilized human being. Bertrand Russell, writing at about the same time as Santayana, shares this sense of noble undertaking that surrounds the philosophic quest for certainty. But with Russell the desperate tones are muted, replaced by measured excitement, curiosity, and the possibilities for enlarged awareness.[3]

Russell exemplifies the heritage of Descartes grown confident, aware that the temporary abandonment of habit and custom is not really so terrible, that even if it doesn't always lead back to the familiar original beliefs the journey is far from dull and the new rationally tempered beliefs well worth the fuss. Santayana's courage in the face of a loss so complete that suicide would be the only proper response is truer to his mentor's mood. I need to capture afresh that first Cartesian terror, the recognition that a problem exists which must be cured by an extreme, decisive act, one that might well backfire, destroying its author instead of the enemy.

In the standard best-selling spy novel no one is above suspicion when the Intelligence Agency finds itself desperately attempting to uncover a 'mole' in its midst. Descartes, like Le Carré's George Smiley, searches relentlessly for the double-agents in his consciousness that are responsible for the error and uncertainty that plague him. Something unknown, but at least potentially identifiable, is the cause of certain ideas and attitudes which, by parading themselves as foundational truths when they are not, have become a source of falsehood and misdirected conviction. So nothing is to be sacrosanct any longer. From masterspy to janitor, from Descartes' belief in God to his data on weather patterns, all that supposedly rings true is to be treated as though it were a traitor to truth until proven otherwise.

None of my former ideas are beyond legitimate doubt. . . . So I must carefully withhold assent from them just as if they were plainly false, if I want to find any certainty. [64]

This strategy of systematically doubting absolutely all truths will expose the traitors lurking in the household of truth, but it does so at a terrible price. I am to doubt whatever I do not trust fully, whatever I do not know with absolute certainty. But more than that, I am to doubt even what I am convinced is beyond doubt. All beliefs, from the plainly false to the plainly true, are to be treated as though they were plainly false. I am to act as though I were in doubt where that in fact is not the case. The traditional components of trust are all abolished. Nothing, anymore, is above suspicion.

The collapse of a world with awesomely enduring mountains and ancient sacred rites traces directly to this bit of self-trickery. It is therefore crucial that I understand why Descartes thinks it so important to purge himself of erroneous beliefs and why he is willing to be dishonest with himself, to distrust his most intimate confidences, in order to do so. But I wonder if the end really does justify the means. I wonder what there is about human experience that thwarts so effectively the quest for certainty and truth, that requires a ruse in order to be circumvented.

Descartes is quite worried by the power of habit. He has been accustomed to trusting his everyday commonsense opinions and to relying on accepted principles of mathematical and scientific inquiry. An intelligent, well-educated gentleman would be ill-advised to do otherwise. But this can no longer continue. To alter the accustomed ways, to call all these trusted beliefs into question, will require considerable will power. Descartes worries that "sloth" might be an overwhelming temptation in such a situation, and might suffice despite his contrary resolve to "bring me back to ordinary life" and to the ordinary opinions that inform it.

Habitual beliefs are so familiar, so comforting, that their abandonment is unavoidably going to be a source of great unease. Likening such habits to the "imaginary freedom" dreamed of by a sleeping prisoner, Descartes notes that such a person would be reluctant to wake up. The prisoner in his sleep dreams of liberty, of walking in bright sunshine amid open fields and conversing with cherished acquaintances. But some kind of pre-dawn disturbance brings him to the edge of wakeful consciousness, threatening to return him to the harsh realities of his imprisonment. Faced with the imminent possibility of being thrown back into that undesired world, his reaction is to resist, to flee from the bleak intrusions full consciousness will bring. He "dreads" [vereor; peur] what might be in store for him. Better the comforts of his dream-world, better a false light guiding his way than the darkness he knows to be the only route away from falsehood. He has no stomach for being forced to grope blindly "amid the inextricable darkness of the problems I have raised just now" [65]. Better security than truth.

In order to break this tight hold of habit, Descartes needs to deploy a counterforce of equal intensity. He must convince himself that it is at least as dreadful for him to linger in the Elysian fields of error as to plunge determinedly into the hellish jaws of uncertainty. Dread must be matched by dread.

One way for Descartes to provide himself with a strong incentive for breaking the friendly habits of a lifetime would be to convince himself that the problems of error and misdirection in his experience were due to some weakness lurking in the first principles of philosophy. If one or more of his foundational beliefs were fundamentally flawed, the result would be widespread damage throughout the whole network of lesser truths, assumptions, and practices. It would be as though my spy novel's hero were to suspect that the traitorous security mole was someone located at the highest echelons of the intelligence apparatus. The organization can tolerate a few errors at the periphery as long as the core of things is trustworthy. But if falsehood has infested the core itself, then immediate decisive action is needed lest the familiar confidences soon become irreversibly undermined. It would be ironic were I or Descartes to tolerate marginal error for the sake of retaining basic familiar truths, only to discover that the errors were not marginal at all but flowed from a center necessary to the well-being of those basic truths. The danger posed by a traitor in high places is sufficient to override the strong temptation simply to let things go on as they are, leaving important friendships and traditional accommodations unquestioned.

But Descartes does not make this claim. He does not attempt to shock himself out of his complacency by arguing corruption in high places. There are no suspicions voiced that some as yet unidentified pillar of truth needs to be unmasked as a double agent. No single source of error is hypothesized and Descartes' energies then directed toward tracking it down. The errors which he says continually plague him, and that he insists plague me as well, are all relatively minor ones. But they are so plenteous that taken all together they add up to a problem far more serious than the presence of a shaky first principle.

Descartes' problem is everywhere, like a disease that has spread throughout one's system. So widely dispersed is the infection that it is unlikely some single cause can be identified as underlying it, some single culprit identified and removed. Any cure, to be effective, therefore, will require a very general approach. Precisely the absence of any single dramatic enemy to truth is what had lured Descartes and myself into a willing acceptance of the approximations to truth and the workable rules of thumb that are authorized by habit and common sense. There is no Grendel to turn our pleasant dreams into a nightmare, so we refuse to take seriously the demand that we face up to the hard truths of wakefulness.

Descartes attacks this unconcern that lurks within him by initiating a bold stratagem. He decides to set aside, for the moment only, as a temporary expedient, two of the instruments of analysis that he and any sensible person would normally take for granted. He pretends that he will no longer accept the distinction between important and trivial truths and, along with it, the related distinction between obvious and questionable truths. He had been drawing comfort from the belief that the important truths are assured even if lesser ones may be dubious or distorted. But if every claim to truth is taken as equal to every other one, then worries that some of them might not really be true make it legitimate and quite natural to call all claims equally into doubt. The comfortable belief that a little uncertainty and error around the edges are acceptable as long as the core of one's hoard of truth is secure collapses. If there is no core and no periphery, no difference between the trivial and the important, then every doubt is generalizable. To doubt any one thing is a sufficient reason for doubting all things.

It follows from this egalitarian assumption that all assertions of truth will be equally acceptable once they have met the basic threshold requirement of squaring with common sense. Even though the seemingly more significant truths can still be given their proper respect, lesser truths are also to be embraced with equal conviction. However important or however trivial it be, a truth is a truth, and this one quality outweighs whatever others it might possess. Thus confidence in all the truths that have met the minimal entrance requirements must be portioned out in equal dosages. If something is true, it is as true as the most certain truth. Distinctions in degree of value and degree of certainty are blurred and all but disappear.

Descartes takes only a simple and easy further step when he proposes to treat all these supposed truths as though they were equally false rather than continuing to treat them as equally true. He has merely reversed the standard judgment from one of unrelieved confidence to one of unrelieved skepticism. Henceforth all agents who are a part of the intelligence apparatus shall be treated as equally suspect. No one shall be above suspicion precisely because up until now everyone in the system had been assumed to be equally loyal but the system had nonetheless betrayed that loyalty.

It is as though there were something polluting the whole realm of Descartes' understanding, something rotten in the Denmark of his mind that cannot be traceable to any kingly deed or princely doubt but still quite plainly exists. Since we are all equally citizens, we must all be equally suspect. Not because of our importance, the significance of our status or our function, but simply because we are a part of the whole. It may seem that kings are special and peasants interchangeably insignificant, but when corruption is everywhere these differences fade into unimportance. To be in Denmark is to be an object of suspicion when Denmark itself is the problem.

Descartes' propensity to find a thousand reasons for convincing himself that his key beliefs are immune to falsehood or distortion is thus shattered by this clever stratagem. Yet by pretending that there are no key beliefs, that all beliefs are on an equal footing, Descartes unwittingly destroys his protections against the consequences of doubt. His beliefs stand exposed to the attacks of skepticism and cannot resist its ravages. The temporary expedient is in danger of becoming a permanent condition. Because some things are without solid foundation, and since there are no important differences among things, it must follow that no thing is assuredly well founded. Unrelenting equality breeds rampant uncertainty, and uncertainty once on the throne does not easily relinquish its scepter. No wonder that

Descartes' mood at the end of his first meditation is so fearful, his venture into methodic doubt become unsuspectedly so fraught with risk.

Once Descartes sets about the task of reconstructing his beliefs on the foundation of ideas so clear and distinct they cannot be doubted, he will reintroduce the dimension of certainty and as its prerequisite the dimension of importance as well. What he has set aside temporarily he will in fact be able eventually to reaffirm. Unrelieved equality in matters of truth is untenable. But Descartes, having blithely opted for equality as an antidote to unconcern, does not at first know what the consequences will involve. The dread that leads him to hesitate before embarking on his voyage into darkness is the worry that he may not be able to reinstate the key distinctions regarding value and certainty he so firmly had set aside. So eager is he to reinstate intellectual importance and security, so desperate, that when he finally does so it will be in a manner not justified by his method.

When Descartes discovers that he cannot doubt that the very act of doubting requires himself as doubter, that *cogito* requires *sum*, he is in possession of a belief that serves as the necessary condition for all of his other beliefs. The *cogito ergo sum* belief has special status in the new world of certainty that he is fashioning, for all else depends upon it. It is not merely one certain belief among many but rather the prerequisite for the certainty the others enjoy. Its importance is its privileged status as the sole disembarcation point from the seas of uncertainty onto the solid ground of certainty.

Descartes is aware of this, for he appeals to the logical priority of this belief in his own existence as part of the evidence to be offered on behalf of its certainty. Moreover his belief in God is of special importance since it is the necessary condition to almost all of the beliefs subsequently validated, beliefs concerning the material world and other minds. Only if the cause of such beliefs is a trustworthy being, one that acts with a good will in creating them and in making them available for his mind to know, can Descartes be certain he is not being deceived by some transcendent malevolence.

So methodological doubt works for Descartes because the certainty he has in his own existence is sufficiently distinctive to assign it the logical and metaphysical importance appropriate to a belief upon which all other beliefs depend. And at the same time his belief in God is not only a deduction from the belief in his own existence but also the source of assurance that his self has been rescued from the subterfuges of a misplaced self-confidence or some kind of cosmic deceptiveness. The instruments of certainty and importance are thus functioning from the very first in Descartes' quest for truth. They have never really been set aside.

Furthermore, as it turns out, certainty and importance are for Descartes not only the preconditions for knowledge but also themselves directly correlate. In the third meditation, Descartes' ontological argument for the existence of God can be read as involving the following line of reasoning: What is more real in its own right [*realitas formalis*] than something else is also more real as an object of knowledge [*realitas objectiva*] than is that other thing. What is more real in itself is more important. God, who is by definition perfect being, must therefore be the most important reality in the universe and so also the most real. Being most real, God must be knowable most certainly.

Thus I am led by Descartes from the idea of perfect being to certain knowledge of its existence as supremely real and supremely important, the eternal source of all created being, all goodness, all beauty, all truth. The more real something is, the more important it is, and the more certainly it can be known. God's perfection is the reason why He can be known indubitably. And similarly, in proper proportions, it can be said that truth, certainty, and virtue characterize the other lesser realities comprising the hierarchy of created entities.

But Descartes' starting point involves the denial of both these dimensions of distinctiveness, not merely their interdependence. Descartes has imported them into his argument despite his claims to the contrary. Thus if I were to take seriously his beginning point for systematic doubt, I would be forced to take his argument in a very different direction, one quite at odds with the one that Descartes intended. If ideas and their objects are both inherently neutral to value and certainty, then distinctions of importance or irrelevance, certainty or dubiousness, must be qualities imputed to reality by the human mind. I am justified in treating my ideas as though none of them has any more value than any other because value is a subjective activity and therefore mine to dispose of as I will. Certainty, which has to do with importance, must be a state of mind rather than a quality of the objective world. It appears in consciousness only when I permit it to, at those moments when my reasoning seems to be going well, when I am confident regarding my beliefs.

By following the logic of Descartes' starting point in this manner, I am led to a radically subjectivist conclusion, one he resists but cannot refute. The things of the world and the ideas by which I know them are equally valuable or valueless, equally uncertain or certain. Therefore they simply are, and in this republic of the actual all citizens are equal. Habit and

convenience introduce whatever further distinctions there might be, including distinctions of importance and of irrefutability. But such distinctions
are artificial, subjective additions. They are matters of appearance, not of
reality. What Descartes feared most has been realized. The abandonment
of a belief in the certainties and importances of common sense can well
mean their irrevocable loss, and with them the loss of the objective world
altogether. The history of Western thought since Descartes has proved
him correct, realizing with a vengeance the worst of his fears.

ii

I am getting ahead of myself, however. I need to allow Descartes to take
me at his own pace on the journey he has proposed. At the end of the first
meditation I am confronted with a challenge. From sleepy satisfactions I
am invited to plunge with him into the dread dark of methodological
doubt. I am lured into this adventure by the assurance that there is nothing to lose and everything to gain. All beliefs are equal; each is as readily
doubtable, on a temporary basis at least, as any other. I step out into this
dreadful unknown. As the second meditation begins, so does the doubting.
All things are questioned, even the reality of this dread journey into doubt.
But I cannot doubt the doubting. *Cogito* and therefore, with non-inferential
certainty, *sum*.

And so Descartes has no difficulty establishing the certainty of his own
immediate conscious activity. By his third meditation he is prepared to
describe it as varied, indeed variegated:

I am a conscious being [*res cogitans*]; that is, a being that doubts, asserts,
denies, understands a few things, is ignorant of many, is willing or unwilling;
and that has also imagination and sense. [76]

I note, however, that everything comprising this being is through and
through an activity going on in the present moment. The *res* is completely
cogitans.[4] There is not a thing that thinks, a reality somehow distinguished
from and maybe even capable of existing apart from the process of thinking.
The thinking, the dynamic, the vitality, is completely and exhaustively
what this thing is. Each different instance of consciousness is a form of
immediate activity expressed in Latin by the '*—ans*' of present process.
Consciousness in any extended sense is only a sequence of such activity, a
conjuries of experiences, of thought-occurrences, *cogitationes*. Thinking
is its thinkings.

Descartes is immediately concerned to identify what it is about this
always active self that leads it into the errors it then refuses to acknowledge.

Very early in his third meditation he manages to classify the varieties of thinking into three broad genera. To be a conscious being is to be thinking and to think is to exhibit one of three kinds of activity.

First, there are "ideas" which are "as it were pictures of objects"[78]. Or, as Descartes should more accurately have said, an idea is *res imaginans*, a picturing but not a picture. Ideas are forms of the thinking process and not static images. Descartes' exemplary list of ideas is marvelously encompassing: "a man, a chimera, the sky, an angel, or God" [78]. But in every instance, to think ideationally is to perceive: to sense or imagine or remember or reflect. The various forms of perception differ with respect to the cause or origin of the picturings that go on, but they are the same insofar as they are all the immediate content of conscious activity.

Besides ideas there are "volitions" or acts of willing, and "emotions." This second mode of thinking is composed of reactions to these picturings, my desire for or revulsion at what I experience, and my inclination to act with respect to what I judge to be the case. "Judgments" are the third sort of thinking process comprising consciousness. They are the kind of experiencing that goes on when I am doubting something, asserting or denying it, understanding something or failing to do so, with reference either to what it is in itself or to how it is related to other realities.

To know the world around me, all three kinds of experiencing must come into play. In the present occasion of experiencing something, I have an idea; and I judge it to be the likeness of an external object; and I commit myself to the truth of that judgment. Error arises whenever my commitment to the accuracy of a judgment is not delayed until that judgment involves a clear and distinct understanding of the idea about which it is making a claim. For me to engage in the form of judgment called understanding, I must experience my idea in such a way that I am aware of every aspect comprising it and am aware of its differences from all other ideas. When this happens, I am experiencing one of my experiences in an especially transparent manner, such that nothing about the idea experienced remains hidden to the judgmental experience.[5]

Suppose that in understanding an idea I judge it in this way to be the likeness of an external object. Now, and only now, is it proper to think willfully, to take up an attitude of commitment toward my judgmental thinking. This means that fully-functioning conscious activity is simultaneously threefold. I am picturing; I am judging what I picture as representative of an external object; I am committing myself to the truth of this judgment. And all three activities are as one. Thinking about thinking about thinking: willing as trustworthy what I am judging as a true likeness with regard to what I am picturing.

Descartes would hasten to insist that the process is more complex in the telling than in the doing. For it would seem fairly simple to avoid error and embrace truth on this analysis. I should never commit myself to the truth of an idea until I understand it clearly and distinctly. Descartes' method for recreating the foundations of science and common sense is nothing more than this straightforward admonition. We should look before we leap: "Perception by the understanding should always come before the determination of the will."[98]

But why then is human existence so infested by error and the painful, tragic consequences of mistaken judgment? Because each of us has a "natural impulse" to leap now and look later. There is in our natures a "spontaneous tendency"[6] to accept the truthfulness of what our experiences seem to tell us.

The intellectual sloth and psychological anxiety that Descartes saw tempting him to prefer familiar beliefs to the methodological skepticism he was proposing turn out, on his analysis, to be rooted deep in human nature. The embrace of error is not the result of a moral flaw but is the expression of a natural propensity, an instinctual response to the deliverances of sense and imagination. No wonder it is so difficult to wake up. No wonder it is so terrible a deed to abandon my beliefs in what is certain and of value for the seemingly unnatural act of methodic doubt.

Descartes appeals to the "light of nature," to rational imagination, to save him from the spontaneous impulses of his own nature. Nature is in combat with nature for the right to determine truth. Descartes says that I should constrain my natural impulses, even though they are expressions of my most distinctive quality as a human being, the quality that places me on a par with God and the angels—my freedom.[7] I should side instead with the light of natural reason which I have to an extent that is pale and feeble when compared to that possessed by transcendent beings.

This is asking quite a bit of me. Descartes will need to argue his case with unusual persuasiveness. Why should I give my allegiance to the light of nature at the expense of my spontaneous nature? Why should I choose rational insight over freedom, exercising freedom to restrict freedom? The answer lies in paying closer attention to ideas, for the activity of perceiving, the process of having ideas, is the necessary condition for judging and willing. My capacity for making decisions regarding truth and falsehood is influenced by the character of the object of those decisions.

Ideas, although they are activities comprising present consciousness, have about them, says Descartes, a strange allurement. They beg me to take them as signs for something else, as representations or pictures of another non-present reality. Some ideas might be innate, inherent aspects of any consciousness. Other ideas might be produced by imagination, which is to say they might be self-generated characteristics of the activity that is myself as a thinking reality. Or they might have their source elsewhere, in a process of thinking that has passively received the characterization it is exhibiting. In each case, however, the activity that is currently going on is all there is of which I am aware, even though one of its qualities is the power to lure me into believing otherwise.

After worrying over the nature and implications of this power of ideas through extended portions of his fourth and fifth meditations, Descartes proposes in the last meditation that I learn to resist the lure to belief by distinguishing between two kinds of perceptions: those that are 'internal', that the active consciousness produces in a manner not dependent upon realities external to it, and those that are 'external', that are caused by the world beyond the mind. In order to be able to identify an external idea and not confuse it with an internal idea, however, a double inference is required.

Some of my ideas have two noteworthy and linked characteristics. They are "much more vivid and prominent" than are other ideas, and they come to consciousness "without any consent of mind" [112]. Whenever these qualities appear in experience my natural impulse is to make an implicit inference that runs as follows: it must be the case that these forceful ideas, because they are so forceful, have taken their origin in something external to me, something with the power to influence my conscious experience in a telling fashion. In equally natural fashion I then make a second inference, claiming that these vivid, independent ideas are likenesses of whatever has been their cause. An external idea is one that has been forcefully and vividly impressed upon me by a reality beyond my consciousness of which the idea is an image.

But cruel experience has led Descartes, as he says it will inexorably lead me as well, to realize that none of these natural, impulsive inferences is foolproof. Hallucinations can be very vivid. In a dream ideas seem to be independent of me but then turn out in fact to be products of my imagination. My sensation of a tower that appears round at a distance will come to be replaced up close by a sensation of that same tower as square, even though the two sensations supposedly both picture the same external reality.

Descartes' primary objective in the *Meditations* thus becomes the effort to devise an alternative to the impulsive inferences of common sense. The alternative must still be inferential, however, for there is no escape from immediate experience except by means of an argument. What is not directly given can only be constructed out of the available evidence. Unlike common sense, the alternative must be logically sound, an inferential structure sturdy enough to command belief even when contrary to habit and custom. The only antidote to the misdirections of nature is the step by step irrefutability of deductive proof.

In order to devise this kind of foolproof reasoning, Descartes requires three sorts of assistance. He needs to assume a principle, to affirm the existence of a special kind of entity, and to make a careful distinction regarding the kinds of ideas there are. By means of this trio of assistants he will be able to make the crucial inference that carries him from immediate experience to the objective everyday world of common sense. To secure access to this commonsense world, to avoid being stranded in the present immediacy of ideas directly thought, Descartes must abandon commonsense inferences. The natural way of thinking is to be set aside in order not to lose the natural world. Present conscious activity must be supplemented by a trinity of special beliefs so that it might yield the world of oak groves and churchly rituals.

Descartes' special principle is one familiar to him from his scholastic studies. The cause of an idea must be as real actually as that idea is real representationally. When the idea of a stone pops into my head, its cause must be something that is as real as an actual stone. This is a version of the principle *ex nihilo nihil fit*; you cannot get something for nothing nor from nothing. This principle can be combined with the premise that some things are more real than others, more able to exist over time and to control their spatial environment, to yield the conclusion that a cause of any reality must have more capacity to persist in time and space than does its effect.

Any finite being such as myself, says Descartes, possesses an idea that there is such a thing as a perfect being, a being in contrast to which its own being is deficient. The principle that causes are more real than their effects means that this idea of perfection entails the reality of a supremely perfect entity that is the cause of that idea. Such a perfect being must have among its attributes the quality of goodness and so would not deceive its creatures. And thus Descartes' judgments—when they involve clear and distinct understandings—can be taken by him as justifying his conviction regarding the truths which those judgments assert. Only a cruel deceiver, certainly not a good God, would endow human beings with the capacity to distinguish truth from falsehood but then corrupt that capacity into its contradictory.

Confident now in his rational, considered judgments, Descartes proceeds to note the presence in his consciousness of ideas that are modes

neither of imagination nor of sensation. These ideas of pure consciousness are marvelously clear and distinct, and they include ideas regarding
extension, number, and change. Again evoking his scholastic principle,
the presence in Descartes' mind of these ideas means that "corporeal objects"
must exist in the sense of extended substance possessing the power to
produce such ideas. There must exist something with sufficient actual
reality to be the cause of such clearly known representations. Furthermore,
given God's nondeceptiveness, the effect in these cases is always what it
seems clearly and distinctly to be: a replica of its cause. Were it otherwise
people would surely not have this propensity to liken the relation between
ideas and what causes them to the relation between pictures and what
they picture.

I do not intend to linger over Descartes' solution except to note how
contrived it seems, how dependent on principles that are devoid of
commonsensical self-evidence. I was told by him to cast commonsense
realities into doubt until by the help of his trio of intellectual convictions I
would eventually be reassured as to their reality. This is a bit like hiring a
supposedly reformed traitor and double-agent to undertake an assessment
of the intelligence apparatus in order to root out disguised disloyalty. It is
not clear why I should trust the instrument of purification any more than
I trust what is in need of purification.

Furthermore, Descartes' scholastic principle embodies a distinction between
the important and the trivial in its concept of degrees of reality. In the
beginning I was asked to set aside all such value structures, to approach
my beliefs, feelings, and ideas as though they were all equally significant
and therefore equally suspicious. In doing so I found myself in difficulty,
for whereas I am certain about the content of immediate consciousness I
am not at all certain about the inferences I make from that content to its
causes. I was asked to resolve this embarrassment by utilizing a principle
that assumes gradations of significance. Having ushered commonsense
importances out the front door, Descartes asks that I immediately sneak
them in the back.

So Descartes leads me into the *cul-de-sac* of immediate experience while
offering a piece of unjustified reasoning as my lifeline back to the world I
seek to know with certainty and live in meaningfully. Yet his legacy to the
Western intellectual tradition is not this faulty lifeline he attempts to offer.
Since Descartes, the efforts of us who are his heirs have been devoted to
devising new and better lifelines in place of the one Descartes proposed.
Some even argue that the trap of immediate experience is not such a bad
place to be in after all. Presupposed by all these varied efforts, however, is

the willingness to accept the trap itself as a given. Descartes' legacy is his invention of this trap in the first place, and his unintended success in convincing me and all those like me that it is unquestionably real. Because of the Cartesian legacy, I have become convinced that present experience is the totality of immediate experience and that therefore the problem of knowledge is essentially a problem of devising proper inferences.

In the course of acquiring Descartes' perspective on the world, I can all too easily forget his original motivation. He feared uncertainty and was willing to resort to any expedient necessary to root it out, to regain a confidence in his beliefs similar to the confidence his ancestors had seemingly had in theirs. With so much at stake, with his whole world of truth and meaning called into question, it seemed quite justified for him to jettison long-standing distinctions regarding value and importance, to treat all beliefs as equally in doubt. Bereft of those distinctions, Descartes was abandoned to the present moment of thinking. It is not surprising that as he finds his way out of this predicament he should merely take up again the distinctions he had supposedly cast aside. Their rejection was ill-advised, after all. If certainty requires the value distinctions made possible by feelings of importance, then obviously the quest for certainty cannot begin by excluding that as a criterion. Descartes' argument is not so much circular as self-correcting. He quietly reforms his premises in order to achieve his goal.

The aim of Descartes' voyage into the dark waters of methodical doubt is to reach the safe harbors of certainty. It would be foolish to begin by tearing down the center mast of the vessel, the conviction that some things are more significant, more real, more relevant to truth than other things, and that therefore all beliefs are in fact not equally suspect. It is ironic, therefore, that Descartes' legacy to modern European civilization, to myself and all like me who seek intellectual and political security, should be this assumption we all share that private immediate experience is the one true certainty and all else is a matter of invention or inductive probability. Descartes' concern to assure me that my most important beliefs are well grounded, despite the criticisms being raised against them by the social transformations of his age, stripped me of those beliefs and handed me over a hostage to subjectivity and the moment.

iii

George Santayana describes this immediacy into which I have been led as "solipsism of the present moment." My solitary and momentary consciousness, now aware of what is here directly as its content, is all there is that can be directly known and so secured against the possibilities of error. Thinking, here now going on.

The story of much of modern and contemporary Western philosophy is an account of the solutions that have been offered to this untenable position that Descartes has led me into but then been unable to extricate me from. In what follows I shall allude to a few of these philosophers and philosophic positions. My broad-brush approach may not satisfy those versed in the issues and technicalities of that debate. My only excuse is that the usual explications and critiques are already plenteously available for those who might wish to explore them in detail. My concern is more naive and more urgent: to feel anew the dread that drove Descartes to his stratagems, to probe and poke among the proposals for avoiding the loss of everyday realities, and to see if an answer can be found at last which rescues me from solipsistic immediacy and recovers the assurances and certainties of the pre-Cartesian world.

For many of the successors to Descartes there is simply no rational escape from this limited certainty. I might seem to have two plausible ways out of this entrapment in the now of consciousness, but both will prove illusory. One potential escape route is by means of my memories of the past and the other is through my awareness of external objects. But when I remember something I had previously experienced, I am merely having a new present experience. I do not re-experience the prior experience; I have a quite different experience which I claim is a replication, a copy, of the earlier one. So remembering the past is exactly like perceiving the external world. What is directly known is an idea in present consciousness, and to this is attached the claim that the idea was caused by something else, something lying outside of present consciousness. It makes little difference whether that thing is said to be at a distance in space or at a distance in time. In either case it is not present and so must be inferred.

A simple primer in logic suffices to make it very clear why the necessary inferences cannot be justified. Our ideas are always particular: this color, this shape, this tone, this emotion, this concept. Recall Descartes' list: a man, a chimera, the sky, an angel, God.[8] But any logical inference requires at least one universal or general premise. Socrates was mortal, Descartes was mortal, Harry Truman was mortal; these and every other person born before 1850 have proved to be mortal. On the basis of this information, what can I infer? To claim that Napoleon was mortal, or Elijah, or that anyone still living is mortal, I must have first the general premise that all persons are mortal. With its help the argument is simple. If x is a member of the set A and all members of set A have quality a, then x must have quality a as well, since possession of the quality is a necessary condition of x's membership in the set.

Without the general premise I can still make my inference but no longer with certainty. By recourse to statistics I am able to extrapolate from a sample to the population sampled. These people are mortal and they are a representative sample of the human race; therefore it is likely that all people are mortal, including this particular person. Insofar as I seek Cartesian certainty, however, this gets me nowhere. From solely the invincible particularity of direct experience there is no rational place to go.

Confronted by this impasse, Hume invites me to a game of backgammon and prescribes a healthy dose of common sense to cure the philosopher's disease. George Santayana seeks the support of animal faith, finding in biology the confidence logic will not provide. John Dewey and the American pragmatists generally attempt to shame me into action. The quest for certainty, they argue, is not only hopeless but wrongheaded. Life is uncertain: substitute Pascal for Descartes. Unless I am willing to take risks, I will never achieve much of importance, and probably will not even enjoy life. The venture into uncertainty is the only reasonable course of action in a world devoid of certainty.

These solutions are effective. They do their job well, but at the price of understanding. My familiar world is given back to me without any explication of its contours. I am surrounded by importances and certainties, but I cannot assess them so as to determine which are true and which only apparently true. Their truth has become a matter of opinion, which is to say they are merely subjective. But this is precisely the same desert island of egalitarian significance on which I was shipwrecked by Descartes. So the irrationalist solution is no solution at all. It is an acknowledgement of defeat. It admonishes me to take a positive attitude toward desert islands. Be content to be alive and to enjoy life; do not ask to understand it as well.

Another approach to avoiding entrapment in immediate experience is constructionist, and is more in the Cartesian spirit. Some intellectual tool is sought, by means of which I will be able to construct a bridge out from immediate experience, over the gulf separating me from everything else, into that world of time and space, objects and persons, that I stubbornly refuse to abandon no matter what the philosophers say are the limits to truth and certainty.

Immanuel Kant offers the most familiar of the constructionist solutions. He claims that consciousness already has the bridges for overcoming immediacy built into its very essence. There are biologically given structures in consciousness that function as runways out from the immediate, that give dimensional location to my ideas and order them into understandable unities and relationships. Phenomenologists in the twentieth century have elaborated Kant's claim by insisting on the intentional character of those structures. They are structures of will and emotion, not merely of judgment.

Hegel proposes a developmental variation on Kant. Neither human infants nor cultures begin with the categorical structures that are achieved by a fully matured consciousness. The bridges linking particular immediacy to wider-ranging generalities still must be constructed by human beings even though they are born with the capacity and the materials for doing so. Thus all experience begins with solipsism of the present moment, but this meager shard of certainty is resplendent with the potential for explicating a richer certainty, one which will lead ultimately to a complete understanding of the structures within which self and world, experience and the sources for experiences, are only abstractions. Marx gave this developmental interpretation a sharply societal reading. For him the process of unfolding adequacy has less to do with intellectual understanding and more with achieving security from the horsemen of the apocalypse.

A third constructionist approach insists on the conventional nature of all intellectual tools. Every category of understanding, every social structure of meaning, is a creation of the human mind. The activities of immediate consciousness can spin for themselves threads of connectedness which will eventually be strong enough to support the weight of truth. But the truths concocted at one time by one individual or society have no privileged standing with respect to alternative truths. Each is to be judged solely by the pragmatic criterion of whether or not it proves to be a trustworthy guide for achieving whatever happens to be the purposes of the persons or peoples who created it.

This approach is categorical and developmental at once. The creation of categories is an *a priori* capacity of the human mind and it is necessary that the capacity be exercised. But any specific system of categories that might be fashioned and endure is an historically emergent fact. It has no necessity and is therefore not predictable. Ernst Cassirer and William James are two important advocates of this relativistic version of constructionism. Its contemporary advocates range from Kuhn and Berger to Rorty and the deconstructionists.[9]

The Kantians and Hegelians both rested their case on necessity. The universal premise missing from the deliverances of immediate experience is to be supplied by principles of order and rules of transformation that are provided to experience by a reality that lies beyond experience. This *deus ex machina* needs to be self-referentially validating, however, or else its proof would require an argument from experience and so once more would founder on the absence of a universal premise.

The conventionalist alternative to this is similar to the statistical alternative proposed as a substitute for deductive certainty. The claim that constructional structures exist and are functional for an individual or a society is itself a construct, a work of the investigator's imagination out of the raw data of experience. From a sampling of individual behaviors and the claim that these are representative, a societal or global generalization is made. The resulting truth-claim is probabilistic. Self-referential consistency requires that it be acknowledged also as subject to the distorting biases of the investigator's preconstructed framework for understanding. Conventionalism leads eventually to mere subjectivism. My preferences guide the construction of the categories by means of which I experience the world. I am once more back on that desert island.

Both the irrationalists and the constructionists deserve my attention, but both have left my primary situation precisely as Descartes described it. I am the ontological prisoner of immediate consciousness. This becomes holy ground for me because it contains the only reality of which I am aware. As all roads lead to Rome, so all knowledge leads back to the present moment out of which it is concocted. Subjective immediacy encounters only a circumferencing membrane that delimits its horizon and indicates a beyond devoid of content or meaning. This isolation in the momentary, this transformation of the fleeting instant of experience into a sacred region before which all else is nothing, is what makes it so terrifying and what makes the various proposals for extrication so important to me and to all the heirs of Descartes. But each of the proposed solutions has its unsatisfactory aspects. The suspicion of *ad hoc* arrangements hovers in the air.

Let me pursue a somewhat different line of reasoning, then, in the hope that a solution to the Cartesian legacy is yet possible. Suppose for the moment that I follow Descartes' suggestion and assume that I am a solitary thinking thing, and that the ideas which comprise my reality, some of them at least, have an origin beyond themselves. Granting these assumptions for the moment, this means I am surrounded on all sides by realities other than myself, realities that by definition lie beyond my experience and therefore beyond my capacity to know them directly. But they are there nonetheless. My subjective immediacy, lived here and now, is separated from other immediacies by an impenetrable boundary wall that demarcates the transition from here to there, from now to then and next.

Supposing the existence of these mysterious realities, how might I ever justify making the inference Descartes made when he claimed that the non-immediate sources of what I know immediately are similar to what they cause? If I can say nothing whatsoever about the cause of an experience except that it caused the experience, how is this different from saying nothing at all? But if I can establish the fact that a cause is like its effect, then my conscious experience relates me to external realities through the symmetrical relationship of mirroring.[10] Descartes' confidence in the goodness of divine reality allowed him to affirm the resemblance of causes and effects when the experience of the latter was clear and vivid. I am going to attempt another, I hope less tenuous, line of argument on behalf of this potent relationship.

The first step in such an inference is to characterize the region immediately contiguous to present consciousness as in some way influential for it. This region of contiguity is the frontier of a strange land that stretches out temporally and spatially in all directions, away from me. It is a strange land because it is not part of my immediacy, not an aspect of my awareness. Its space is other than the space of here: it is there-space. Its temporality is other than now: it is once-time or eventual-time. In every relevant respect it is something other than what I know with intimate confidence, and yet it is something which I have claimed influences that knowledge. This region of contiguity is alien to me and yet intimately related.

My metaphor of the non-immediate as a land stretching out toward distant horizons is misleading because it implies continuities in terrain. The metaphor tempts me to assume that here and now is the same sort of reality as there and then, that immediacy is a transient overlay on more permanent continuities. It permits me to claim that 'here' and 'now' are relative terms, defining by reference to immediate consciousness what can be defined in more neutral ways by means of a geometry of space-time. But this is precisely to make surreptitiously the Cartesian assumption about similarity that I am attempting to validate.

All I am really justified in saying is that when I cross the boundary into the frontier regions of non-immediacy I enter *terra incognita*. In stepping over the border I must divest myself of the only space I know, here-space. I will be losing hold of the only time with which I am acquainted, now-time. The only environment of which I have any experience, the environment of immediate experience, will be absent. Descartes finds himself in the *Meditations* already using a phrase that John Locke later makes famous. This region that is non-immediate non-here non-now: it is—what can one say?—it is *je ne sais quoi*. I can infer from here-now-awareness to this other region on the basis of general principles such as the assumption of similarity, or I can construct some form of bridging instrument, whether it be biological, developmental, or conventional. But I cannot simply go there and turn its objectivity into subjective immediacy, its there into here, its passed or yet-to-pass into presence.

I have no choice but to limit my encounter with the non-immediate world along a thin edge of otherness. The contiguous regions, the marches of that land, are already alien to me. They are as unknown as its heartland. The solipsism of my present moment is indeed invincible. But insofar as I continue to cling to the assumption that I am a solitary subject having momentary ideas and that the source of many of my ideas lies outside of present consciousness, I shall know this much about that strange world beyond my horizons: there are transmission lines linking its unknown and my known realities.

There is transmission of character going on, and so there is at least the theoretical possibility of tracing that character to its source. By means of the connecting process between source and outcome I might be able to arrive at a picture of the long ago and the far away by means of its present evidences. Modern science, both natural and social, relies in a fundamental way on this pattern of inference. History and paleontology are obvious exemplars. All modern intellectual disciplines, indeed, work from this assumption in their efforts to reconstruct realities absent from their direct sense awareness.

The transmission thesis entails a denial of action at a distance. Influence is always from one entity to its contiguous neighbors, and then by a series of transitive relations to non-contiguous entities. But here my quest for a mirroring relationship between causes and their effects encounters a discouraging obstacle. Transmission creates an asymmetrical and irreflexive relation between its terms. Influence is in only one direction and requires sequences of ordinal continuity from event to event. The mirror of similarity is not able to define what the relationship is between the content of consciousness and the makeup of the world independent of consciousness. In saying that the two realities are linked by a transmissional structure with specific characteristics , I must surrender my notion of picturing for something more complex, more obscure.

Like a river's narrowing gorge, the influences flowing toward an event converge at the point of the event's occurrence and then, escaping the confines of the strait, fan out as the distance from that event increases. Thus from any given point I can construct a double cone of cause-effect connections. The lines of transmission by means of which information about distant realities is conveyed to my consciousness will coalesce as they near the present, and the influence of my present activities will spread out in increasingly divergent ways as they rush toward the future. The geometrical progressions involved mean that I can quickly lose track of the influences and influencings, but the web of connections and interconnections is as obviously there to be discovered by patient inquiry as are the names and dates needed to fill in a genealogical table.

What is true for my own experience can be applied by extrapolation to any occurrence in space and time. Each defines a causal matrix, a double-cone for which it is the intersection. By treating that central occurrence as what the Cartesian center of immediacy really is, the causes and consequences of its experience, or merely of its existence if it be incapable of experiencing, can be traced out. As these networks of influence are filled in, an interconnected world emerges, one stretching out in space to the further reaches of the astronomer's radio-telescope, focusing down into the spatial densities available to the biologist's electron microscope and the physicist's particle accelerator, reaching back in time from the historian's parchments and the archeologist's shards to the paleontologist's fossils and the geologist's sediments, and reaching forward to the predictive claims of the natural scientist and the statistical extrapolations of the social scientist.

Despite all of this ramified network of influences, however, only the immediate causal antecedents of subjective consciousness are present to it. Direct transmission occurs only between the immediately contiguous causal circumference and present consciousness. By means of my putative belief in transmission lines, I am able to build up a surprisingly detailed picture of the alien landscape that lies beyond the here and now. But the tool for doing all of this remains an act of inference, plagued by all the same old problems.

And so I am no better off with regard to certainty than those who do not accept the transmission thesis. I am aware of the marches of this other land, for they press upon the borders of my consciousness. But the rest is rumor, knowledge by description but not by acquaintance. Like Moses, I am not permitted to cross Jordan into this land with its milk and honey of enlarged experience. I remain in the desert isolation of a self-contained selfhood.

iv

Contemporary science has given a new twist to the transmission thesis by abandoning the assumption that the transmitters of influence are enduring realities. As a result, my isolation is once more complete despite having granted Descartes his assumption that objects external to experience exist and influence it.

The belief that any agency of influence must be an enduring substance was taken for granted by Galileo and Newton, a self-evidence taught them by Aristotle and his successors. They were convinced that the atoms comprising the material universe, and interacting in accord with laws of transmission which it was the task of science to identify, were agencies that pre-existed their acts of transmission. Any causal transaction required an agent with the power to effect the interchange and a recipient altered in some manner by the transaction.

The world, on this Galilean interpretation, is a vast amphitheatre filled with substances—atoms, photons, or whatever—all existing simultaneously. Each is undergoing constant alteration as it acts or is acted upon, but its relation to other enduring substances is limited to such transactions. Were it possible for these entities to become absolutely quiescent, they would comprise a vast pile of self-contained units, each unrelated to the others. Essentially, therefore, both those entities directly contiguous to my immediate experience and entities distant from it in time or in space are all equally real and equally independent.

Within this Galilean sort of universe my problem is how to get to know realities that are absent from my presence. Their existence is assumed. These realities are present to themselves at the same time I am present to myself, but it may be that neither of us knows that this is so nor knows what the character of our different present experiencings is. The strange land lying outside my immediate experience is there, much as I am here, despite the difficulties of communication. It is as real as I am real, even though not as well known to me, even though not known by me at all.

Einstein and Heisenberg have led contemporary scientists to abandon this notion of enduring, self-centered substances and to replace it with a theory of events. Matter is energy and energy is activity, eventfulness. An electron is a way to describe how electromagnetic energy is distributed within a force field. Sets of energetic occurrences replace atoms in motion as the fundamental realities in the universe. It is as though at last Descartes was taken seriously in his insistence that the self is essentially its activities, with the added proviso that material realities are just like selves. Bertrand Russell and Alfred North Whitehead have, in quite different ways, attempted to elaborate the philosophical commitments presupposed by this contemporary rejection of enduring substance. For both, the problem is how best to describe acts without actors, influences without influential agencies.

Russell[11] stays close to Descartes, relying on my old friend the similarity assumption, but now it is aspects of contiguous events, not things and ideas, that mirror one another. The consistent repetition of certain qualities in event after event, Russell argues, allows that set of events to be taken as comprising a 'causal line.' Causal lines, once postulated, permit an inquirer to weave a number of them together into the commonsense cloth of enduring objects. But these chairs and trees and persons are not concrete events. They are abstractions from sets of underlying events. Myself as enduring through time and moving through space is likewise an abstraction from a set of here-now immediacies.

David Hume had recognized this as the unavoidable consequence of Descartes' method, and with Russell official science and philosophical epistemology are at last brought together. Thinking for Descartes was a kind of activity but, since that activity is contained within the boundaries of the momentary, Russell argues that thinking substances cannot be said to endure although their characteristics might well recur again and again. But if on Russell's analysis an extended substance is a causal line that has been constructed from momentary events by the mind of an observer, then any enduring object has to be an idea characterizing a thinking process.

It is impossible, therefore, to avoid the conclusion that substances too are completely activities or aspects of activities. For Russell thinking and extendedness are, fundamentally, both characteristics of momentary happenings. The specious present of consciousness and the space-time events of nature are more or less instantaneous. From these fleeting realities my world and its permanences are constituted, by means of inferences that have been driven deep into my animal instincts and cultural habits.

Ah, yes: a familiar argument. Russell offers me irrationalism once more, this time dressed up by the use of mathematical set theory, as the way to extricate myself from solipsism of the present moment. Why the members of a particular set should include certain events rather than others is left unanswered. An enduring substance is a collection of similar events the similarity of which is a mystery. Furthermore, accounting for the likeness is a matter of indifference to Russell because it is not necessary for purposes of scientific prediction. The purpose of science is not to understand the world but to control it.

Whitehead[12] takes the further needed step of attempting to provide an account of why a particular occurrence exhibits its characteristics, and therefore why a causal line comes to be generated. Whitehead's concerns are metaphysical as well as scientific. His account of causal influence is thus part of an attempt to bring together into one interpretative generali-

zation the influences felt in human conscious experience and the influences that seem to be at work in the consistencies exemplified in the
events of nature.

Thus Whitehead's account is one in which the actual world is composed of a plethora of happenings, each one a complex transaction of
inheriting and integrating and influencing. A subjective immediacy, which
is the present moment in its brief dynamic flight of awareness, experiences the character of its interface with non-immediacy, then transforms
that inheritance into unities which are objective enough to influence what
happens to subsequent immediacies.

The details of Whitehead's speculations need not be rehearsed here except
to note that they are a more fertile soil than Russell provides for finding
my way out from the *cul-de-sac* of solipsism. An entity that feels the
direct influence of its antecedent world has the immediate past as a part of
its present and so is not encapsulated in an instantaneous now. But the
gain is a small one because those antecedent realities have no immediacy
at the point of their transaction with the present occasion. Where enduring substances and agencies are only abstractions from briefly existing
immediacies, the moment of transmission is all that there is.

In the world of Descartes and Newton, enduring agencies had to exist
in order for there to be transactions. As soon as I am able to prove or
otherwise willingly embrace the thesis that transactions are taking place
between my present consciousness and something outside consciousness, I
am able to infer the existence of some kind of non-momentary persistences.
There are agencies that endure at least long enough and with sufficient
power to cause in my present consciousness the qualities I cannot attribute to my own powers. Indeed, I too must persist as more than my present experience in order to be the agent of those qualities not externally
caused. There is thinking going on. Therefore a thinker exists through a
duration at least as great as that of the thinking.

On this classical view, the moment of experience is not absolute, for in
addition to it there are its agencies as well. When certain characteristics
of a given momentary experience recur, it is not unreasonable to assume
that a single agency is responsible for the recurrence, that it endures through
the period of time in which the moments of experience are reiterated. To
argue that for each moment of experience there is a new causal agent is to
defend a more complex and at the same time less plausible alternative
inference. When under a strobe light I see a red shape at each of a number of sequential moments, I might conclude that a series of ripe tomatoes,
each flickering into existence and then perishing, is the cause. But as

Kant demonstrates, it would be simpler and more rational to assume that it is merely one long-lived tomato. There is more permanence to the world than to my perceptions of it.

In the contemporary worldview reflected by the philosophies of Russell and Whitehead, however, a single agent will not do. Momentariness is fundamental; the only thing that endurance can be, therefore, is an abstraction. Consequently I cannot argue, on the basis of the claim that there is a causal transmission of influence from the non-immediate past, that this past is composed of enduring entities. The transmission processes themselves are irreducible realities.

For conscious immediacy there is the fact of influence but not the fact of another independent consciousness which is the agent of that influence. Whitehead's speculative metaphysics permits me to argue that the influence occurs because processes marked by subjective immediacy culminate in an objective content that carries traces of that influence. But the influence is an object for immediacy, a characteristic of the present to be taken account of by that present. It is, in being this, not a characteristic of the immediacy which fashioned it. One moment with its unique subjective immediacy has perished; it is another moment characterized by another immediacy that now emerges.

My conscious activity on some occasion constitutes an emergent moment of awareness. This activity of mine can be said to involve a transmission into its formative processes from a source that is external to it, that is in its past. But the moment which is now past has passed away. Only its influence lingers on as a factor for present consideration. My present conscious activity is a matter of immediacy. The immediacy responsible for the influence felt by me as an aspect of my present awareness, however, is no longer immediate. It is not an immediacy other than my immediacy, influencing it from a distance but nonetheless concurrent with it, two immediacies in causal relationship. No, indeed. That other immediacy is now as an immediacy nothing, although once it was everything. There is only my immediacy which is an occasion characterized in a way that has been responsive to the characteristics present to it because of the existence of an immediacy no longer existent.

When I abandon a belief in enduring substances and insist that the fundamental entities of the universe are events, I cannot avoid this kind of conclusion. No immediacy exists except present immediacy. No objective reality exists except as present to an immediacy which experiences it as part of the content of its here-and-now. Contemporary metaphysics gives ontological reinforcement to the epistemological solipsism I inherited from

Descartes. Subjective immediacy, including its thin circumference of causal contiguity, exhausts the demography of the actual universe.

V

Descartes had led me into solipsism of the present moment by recommending that every item in my conscious experience be denuded of its valuational patina and treated as though its reality were as suspect as the most trivial puff of self-indulgent fantasy. From such skepticism there proved to be no escape. Consciousness here and now was the extent of my knowable universe.

I then relented a bit and permitted Descartes to convince me nonetheless that some kind of transmission theory was justified. This seemed to promise a way out of solipsism and, even though the particular proposals for how the transmission works were less than satisfying, I embraced it. In doing so, I thought, I would be no worse off than modern science which depends for its explanations and predictions on a theory of causal influence.

By means of inferences from effects to their causes, I began the arduous task of pushing back the horizon of my collapsed universe to include, first of all, the contiguous agencies of these presumed transmissions. By extrapolation I progressed from these neighboring causes to their causes and to their causes' causes. My confidence in what I was claiming to know grew thinner, however, as I progressed away from present immediacy both temporally and spatially. But whenever I began to wonder how far I could go on expanding this balloon of understanding before it would explode, Kant would reassure me that no scientific data nor logical inference can ever decide one way or the other whether the horizon of true knowledge has an absolute boundary or whether it is as vast and as detailed as my extrapolations were powerful and clear.

Nonetheless my understanding began to collapse in upon itself, a house of cards too fragile to withstand the onslaught of the scientific enterprise that constructed it. For it became necessary to abandon the notion that substantive atoms and egos comprise the building blocks of reality and to replace them with electromagnetic events and psychic occurrences. Once again all that there is for me has been reduced to what is now occurring before me. The moments of immediacy that comprise each here-now constitute the whole of the existing universe. The contiguous past directly transmits its influence to this existing universe, and through it the remoter past, but no longer as an independently existing and co-present immediacy. The events of the past have perished so that their influence might emerge as factors in the activity which is the living present.

I am stranded once more in immediacy. The past is a factor in that immediacy and so is the future. But neither past nor future exists except as an ingredient in the present. There are no events with their own separate immediacy that exist apart from and influence this present immediacy. This is so precisely because such occasions would have to be present in order to be immediate and so would be features of my immediacy rather than influences upon it.

Whitehead succinctly formulates this unavoidable conclusion in what he calls the "ontological principle."[13] What happens does so either because of some characteristic of immediacy or because of a characteristic found in the actual world of that immediacy. Descartes offered me a world I could know only inferentially, but it was a vast domain extending indefinitely in time and space beyond the outer limits of present consciousness. If this beyond was not accessible to me directly at least it really existed as the objective correlate to my metaphysical and scientific inferences. I might not know its characteristics with sufficient clarity and distinctness. I might not know them at all, but even *terra incognita* is *terra firma*. Whitehead, in contrast, withdraws the objective correlate. In an eventful universe there is only the present in process, along with whatever of the past is directly available to that process for determination. The present is holy because it is heaven and earth combined, the sole locus for everything there is. What lies beyond is not only inferred but in large part invented.

Descartes closed his first meditation with an expression of terror. He dreaded the venture into darkness that he was about to undertake, preferring instead the familiar comforts of a well-lighted and commonsensical universe. He recognized its limitations, its illusions, its errors and tragedies. But it seemed much more preferable than the void into which he was about to leap by calling all those familiar truths into question. Dogmatic slumber was a powerful alternative to doubt. Nonetheless Descartes took courage and embarked in quest of certainty.

He was wise in dreading the venture, for, following his starmaps and utilizing his modes of transportation, I have sailed on and on and I have found no further shore. What is real turns out to be very meager, a desert island of immediacy. All else seems mere invention, a mirage.

In accord with Descartes' recommended procedure, I began in self-deception. I find now at the end another reason for self-deception. Then I sought to avoid error; now I seek to avoid a truth too devastating to face. My voyage into the dark has found no safe harbor of the sort Descartes hoped to reach. A journey without an end, doubt that finds no rest in certainty, is terrible indeed.

All of this is a long way from ancient hills and crumbling gravestones. The meditations of the philosophers seem to have opened out a ravine of difference separating systematic analysis from common sense. The philosophers give me a world of bare immediacy and yet I continue to walk along wooded pathways into distant hills and wonder at dusk about death and transcendent deities. I need to begin all over again, to take stock of what resources I might have in this universe of perishing occasions that could save me from the pure light of an eternal present. How is it possible to avoid the terrors of philosophy and to accept as obvious a world of actual distances and previous times, a world of real significance for me and transcending me?

Each of the various constructionalist theories I mentioned earlier attempt to constitute an external world from the manifold of experience by bringing a principle of order to bear on it that is powerful enough to transform immediacy. By means of this principle it was said that I will be able to recognize characteristics in my experience that are characteristic of other experiences or any experience.

Suppose such a principle is contained within immediacy, however, and not merely available to it. Suppose that what transcends the present moment is present in that moment as an aspect of its inherent quality. Then I would not need to rely on an inference from experience to what lies beyond it as its precondition. Instead I would be able to construct within my own individual experience a structure that is general to all reality or at least to all relevant human experience.

The dark night of solipsism can be overcome by the discovery of structures that authorize belief in the reality of an objective world by making me directly aware of that world. Such a salvaging operation would be quite literally soteriological. It would save me from the meaninglessness of a life lived under categories of self-deception. It would destroy the idolatry of treating mere immediacy as holy. It would lead me to the truly sacral meanings I have been seeking.

The constitution of an external world is dependent upon the constitution of an historical world replete with the norms and values that make possible civilized experience. If such experience is to be saved from the nihilism of the momentary into which Descartes' method leads, then the past must be shown to be present in the present in some significant fashion. In this way the terrors of history as well as those of philosophy can at last be overcome. The sound and fury of the daily struggle for survival and dignity can be rescued from the dreadful possibility that they might signify nought.

Three

SOLID GROUND

In every consideration of a single fact there is the suppressed presupposition of the environmental coordination requisite for its existence.
A. N. Whitehead, Modes of Thought

i

Descartes' method was supposed to rescue me from the uncertainties plaguing my quest for knowledge and from the risks threatening the success of my practical activities. Descartes gave me certainty and security, but his service fee was solipsism. This terrible isolation in the momentary present need not be endured, however. I come scampering back to the pre-Cartesian world, to experience innocent of the rules for inquiry proposed by the *Meditations*. My presence to this world must be examined.anew to see if it might provide the resources to which Descartes' method has blinded me.

I continue to share Descartes' concerns about truth and peace, about understanding my world and living the good life. But perhaps these are aspirations that can be fulfilled precisely by refusing to exclude the pre-judgments and assumptions that methodological doubt castigates. There is something artificial and stifling about reflections limited to what is experienced under the tutelege of scholastic philosophers while sitting in a study. I shall return to the mountains and oak, to winding trails and carefully tended churchyards. These experiences, I shall discover, harbor the feelings of derivation that are my Ariadne's thread for avoiding the Cartesian minotaur.

43

The content of my immediate experience is primarily emotional and the color of the emotion is derivational. What I am experiencing is experienced as having arisen elsewhere. It comes at me and must be taken account of. I feel the coming-toward, the welling-up, the confrontational impact. I may have no comprehension, no feeling or thought, regarding wherefrom this coming, nor why. But when I girdle an oak with my arms the sensations that flood consciousness are not mere flecks of color, shape, texture, and tensile strength. Sheer presence floods in, presence intruding its demands at the expense of my preferences and doing so in virtue of its established reality.

My arms hug this oak tree tightly, barely reaching a third of the way around its circumference, the bark printing its coarse patterns into my skin as I try vainly to squeeze the oak into a size I can in fact encompass. I am resisted and so know that I am in the presence of what is not myself, not my present awareness and its freedoms. This intruding presence is something I sense as stretching back indefinitely along a temporal route from which it now arises to meet me. Its stolid resistance implies continuance, points to a presence that will persist beyond this brief meeting into some indefinitely distant future. It may be true that my sense organs are the proximate transmitting agencies for these feelings, that they have been influenced by agencies external to them, that the character of this medium must be taken account of in order to characterize those agencies. But these are all matters of interpretation and are fraught with possibilities for error and confusion. The experience itself, the sensation of impinging otherness, is direct, unmediated, unavoidable.

The great American pragmatist Charles Sanders Peirce takes sudden encounters as paradigmatic of the direct experience of derivational reality. For example, "a man carrying a ladder suddenly pokes you violently with it in the back of the head."[1] I am thinking about something, enjoying the scenery, daydreaming. A sense of control, of being able to determine what is to be thought about or seen, has me full of myself, confident in the privileged position of my own conscious activities. Such moments are the ones Descartes had in mind when he insisted that all anyone can know with direct certainty is the thinkings of a solitary thinker. Suddenly I am struck in the back of my head by a rigid aluminum bar. This "strange intruder," as Peirce calls it, is the experience of something which has the power to interdict my musings, to obliterate them or push them aside, and to force me to take account of something I had not intended to. What was gloriously solitary and therefore susceptible to solipsistic tendencies has suddenly become dyadic.

This "double consciousness," an awareness of both myself and what is decidedly not myself, is vague with respect to details. When the ladder bashes against my skull I am not aware that it is a ladder. Indeed I have no notion at all of what might be the source of the intrusion. It is as though there were a thief in the night. I know he was in my house, but I have no idea what he looked like or when he came or even whether he stole anything. I can know *that* there was a thief and have absolutely no idea about any of the relevant questions that need answering: who, when, where, why. Developing hypotheses concerning the likely answers to these questions and then verifying them, so that the thief might be identified and caught, is an activity best left to the police detective with his technologies for data collection and inference. Or perhaps it is a task for the little grey cells of a mustachioed Belgian.

Make no mistake about it. I know an intrusion occurred and that it came into my world, my house or my consciousness, from elsewhere. The character of this intrusive presence, this pain, these rummaged shelves, could have been self-induced. But the power that is the intrusiveness itself comes at me from elsewhere. When I am broken in upon, when my mastery of the world is resisted by a counter-mastery, I am as directly aware of the resistance and its reality as I am of myself and the sudden need I have to reassert my control. Whatever else may be the case, this much is evident: I am not alone. As Peirce remarks, "A man cannot startle himself by humping up with an exclamation of *Boo!*"[2]

Whitehead's paradigm for derivational feeling is drawn from the opposite edge of the experiential spectrum:

An inhibition of familiar sensa is very apt to leave us a prey to vague terrors respecting a circumambient world of causal operations. In the dark there are vague presences, doubtfully feared; in the silence, the irresistible causal efficacy of nature presses itself upon us; in the vagueness of the low hum of insects in an August woodland, the inflow into ourselves of feelings from enveloping nature overwhelms us; in the dim consciousness of half-sleep, the presentations of sense fade away, and we are left with the vague feeling of influences from vague things around us.[3]

Insofar as I am alert, wide awake and bushy tailed, my relation to the world around me is open to Cartesian exuberance. I utilize the full complexity and subtlety of my sense organs and brain to focus in on the character of things. Inferences are being constantly made, ambiguities and vagueness overcome for the sake of clarity and precision, interpretive frameworks elaborated. I inhabit a perspective of which I am chief architect, and like my designer jeans it carries prominently its maker's label: 'ego.' The contribution of other minds to the fashioning of my design, the story of the origin and transport of the materials used, is readily neglected. I am as the gods, even though sober analysis may disclose my kingdom to be confined to the dimensions of here and now.

The day fades; I grow weary and the light grows feeble. I can no longer distinguish clearly one tree from the other, nor identify a specific sound with a definable source. The neglected aspects of experience begin to reassert themselves. "Vague things" populate the landscape in place of things with definite names and describable characteristics. With the vagueness comes a fuller realization that the content of my experience arises from beyond my enjoyment of it. I feel as though the *diminuendo* of a lively melody had just revealed an underlying *basso profundo* I had been neglecting. It was there all along, but the discrete vitality of the tune it supports had captured my interest. I had defined importance in terms of what was immediate and vivid rather than in terms of what was foundational. It is time now to reverse that judgment, to repudiate the allure of Descartes' pied piper methodology.

I am bothered by these vague presences in the August woodland or in the gloaming of false dawn, because they escape from me while at the same time influencing me. They intrude, but not in sudden fashion. There are no surprises. I should have plenty of time to take stock of the situation, to get a fix on the intruders, to retain control over this world of mine against which they press from elsewhere. Yet as soon as I attempt to identify them more precisely, to remove their vagueness, their circumambient hum, they fade away. My instruments for all their subtlety are far too coarse. Like Midas, my touch destroys these "vague presences" precisely because it must remove their vagueness in order to obtain understanding.

So I cannot understand, and therefore cannot control, what is nonetheless pushing its way into a realm of which I thought myself the absolute monarch. Once again, just as with Peirce's example, it is the persistent pressing in that establishes the otherness of this aspect to experience. Insofar as I characterize it, it becomes a part of the conscious realm over which I rule. By being only a that, however, an intruding power that never discloses itself and so is not characterized, I cannot tame it and hence must always confront it as a challenge from elsewhere. Its primitiveness, moreover, the feel of it as antedating and underlying the foreground of conscious awareness, establishes it as not merely an other but as a fundamental other.

Whether violent or subtle, a bump in the back or a moodiness at sunset, the experience is of unavoidable otherness. The content may not yet be analyzed, its origin or import may lie veiled in obscurity. But the presence of derivational otherness in experience, the presence of something having a content, origin, and import not confined to its presence, is felt as unmistakably real. Such feelings of derivation abound within the immediacy of experience. They have two distinguishable qualities. Even though they seem purely realities to acknowledge but never understand, thises but never whats, their very presence says two things about them. First, derivational feelings have directionality. Second, they have importance.

This otherness which is impinging upon my present consciousness is felt as coming from elsewhere, but the 'where' is first of all a 'when'. Since the intrusion is something that comes to presence, that emerges into the region of my immediacy, I experience it as having endured from some time previous to that presence, from a time when it was existing independently of me and apart from me, up until this moment in which it now arises as something no longer apart from me yet still independent. The source of that blow to my head is characterized by its pre-existence and its power of emergence, not by any specific point of origin or by the shape of a trajectory that brought it to my presence.

First I have the sense of meeting up with what has been there awaiting me. It explodes into consciousness as a power of which I have not been aware until this now when its reality is revealed. It was shuttered up until now from my awareness of it, but in this moment it has been revealed for what it was all along. My experience of its otherness is the experience of it as a reality that derives the very fact of its presence to me, of its resistance over against me, from something about it which was not present to me but nonetheless had the power to reveal itself as present. I experience the blow as deriving from a power that rises up out of the past into the reality of that blow.

Derivational feeling entails the past in the form of an experience of what has passed from not-here not-now to here-now. Only subsequently is this sense of temporal directionality given any specificity. The painful tactile sensations come eventually to be felt as concentrated in the specific bodily region of my head, and the power of the impact is translated into a trajectory of causal influence for which the intersection with my cranium is the concluding member.

Sometimes it is only when the intrusion is well past that it can be identified as having a clear and distinct location within some historical route of influences leading from the contemporary experience back first to its occurrence and then to its origins. My throbbing headache leads me back into the past until I have identified my skull as the point of contact between my body and something else, and have some sense of when that occurred as the sudden interruption of my Cartesian daydreaming.

Complicated assumptions are involved in this effort at specification. To distinguish one intrusion as later than another requires some kind of chronology, a system for giving serial order to feelings felt and remembered. To locate my skull rather than my foot as the point of impact entails a metric system able to organize a geometry of lines and planes in which locations can be uniquely specified. Derivational direction can be to the left or right of here, just as it can be prior to or after now. These various spatial and temporal orderings can then be correlated so that influences can be specified along causal lines that move away from both here and now, to locations long ago and far away, to future millenia and other galaxies. Particularly sophisticated is the construction of a relationship of simultaneity in which space-time locations are linked that have no derivational connectedness.

This systematization of distance and duration is so fundamental to human experience that Kant was convinced it is innate, prior both logically and experientially to our knowledge of mathematics or physics or history. But the systematic specificity is biologically and developmentally secondary, a clarification for pragmatic purposes of an encounter with otherness that is far more primordial.

My sense of the past is not just an experience of directionality, however, of something fading away from presence into obscurity. The receding character of efficacy gives my temporal horizons their geometry. But if that were all I knew of the past, were it merely for me spatial extension into a fourth dimension, I would have made little progress out of Descartes' trap. Events would continue to be self-contained, related to one another only by their location in the causal lines being geometrically extrapolated from immediate experience.

The layers of past influence would be like road signs along a highway. The more distant ones are obscured by the nearer ones. I can guess at them based on my dim sense of their far-off characteristics and my judgments regarding their likely similarity to what is immediately before me. But the signs have their own integrity and are essentially equivalent in all but content. Were I to drive along the road so that each sign in its turn was immediately beside me, each would be as vivid as the others. Each would be capable of being understood on its own terms, without significant reference to the other signs. A time machine, or an accurate historical reconstruction, would make past events all equal in precisely this sense.

Such a monochromatic experience is precisely what Cartesian doubt created. If derivational experience were only to be directional, I would remain stuck in Descartes' tar baby universe. I would have escaped solipsism of the present moment, but the causal chains I replace it with would be merely a series of solipsistic experiencings yoked together by a feeling of their seriality. The past as I experience it would be a string on which to thread experiential beads. But it would not be Ariadne's thread. Instead of leading me out of the maze of Cartesian scepticism, it would add on a temporal dimension as well.

Fortunately the structure of derivational feeling is in fact not so arid. My sense of what is present in experience is of its arising there because a prior power has effected that arising. I am vibrantly aware of this power as the reason why the upsurge of experiential content is characterized in the way that it is. My present experience of the past is the experience of a relevant background to the present which is ordered in such fashion as to account for the present that has superseded it.

The relevance of the experienced past is not defined merely in terms of distance, closest-to-presence being most relevant and irrelevance growing as the directional linkages recede toward the horizon. Herbert Butterfield, in *The Whig Interpretation of History*, lambasted historians who construe the historical time-line of British history in just this fashion.[4] What is most ancient, said the Whigs, is most in error, rife with superstition and irrational practice. The movement through time toward these present days is a progressive transformation of wrong into right, bad government into good, unreason into enlightenment.

Were my experience of the past only an experience of its directionality, I would be forced to a Whig interpretation of all temporality and not just British history. What is impinging would be relevant to present experience in virtue of its direct influence, its unobscured efficacy. The elder events in a causal sequence would be relevant only in virtue of their influence on successors, and the more indirect the influence the weaker. Hence the past would recede in influence as it receded in immediacy.

In a world where all events are formally equal, I can see my way to no other conclusion. I might wish to impute relevance to past events in a way that upsets the hierarchy defined by directional distance, but such an act would be a subjective overlay, an artificial construct similar to the hypotheses constructed in science. It might prove useful for some purpose but it could not convey descriptive truth.

But my experience of relevance is not simply a function of temporal location. I experience the past as a content organized for me in terms of the capacity of that content to account for the present. Relevance is explanatory power, and explanations are more than roadmaps for experience. They are also its interpreters and judges.

This relevance which the past has for the present is the second fundamental aspect of derivational feeling. Relevance means importance, and what is important is so independently of whether it is recent or ancient. In *Modes of Thought* Whitehead defines importance as "that aspect of feeling whereby a perspective is imposed upon the universe of things felt."[5] When I create a perspective on some given content, some array of things or qualities or events, what I am doing is organizing them in a systematic manner. This requires distinguishing them by type or by gradation within type. There are mountains and there are oaks, and among the oaks are some larger ones and some smaller ones, some awesome in their beauty and some repulsive, some of passing interest and some that require my unstinting consideration.

Involved here, of course, are judgments of relative importance. For me to group the trees, for example, as oaks and not-oaks is to select out their leaf structure or trunk texture as having a significance not accorded, for this task at least, their location on the mountainside or the degree of fungus infesting their underbark. And even in focusing on a single leaf, I am interested in the degree to which its bays are indented or its lobes pointed, but not in its color or smoothness nor even in whether it comes in rosettes or is stalked. It is the former and not the latter qualities that permit me to accomplish the needed sorting into oak and other.

Thus a number of items of matter-of-fact are singled out from the expanse of given content and grouped together. Something about them is utilized to effect this selection. That 'something' is made salient by its role as an instrument for grouping the items in a particular fashion, and the items are made salient by the spotlight thrown on them through their newfound membership in the group. My effort to identify the oak trees present in a forest fills experience with leafiness and pulls those leaves possessing deep bays and sharp points into special prominence.

Whenever particulars are fused with some larger generality, judgments of importance are at work and the result is a perspective on those particulars. "This is a grove of oak" or "this is lovely" or "this is a member of the set of all n-tuples" are all instances of perspective-making assertions. In statements I make about oaks, my mention of their jagged-leafed, furrowed-trunked appearance will single out those characteristics about them. The content of my experience, of anyone's who is guided by my comments, will be so construed as to give pride of place to certain leafy and barkish qualities and to the lineaments of difference within experience that are thereby implied. The relationships of importance that are defined in this manner are what a perspective is.

Other perspectives are always possible. A botanist might wish to identify oaks in terms of cellular structure and genetic makeup rather than in terms of visual cues. A lumberjack might be more interested in the size of trees than in their kinds. An artist attends to the play of color splotches in a region of forest, unconcerned as to whether the colors are cast by the leaves of an oak, by neighboring underbrush, or by the ground. Which is most important: taxonomic classification or expended labor or aesthetic enjoyment? It depends on my perspective. But there is no such thing as having no perspective on experience. If importance is the agency for perspective-making, then something or other is always of importance to me.

Thus derivational feelings give me direction within a past fraught with importances. My direct experience is of this dimensional depth and its variegated significance. The non-inferential world is perspectival and therefore rich in the qualities of which Descartes deprived me. My desert island stirs with the possibilities of life, of the buzzing blooming world philosophy should explain but never be allowed to explain away.

ii

Freedom is present wherever there are perspectives, for a perspective can be fashioned by the exercise of choice and in every experiential moment there are always numerous choices to be made. What becomes important for me in direct experience is a function of the perspective serving to organize that experience, and on many occasions I am its author. The grove of oaks stands out as significant among the flora of the hillside because I have selected deep-bayed, sharp-pointed leafiness as a key principle of organization. In my woodland walk these leafy qualities have become an instrument by which, for the moment at least, I manage to distinguish background from foreground within experience, the center from the periphery. Were my mood while walking less scientific and more artistic, the oaks would fade into the general background of relevance, equal in significance to the other sources of color and texture. The relationships among those hues and tonalities, rather than among their sources, would now take on importance.

When by means of my creative powers I have raised up a fully exemplified structure, a perspective ordering the complete content of immediate experience, including its derivational aspects, into hierarchies of importance, then I can be said to have made me a world. I use my freedom to make personal worlds for myself within which to live, within which to act and understand. The inverse is just as true, however. My experience of centrality and peripheralness, my awareness of aspects of importance texturing the content of direct experience, might identify for me the appropriate principles in terms of which that experience is organized. The salience of the oaks then calls my attention to the importance of their leaf structure, discloses it as the way by which they obviously differ from the trees around them. They organize my world for me, insisting that I approach their environment out of a perspective that affords primacy to oaken shapes and textures. Here I do not create a perspective nor choose one, but instead find myself encompassed by its independent objective reality.

To encounter importance first and its principles thereafter is to find myself confronted by a world of which I am not creator. Perspectives are not always matters of subjective preference, of the will shaping a docile experience to suit its purposes or merely its fancy. Sometimes the perspective is thrust upon me. I encounter it, threatened or delighted by what I have found, but very aware that I have found it and not fashioned it. In these moments, invention makes way for discovery.

The importances I discover in experience lead me to search for their cause. I explore the contours of a world I have not made, a perspective I have had thrust upon me. Yet my freedom remains actively engaged, either insofar as I choose to conform to the opportunities and limitations of the world into which I have been thrust or insofar as I choose instead to defy it, to alter, abandon, or abolish it. The mountainside presents itself as dominated by its mantle of oak, but I might nonetheless insist on a more subtle analysis for purposes of my ecological survey. Or I might simply bracket out the oaks and all flora as irrelevant to a perspective that defines importances in terms of geological rock formations and their mineral deposits.

My actual experience encompasses both relationships. I decide what is important on occasion; on occasion I find it thrust upon me. The role of creator sets me over against the world I have organized around me, whereas the role of recipient locates me within an organization of things transcending my personal choices and understanding. Both have their truth, it would seem. My perspective on perspectives must be bifocal. But it would be tragic were I to mistake as my own creations what were in fact accomplishments predating me, were I to be blinded by my own powers of worldmaking to the presence of a world of importances to which I owe that very power of mine. Descartes' method is just such a blinding. The fate of Oedipus or Lear is the penalty of overconfidence in regard to the source of the world's importances.

Whatever the origin of my worldview, the function of importance is to give it meaning. My world is a perspective on experience, an ordering of its content into regions grouped by the relative importance of certain shared aspects, those regions grouped into larger regions, and ultimately the subordinate groupings united in a total structure of relationships in which each has a definable relation to all the others. In this sense my world is a coherent perspective, a presentation of reality as meaningful. The relationships that give experience its coherence play the roles they do because of the principles of organization they entail, and those principles are either judgments of importance or presuppositions of importance.

These principles thus provide me with an account of the order that is experienced, an explanation of why it has the character it has rather than some other. The meaning of my experience, the sense things have within my world, is because these organizing principles are at work. What makes them important is that they explain things. What gives them explanatory power is that they are important. Order and importance, structure and value, are coimplicates.

In both the present as I directly experience it, and in the past as it is given for me in present experience, I encounter clusterings of the characteristics that comprise its content. These clusters or groupings are rooted in distinctions that imply gradations of value. Those characteristics that define a grouping, that distinguish it from everything else, are more important than characteristics which do not. Even more important are linking principles of every sort, those characteristics in experience that knit groupings together, that unite what has been distinguished. The relational structure of experience thereby revealed is in part directional, a matter of the serial orderings that comprise the geometry of space and time. But it is also unificatory, transforming bare content into distinguishable enduring entities, into the thises and thats of a coherent world.

This argument of mine, that feelings of derivation bring direction and importance into immediacy, is reminiscent of Kant's arguments for why *a priori* elements are present in experience. The structure of experience, says Kant, involves a space-time matrix and principles constitutive of the objects of everyday and scientific experience. But whereas for Kant these categories necessary for the experience of a world are given to consciousness *a priori*, my meditation on experience has led me to find relational principles in the very manifold of the sense experience that is in need of being constituted as a world. This means that despite the similarities, despite the agreement on the constitutive role of principles in the formation of experience, Kant and I hold sharply divergent views.

Once it is agreed that principles and structures of importance are key to the emergence of meaningful experience, the question becomes one of determining whether the past is constitutive of the present or vice versa. Do the organizing principles for the present arise from the past, as I have been arguing, or, as Kant would argue, do they appear in the present as instruments for constructing the past? Are human beings worldmakers, fabricating the raw materials of the present moment into a perspectival order complete with temporal and spatial dimensionality and with objects and events populating the occasions defined by that geometry? Or is present conscious experience, with its space-time horizons and its objective content, a creation of the past? Am I a product of the past or its author?

The answer is that I am both. The contemporaneous world that I experience is a straight-forward extrapolation from my knowledge of the past as it impinges upon me from its elsewheres and elsewhens. In this sense the world I inhabit is primarily a creature of its inheritances and I am a mirror that focuses them into a perspective. But that very past is itself a complicated inference from the derivational and non-derivational whisperings of immediate consciousness. In that sense I have played and play a crucial role in making the historically dimensioned world amid which I live.

If each of these conflicting positions taken by itself seems too one-sided, their simple reconciliation seems fatuous. I can rightly claim that the inchoate and as yet uninterpreted power of the past melds with the derivative power of its interpreted structurings to provide the data for my efforts to reflect and to reshape its received reality. Always the maker is already in part a product of the reality to be fashioned; always the raw material of creation is already partially cooked. But even though I may well be both creature and creator, I am not so in equal proportions. Kant's Copernican revolution was an act liberating the human spirit, a recognition of its creative power, its sovereign lordship over the shape of human experience. But it is also painfully obvious that Kant was very much an expression of bourgeois *hubris*, bent on glorifying the individual entrepreneurship of will. His belief in the victory of human consciousness over what it knows can be seen, ironically, as a brilliant exhibition of the workings of the pre-existent world that fashioned that consciousness. The revolutionary who decries the times is an expression of its ideals, not their inventor. I am thrilled by the call to liberty first issued by Descartes and then echoed by Kant. But if I am to recover a world in which I can live a meaningful life, I will need to reaffirm more humble understandings of nature and the efficacy of the conscious ego.

The present arises from the past. It is this present whether I like it or not. It imposes itself upon me, not needing except in marginal ways my permission before structuring my experience into a world I am aware of willy-nilly. The past is that region of power which accounts for the present arising from it. The character of the past is such as to explain why the present is characterized as it is. The past explains the present, makes sense of its content, gives it a context within a perspective that extends into the recesses of indirectly experienced predecessors and foreshadows the possibility of successors. This explanatory power of the past, which is at the same time the evidence of its creative power, is why the past is important to me and why my own creative powers are in comparison so meager. My interpretations of the past and present are subjective and open to disputation; the past shapes the present in ways that are widely acknowledged, unavoidable, objective.

Even after rejecting my role as in any fundamental way that of worldmaker, I would still be succumbing to Kant's revolutionary lures were I to continue believing that I am at least a value-maker, that the importance the past has is something that I ascribe to it on the basis of its usefulness. The convenient distinction between a fact and a value, the world and its importances, is a false and pernicious one. What makes a world makes its values too.

In recognizing that I am born into a perspective made by predecessors, I must thereby recognize that the question of what is important for me is overwhelmingly answered not by me but by the character of my inheritance. The power of the past is due to the importances it harbors. It is the source of meaning and efficacy because it is important, not vice versa. I occupy a world with its structures of relevance, its organizing centralities, its predominant characteristics. That world prefigures for me the valuational distinctions that make sense of experience. Not I alone, nor even I in league with my comrades, but rather the importances of the past create the present significance of my world, including its potential for new significance.

Descartes proposed that I strip the qualities of experience of their varied degrees of importance. The obvious truths, the sacrosanct procedures, the commonly agreed upon customs, the habitual actions, were all to be reduced to the same level. They were to be taken as merely descriptive content devoid of value. But this stripped them of their derivational character, for their durational complexity and significance were inextricably entwined with their existence as realities independent of my efforts to know them or interact with them. Descartes' method turned vector experience into scalar, substituted contiguity for efficacy, and dropped me suddenly and surprisingly into solipsism of the present moment.

Descartes then tried to avoid the terrors of this entrapment in the immediacy of consciousness by a search for world-constituting principles. The ones he found took their authority from his confidence in the reality of God and therefore the existence of a good Will that is the constituting power that sustains the objective universe. The beneficence of God replaced that past as the ground for the dimensionality and efficacy without which there can be no meaningful world.

The successors to Descartes have offered other candidates for worldmaker. Kant proposed that we dispense with the gods and credit ourselves with the requisite constitutive powers. Kant's disciples have shifted the location of these divine powers from the *a priori* structures of our consciousness to our cultural proclivities and finally to our arbitrary willfulness.[6] But throughout, it is a worldmaking will that rescues the present from its solipsism, and therefore the results of the rescue operation are artificial, concocted, essentially arbitrary.

As Nietzsche insisted, the logic of Western thought since Descartes has led increasingly toward the glorification of will. But the will that is said to constitute the world is on this view itself no more than an element of the immediacy with which it works. The godlike thinking agency that wills the content of present consciousness into a world, and that then affirms its handiwork as good, is no more permanent than the moment of its willing. All that this comes to then is the stark conclusion that my world is a fabrication of will, an invention out of the content of the present. I have the illusion of there being a vaster scope and significance, but all that is real is the willing-now-here that is the solitary Cartesian self.

My abandonment of the Cartesian method meant refusing the initial bracketing of uncritical and presupposed valuations regarding importance and relevance. The arbitrary exclusion from experience of this central element in experience is the reason for the eventual arbitrariness marking Descartes' approach to truth. By unbracketing these excluded dimensions of experience, I was able to discover the derivational structure in experience and so to identify the reality of the past as it is present to immediacy. My inquiry into this reality has led me to characterize it as organized into regions of meaning able to give significance to the present. These importances in the past are why the present is a meaningful world, a world

environed by traditions and possibilities whose scope stretches outward to
the limits of human comprehension and whose profundity is unfathomable.

iii

I have decided to pay a visit once more to the grove of oak trees on my
mountainside. I am standing right now under one of the tallest trees in
that grove, pressing my palms against its trunk and feeling the resistance
it offers, sensing the mottled imprint it is etching into my skin. I try to
girdle the furrowed trunk with my arms and feel kinesthetically the meager portion of a circle inscribed by the reach from one fingertip to the
other. How many more linked arms would be required to complete the
ring? I must be careful not to stumble over the roots. They offer a rough
and uneven surface for standing, and my ankle tendons are beginning to
hurt from the strain created by the constant upturn of my foot, as though
I were perpetually climbing a hill.

Now I gaze up into the crown of the oak and observe the complicated
pattern of the branches. I even jump up and grab onto low-lying limbs,
lifting myself up into the tree. Once I am within the pattern of the branch-
ings I realize how it makes for easy climbing, and so I work my way up
very high, near the crown. The gentle sway is a bit unnerving but worth
tolerating, for from this vantage point I can see the architecture of gradually
thinner and more supple branches, each forking off from relatively thicker
and more sturdy branches. I see how this creates a framework for maxi-
mizing the access of the leaves to sunlight while at the same time providing needed flexibility to withstand the onslaught of wind and weather.
The leaves themselves deserve closer inspection, for they continue the
forking framework pattern to an ever more minute degree.

The sheer massiveness and the complexity of this oak are unavoidably
experienced in this intimate encounter. The tree resists me, sustains me,
surrounds me, engages me, and on a scale that I find somewhat
overwhelming. In an encounter of this kind, I am not likely to question
either its reality or its power to shape its environment and thus, for the
moment at least, to shape me and my purposes as well. Compared to the
mountain or to the planet, my oak may be minuscule, but compared to me
it is mammoth and complicated.

Because these aspects of its reality predominate, it will require a more
subtle eye to notice how the shape of the oak is proportioned to its
environment. If I take the time to look closely, however, I can see how its
branches are smaller and less frequent on the side away from the after-
noon sun, how it bends outward at an angle to adjust for the slope of the

mountain and the typical slant of sunlight, how its canopy is fullest where it reaches above the other oaks surrounding it. My tree is adapted to its surroundings, accommodating the limitations they impose, taking advantage of the opportunities provided.

Under the tree a serene calm prevails. It and its neighbors in this stand of oak provide shelter from the wind or rain and shade from the sun. Various insects come and go, in contrast to the tree's stolidness. There is an absence of visible change in this creature of the forest. Its leaves rustle but then are still; it sways around an equilibrium; the transformations of sunlight and soil nutrient into new growth go on placidly beneath my notice. This all conspires to give the oak a feel of being long enduring, rising calmly above the quick changing tempos of the moment. The weight of precedence is overwhelming, of achievements repeated, endlessly sustained with only the slight modifications required in order to incorporate new achievements.

This oak has been around a long time, I'm convinced of that. I would not be very good at guessing how long ago it was a struggling sapling. I might not even know how best to find out. How do I set about counting its rings? What are the appropriate botany texts to consult? But I have no question that it is old, older than I am, older than anyone I know, outlasting my personal world and maybe outlasting that of my parents and grandparents too.

These feelings can readily be cast into a valid sequence of inferential reasoning. I have, for instance, the immediately observable fact of the tree's volume, its circumference and its height. A tape measure and a bit of triangulation could give me these dimensions in a fairly exact form if need be. Then I require some kind of covering law, some formula for calculating the growth rate of oaks. They are a slow growing tree, according to the reference books, although they can easily reach a height of 10 meters within a score of years and thicken at an average of 5 mm a year. This would give me a two-variable formula for computing the tree's age, but in addition I would probably require a series of codicils regarding the effect of climate, soil, and location upon typical growth rates. Limiting myself to girth only, however, if oaks around here grow at about 5 millimeters a year and this tree is about one meter in diameter, then (long division, please) the oak must be approximately 200 years old.

If the tree has been cut down, I can confirm these rough and ready estimations by counting its rings. In this case the factual data are precisely and simply ascertained. If I want to be absolutely sure I can even photograph the ring section and study its magnified image. The relevant covering law is a well-tested hypothesis claiming that biological processes going on in a tree during one season result in an expansion of its cambium and that this is distinguishable from similar expansions occurring in subsequent or prior years.

I might want to undertake other kinds of inferential reasoning, drawing from data regarding complexity, shape, environmental placement, and the like. Quite a number of different covering laws would also be involved. I would hope for agreement among these variously calculated answers regarding the oak's age, and I would continue my analysis in the absence of a convergence accurate to some appropriate degree. When I was at last done I would have knowledge about something not experienced: the moment when the acorn from which this oak developed first sprouted its tender shoots and took root in the awaiting humus. This knowledge would be based on things for which I have first-hand experience, observations regarding height and shape and location, plus some general statements about natural processes which I trust solely because they allow me to make inferences that experience has shown to be useful.

My inferential reasoning has put in place an artificial scaffolding of general statements and of particular facts known only indirectly through those inferences. This knowledge is quite different from the direct experience I had when I first walked up to the tree and tried throwing my arms around it. The inferential approach is a labor required by the demands of precision. It is a way to pinpoint the oak's birthdate with relevant accuracy.

As Aristotle would hasten to remind me, accuracy in these matters is desired because it is needed as an instrument for accomplishing some specific purpose, and so it need be only as accurate as is appropriate to that purpose. If I am employed by the Forest Service and intent on marking the oak for the next commercial harvest, its age need only be accurate within a decade and may not be relevant at all. If my commitments are to pure science and I seek the oldest tree in the forest in order to use it as a benchmark for determining the rate of ecological change in the region, then precision regarding the tree's age will need to be greater. The facts and the generalizations relevant to the task, as well as the instruments used to gather the information, will alter as the degree of required accuracy alters.

My direct experience of the oak's antiquity, in contrast, serves no purpose. It is simply part of the experienced character of things. It is low on accuracy. "That oak, it sure is old!" I exclaim. "Yes," my companion agrees, "it's been around for quite some time, I suspect." The fact of the antiquity, not its calibration, is a deliverance of immediacy, of the derivational qualities constantly exhibited by immediate experience. Only as the purposes that define my practical orientations come clamoring for precision will the sheer presence of its endurance become transformed from a vague something enjoyed into a specific fact to be understood and utilized.

Another kind of inferring can also draw my curiosity, leading me from an awareness of the oak's long duration to the realities that have made it possible. This oak of mine, now here within the grove and here as well for many a previous now, derives its sustained existence from an environing past sufficiently extensive, complex, interconnected, and persistent to provide for the emergence and continuance of what is now experienced. The oak in its previous stages of development, and the environment for the oak at each of those stages, had a powerful enough hold on regions of the world in continuity with this current here-now region so as to exclude other competing possibilities, possibilities that if existing would have destroyed or otherwise reshaped the order of things that is this oak as I now know it. The mountains must have been providing nurture over centuries to this forest for it to have been able to sustain such an extensive stand of mature oak, amid which my familiar oak integrally dwells.

How breathtaking to realize that the past has somehow conspired to make this oak exist in all its towering majesty! For vacuous space, no special derivational structures need be exemplified excepting temporal directionality. To make an emptiness, almost any past whatsoever will do insofar as it is marked by the absence of sustained order, by the failure of momentary achievement to translate itself into forms of regional control. In contrast, the efficacious environment accounting for this ancient oak is a tribute to the persistence of a comparatively narrow range of conditions. Perhaps that is why there is so much empty space in the universe and so few oak forests. Were I a stranger exploring the region dominated by these conditions, the contrast between this forest and what random variation and spontaneity might offer would be striking. The importance of this past is its power of endurance, and my oak along with its neighbors is proof of that importance.

Importances are regions of the past that order my vaguely felt sense of derivational content into perspectives that give sense to the present. The region I identify as the causal environment for my oak is a region of importance because of its power so to construe my experience that the present is filled with my awareness of this oak as having stood there from time immemorial as a witness to the fertility of this land. An importance concentrates the indefinite elsewhere, conflates its diffuse linkages, focuses them into a coherent order. In virtue of the functioning of this importance in experience, the past as an indefinite elsewhere is exhibited as comprising definite lines and planes of inheritance, matrices of antecedence that give temporal thickness and dynamic to the present, and therefore give it significant differentiations, relevancies, its own importances.

The greater the range of the inheritance lines that conspire to account for a present reality the more significant it must be. Where the whole wide world in all its specific configurations is necessary to comprise the sufficient condition for some new emergence, then I am in the presence of something with universal significance. What child is this that has the whole earth as its mother, the full-vaulted sky as its father? How noteworthy the ancient oak that requires two centuries of environmental nurture to become what it is.

Conversely, the greater the range of outcomes deriving from a single region of inheritance, the more important that source. And where a single region of importance might be identified as playing a necessary role in the emergence of each of the multifarious elements comprising the present world, then I am once again in the presence of something universally significant. And this all men call God. How noteworthy the mountainside that over two centuries has nurtured not only this magnificent stand of oak but the complex ecology of this flourishing forest.

The essence of a thing is that about it which is necessary to my identification of it as this thing and not another. But if some reality, X, is a sufficient condition for the existence of some other reality, Y, then Y is necessary to the definition of X. If there is no Y, then X cannot exist; were X to exist, then it would be necessary that Y exist as well. Suppose I were to imagine something, therefore, so deeply linked to important realities in the universe that it would be said that these importances, call them X, were sufficient for the existence of this something, Y. I would be imagining that the universe itself had made this reality, Y, necessary. For universe X, Y is of its essence. Given that past, with its structures, this present reality had to emerge. Therefore it is crucial to my full understanding of the past that I understand how and why it had the power to give rise to this present necessitated by it.

This is merely the logic of causal necessity when it is defined in terms of material implication. Were this a fully deterministic universe, where the whole of the past was always the sufficient cause of the present, then that particular present, given that particular past, would be necessary. In such a world the present would be part of the essence of the past. When the past was present, the future now become present was only a possibility, but it was a possibility that would have to be realized because its realization was grounded in the very essence of things. As William James puts it so elegantly, in a deterministic world there are no possibilities in excess of actualities.[7]

At first it might seem that such a LaPlacian universe is something I should be glad does not exist. Surely I would much prefer the breathing room afforded by an indeterminacy of causal connections and the freedom of present choice. But freedom means risk and uncertainty, confusion in the midst of a chaotic present and trepidation at the prospect of an unknown future. I do not like the world's uncertainties. I am still enough a child of Descartes to be unhappy with their presence, and so I am attracted to the deterministic model in my quest for a world I can understand and live in securely. I search diligently for strands of connection that are deterministic, specific aspects of the present that are necessary given a specific structure exhibited by some specific region of the past. If I must, I will settle for probabilities instead, connections that create certain tendencies, that constrain the range of possible outcomes even though they do so without forcing closure to a single possibility that can then be counted on to occur. Despite all my efforts, however, some things still seem arbitrary, spontaneous, flickering into the present without regard for the specific orderings of the regions from which they derive. Such things escape my control and my understanding, and so they terrify me more than they liberate me.

Consequently I am always on the lookout for the more essential among the host of realities that are given in experience. I am interested in finding out what there might be in my world that is so linked to the derivational powers defining that world that its absence would require widespread and fundamental transformations in the character and even the existence of those powers. I am particularly on the alert for those things that derive their reality from as full a range of powers as possible, maybe even from the totality of powers, and so would perish only if the universe itself were to be pulled apart. Such things are part of the essence of the universe. Where more and more of the importances of the past conspire to create and sustain a certain present, the importance of that present grows as well, its importance both in its own right and for the future which it will constrain.

The scientific laws of nature describe the structures of some of the importances of the past, ones basic enough to the present that they are called universal laws. I recognize that it is likely there are imperfections in my understanding and formulation of such laws, and so I will tolerate the existence of a history to the propositions of science with respect to nature's laws. How those laws were described in the time of the Ptolemies is different from how they were described in Tudor times or in the Bismarckian era. But nature's laws themselves, the network of natural importances, need to be unchanging across time. They surely must be as old as the universe if not, in some undefined sense, timeless. It would take a bold flight of speculative imagination to conceive of an evolution in these laws rather than merely in one's understanding of them, for a change in the laws would mean that a slow transformation of our universe was taking place, changing it into a quite different universe. I would prefer leaving to science fiction the exploration of such an unsettling possibility.

The battle still rages as to whether the seeming permanence of the most basic structures in the universe can be extended to include organic behavior, more specifically the behavior of the higher primates, and even possibly the culture-creating and sustaining behaviors that are the distinctive feature of *homo sapien sapiens*. At issue is the degree to which the importances of the past constrain the practice of those realities that are endowed with the power of choice. Most pointedly at issue is the degree to which such importances shape the way in which that power of choice is exercised in its fashioning of the artifacts of freedom. Can there be necessity beneath the apparent arbitrariness? I wonder how important the past is to the appearance and endurance of cultural achievement.

To answer these questions, I find myself once more beside that churchyard in the hills with its liturgy being performed by the congregation on a Sunday night. As the worshippers work their way through the service, I am struck by the way their actions flow smoothly along complex patterns, their words tracing a highly stylized cadence and content. The participants are rising, kneeling, moving about in a way that seems to involve no hesitation and no disharmony. Their words are occasionally spoken in unison, and actions suited to the words anticipate or echo them. I realize that this is a ritual with which I am myself familiar, so I pick up its cadences as one might join a dance, adjusting my individual rhythms to its structured tempo. I move by shades of adaptation from separated idiosyncratic behavior into the pattern shaping the behavior of the group.

Mental and emotional adjustments will be necessary as well. As I pick up the cadence of the liturgy I move from an attitude of bemused observation or alienated separation into an attitude of worship, of corporate involvement in a ritual that has a specific purpose. I praise, confess, absolve, reaffirm, commit. By words and deeds I enact a belief that locates my life within a context of meaningfulness. I establish or reestablish an orientation in the present in terms of a felt and perhaps even rationally articulated sense of the basic significances defining that context and authorizing its appropriateness.

The aspects of continuity present in this participatory experience are similar in kind to those present in my experience of the oak. There is complexity, subtle intricacy, a complicated pattern of realization. There is durational texture, the feel of the liturgy as practiced, as familiar to the point of not needing to be attended to in order to be performed. I am also immersed in the liturgy as though in a wide-spreading sea of harmonic resonance. My activities are not only a behavior common to the participants crowded into a mountain church some certain evening, but are shared also by others having no known connection to the people of that church or to that evening. A stranger might enter the sanctuary and nonetheless fall into step with the congregation without missing a beat or even exchanging a word of greeting with his fellow worshippers.

As with my oak tree experiences, this visit to the church could be interpreted as an inference from present experience by means of general laws to the conclusion that these behaviors must be expressions of a cultural custom and not something spontaneous, and that this custom is of long standing. The matters of fact in this instance, to be sure, are more idiosyncratic than those encountered in the presence of the tree. There is less repetition from subregion to subregion, less similarity in the comparison of this to other realities. But perhaps that is only to say that the covering laws are harder to detect.

The liturgy is a ritual behavior of which there are ample other instances, and I can probably manage to come up with a generalization about the cultural function of community rites that would allow me to infer that a ritual exists among these mountain folk and that it has certain characteristics in common with rituals practiced in urban settings elsewhere, in primitive cultures, in the ancient civilizations. I would be harder pressed to generalize concerning the specifics of the ritual, to find a formula that might allow me to predict what words to expect in the chant, what movements to anticipate in the actions of adoration or confession. Are these generalizations simply harder to find than the laws of inanimate nature? Are there in fact no laws at all governing cultural behaviors? To answer "yes" to the first question would seem to strip culture of its freedom, to put me on a par with the ants and bees. To answer "yes" to the second question, however, would seem to strip my cultural existence of its meaning, to make my actions into surds, spontaneities without importance because without explanation. Between the sociobiologists and the Sartreans, I must find a middle way.

Yet in whatever way I work this out, my results are a theory about cultural causation and human liberty. They are attempts at precision in the matter of the origin and development of consciousness, the rise of humanity, the appearance and spread of civilization. My direct experience of the cultural past is another and a prior matter. As with the antiquity of the oak, so also with the antiquity of religious ritual—I know it as ancient by the derivational feelings it evokes in my direct experience of its current manifestations.

There is a difference, however, between the durational texture of my feelings as I experience an oak tree and as I participate in a liturgical service. I know my freedom intimately as the name of conscious immediacy. And as I sense myself to be in the presence of realities grounded in that freedom or in another freedom, I cannot help but feel their derivational aspects as vulnerable in a way not felt in the presence of an oak or the mountains. This specific reality, this prayer being chanted by a kneeling congregation, exists thanks to a principle of order at work in its antecedent environment. Insofar as this prayerful practice has endured across the generations, the causal conditions for its existence, the structures giving it social salience, have persisted.

But these sources of endurance are the products of freedom. Human beings in their varied choices have come to prefer a certain mode of behavior under specified conditions, have opted for it again and again under conditions where alternative choices were possible and even compellingly attractive. Amid so much potential volatility there has been this consistency. Wherein lies the power of this ordering principle such that people have exercised it where they need not have, and have done so with such consistency that it has taken on the quality of unreflective habit, accustomed response?

I am in the presence of a derivational power that is essentially the power to change: to uproot, to create, to alter, to diminish, to destroy. Freedom is the power of innovation, of novelty. Yet it has been exercised contrary to itself, has become the power to preserve. Freedom has taken on the shape of natural necessity. The social past constrains my present even though I am inherently free. The formation of cultural importances in the past is thus far more astounding than the formation of natural importances.

It is of the essence of nature that it persist; it is of the essence of freedom that it innovate. And yet sometimes freedom constrains itself. Why is this so and how is it possible?

iv

Let me see where I have come so far. I have found in my experience of the environing world, the world of oak trees and church liturgies, an encounter with supporting depths. The conditions of conscious immediacy have thickness, dimensional massiveness. There are regions within the past, indeed the past is a region of such regions, that are so structured that they give importance to what they support. My experience of transitory occurrence is matched by an awareness of orderings that endure and that can rescue mere occurrence from slipping into triviality.

The basic natural structures of inheritance reach back into the obscurities of the indefinite past without alteration. They seem essential to the universe, structures that comprise its foundation. Less essential natural orders also exist and constrain regions of the past, but these lesser orders derive from the truly essential ones. The laws of geologic and of organic evolution, for example, both depend upon the laws of physics and chemistry.

The social structures of inheritance may in some instances be natural and may reach down into universal essentiality. But social order, and that in the past which gives it consistency through time, seems essentially rooted in more unstable soil, in a ground that is essentially momentary. Social order, it would seem, is not foundational at all. And yet some of these orderings endure and some stretch back into the human past as far as the eye of understanding can see. This wonderment, the persistence of the fruits of freedom, must now be explored.

Four

THE HISTORICAL PAST

Every active epoch harbours within itself the ideals and the ways of its immediate predecessors.

A. N. Whitehead, "Memories"

i

I live together with other human beings in a community that has distinctive traditions. Those who comprise my social group share particular convictions and undertake or permit characteristic activities. We believe certain things to be significant, and we act on the assumption that certain things are right or useful or opportune. Other communities of people arrive at quite different conclusions, accepting beliefs which we reject, legitimating actions which we prohibit.

Our more reflective members, or sensitive observers from other communities, would be able to distinguish between the implicit criteria by means of which my own community and those others make their differing judgments, the special principles of organization inchoately underlying each community's distinctive activities. A comparative analysis might even disclose more similarities than at first were thought to exist. For us who use them, however, these foundational structures of our community are not felt to be in any sense arbitrary or culture-bound. We do not even think them generalizable.

I must account for the emergence of values which constitute historical regions of consensus, which unite individuals by means of the degrees of relevance and levels of importance which they take as inherent in their experience, and yet which simultaneously cut them off from others who do not share those assumptions.

The natural scientist finds justification in experience for asserting principles of organization that are powerful enough to make intelligible the whole domain of natural phenomena. The authority of such principles lies in their universality, hence their trustworthiness and their capacity for generating accurate predictions. The organizing principles of a society, in contrast, are too weak ever to achieve this sort of universal acknowledgment. Yet they command their limited consensus with an authority at least as intense as that of scientific law. I must account for this authority.

In the social world there are at least three declensions of importance, three regions in which the derivational consistencies explanatory of present social experience take on a special urgency. These are person, place, and deed. Born and raised in community with others, I emerge into consciousness surrounded by persons of differing ages. I share with them a place of habitation which they and their ancestors have occupied for varying lengths of time. I am expected to interact with these people and utilize these places in the same distinctive ways they do.

In order to function effectively within this community, I must be sensitive to the historical texture of these three dimensions of social existence. I must know and know how to relate to the social meaning of the objects, events, and people around me. This knowledge can be acquired only insofar as I can grasp the proper linkages between what is immediately given to my experience and what the appropriate realms of importance are that organize that private experience into a world where others dwell. Even though the linkages be made intuitively and affectively, devoid of any critical reflection or intellectual deliberation, they are necessary to my survival and well-being. In the absence of a sense of social meaning, I would simply pass through the community as a stranger, an alien presence.

Indeed, a stranger by definition is one who does not share the meanings that organize my social world. A stranger is one who does not participate in the shared perspective by means of which the members of a community are able to think and feel and act coherently. To be estranged is to be outside the web of coherences, to be a surd that does not fit in with the assumed scheme of things. A total stranger, an entity sharing absolutely nothing with the members of a community, could not be dealt with on even the most rudimentary level. Such an absolutely alien reality would be, for the community, no reality at all—a phantasm, a madness, an impossibility.

My world and its importances define reality. They do not conform to it; they make it. Suppose I enter for the first time into a community not my own. Of the three dimensions of social importance—people, places, and deeds—the first is surely the most salient. As I begin meeting people, begin participating in their lives, in the ways of their culture, I will need to be sensitive to characteristics that serve to define the reality of the situations in which I find myself.

If the culture I enter is Japanese, for instance, I will be expected to reflect this sensitivity by the way in which I utilize its system of speech levels and styles of discourse. For instance, I must be aware of the important differences between myself and the person to whom I am speaking, differences in our social position, our sex and age, and the extended family groupings to which we belong. I must also take into account differences of the same sort between either of us and any person who might be the subject of my comments. Any topic, in fact, has a level of importance I must take care to reflect linguistically, and the purpose of my discourse, whether I come to ask a favor or mete out a reprimand, must also be reflected in my linguistic choices.

I have the prefix 'o-' available to indicate my sense that a person or topic deserves homage, and I can attach it as I choose to any noun or verb, indeed to any part of speech. *Sake* (rice wine) thus becomes *o-sake* if I am making a remark about its fitting role in the meal I have just completed.

Verb forms allow a far richer variety of shadings, however, than nouns. Along the 'axis of reference' expressing my attitude toward the subject matter under discussion, I can use any of five differing verb endings in order to indicate whether I think it a humble, neutral, respectful, elegant, or exalted topic. Thus in referring to an act of writing, perhaps to a *hiku* that has just been composed, I would use the verb stem *kak-*. If I wish to suggest that the poem is a trifling piece, I would attach the ending *-u*, thus using the verb form *kak-u*. But I would indicate a more respectful attitude toward the verses by using the verb form *kak-areru*.

At the same time I must be sensitive to the 'axis of address' which has three verb endings with which to indicate my attitude toward the person to whom I am speaking, in this case the person being offered my assessment of a *hiku*. In the presence of an equal I would use the plain form, identical to the neutral form of the axis of reference: *kak-u*. But I also have a polite form available, for instance when addressing a stranger or a superior: *kak-imasu*. For some verbs there is also a deferential form midway between the plain and polite forms.

By combining the axis of address and the axis of reference, and by gracing this as appropriate with the prefix of homage, all of this being simply second nature for me, the available linguistic alternatives become almost endless. For instance, *o-kaki ni naru* would be the appropriate prefix and verbal form to use in order to express my conviction that the act of writing which resulted in this poem was an elegant accomplishment. But if I at the same time wish to indicate my deferential respect for the person to whom I am providing this bit of literary criticism, I would interpolate the polite form into the elegant: *o-kaki ni nar-imasu.*

Nor does this suffice, for my sensitivity to the status of the persons and subject matter involved in this conversation can also be indicated by stylistic means. In addressing a stranger or superior I would tend to use grammatical constructions that involve negatives, my phrasings would be elaborate and lengthy rather than terse, and I would avoid words or constructions typical of the non-standard dialects while gladly introducing Japanese words that have a Chinese origin. So varied are my options that in an experiment involving 246 Japanese women, asked to respond verbally to a simple situation stimulus, no two verbal responses were identical or even nearly so.[1]

American English is less precise, but the distinctions are more plentiful than we who use the language habitually might imagine. It's cootchy-coo talk to the baby, formulaic repetitiveness for the dog, Basic English vocabulary when speaking to a 5-year-old, casual argot for jiving with the teenager, teasing intimacy with one's spouse, respectful comradeship for the section boss, vulgar camaraderie with the locker room crowd, polite formality when speaking to the business contact, latinizing complexity for the scholarly colleague, intimate respect for the aging parent, over-loud deliberateness to the foreigner. Sometimes words, sometimes tone, sometimes body language, sometimes meter and pace are what is crucial. The dimensions by which the distinctions are subtly shaded are enormous. A mistake could mean embarrassment or social disaster, and so mistakes are rare among those for whom the world that defines the mistakes is second nature.

Not only do I greet different kinds of people in differing kinds of situations differently, but the character of my greeting also changes depending on the sort of person I am. Were I a boy, my address to other boys or to the mayor of the town would not be the same as it is now that I am a middle-aged man, nor as it will be when I am one of the white-haired elders.

The central reason for this rainbow of appropriateness in my responses to people has to do with the social meaning embedded in their status or gender or age. I respond to people because of who they are, and who they are is a fact about them defined by the cultural realities in which they participate. If in my society the bare fact of an old woman's white hair or wrinkled brow is taken as meaning the presence of experience and the wisdom of long-livedness, then my behavior in her presence should be properly deferential. Yet the wisdom which is the imputed basis for this deference is neither directly experienced nor inferred.

I bestow it on the elderly woman with whom I am talking without any need for evidences of her sagacity, simply because wisdom is the social meaning of age in my community. The same historical background that made possible this old woman's longevity has also made possible its worth. My experience of the derivational extensiveness of her life, felt in the texture of her skin, the bend of her body, the way she walks, and the way she uses language in speaking to me, includes my awareness of her as a source of wisdom and advice. I treat the length of her years as an important fact about her because of the wisdom it has permitted. And yet at the same time I treat her wisdom as her outstanding feature because it has made possible the temporal massiveness of her experience.

In such a culture, wisdom and age are yoked, each the cause of the other, each having the other as its meaning. For me, were this my culture, such would be just the way the world is. Wisdom and longevity are one single fact, as though in Spinozistic fashion they were two attributes of the same substance, each a full articulation of the same reality. The old woman imbibes the same social meanings, of course. So as she grows older she expects to become increasingly sagacious. And so she does, for her age exhibits it.

In other communities, to be sure, the linkages may be quite different. In another world a person's age might be denigrated for its brittleness, for its inability to adapt to changing times. To be old would then mean to have become inept. This old woman might in that other culture no longer rock peacefully before the fire, content to impart the fruits of her experience to all who seek assistance. Instead she might come to note her fading importance and then simply walk off one night into the dark of irrelevance.

As a stranger to some town or land, I must be sure that I know the proper expectations in dealing with other persons. It would bring a blush to my face, or maybe a rope to my neck, were I to misread the social world and revere what is merely ineptitude or show callous disdain for what is in fact wisdom.

Almost any characteristic of a person can be linked socially with the derivational properties that vest it with significance. Obvious bodily differences are a prime point of linkage precisely because they can be grasped by even children and fools. Skin pigmentation conveys a sense of biologically inherited derivation from an environment both unimaginably ancient and distinctively selective. People with brown skins obviously must share common brown-skinned ancestors stretching all the way back to the dawn of humanity when they were first set apart from those whose skins are of another color. This shared distinctiveness in skin coloring can then be further linked to long-standing rights and privileges. Separate is never equal. The brown peoples have first rights on this land, its water and its salt, because it was their ancestors who first settled here.

In a fully developed racism the direction of linkage between visible traits and their ancient meanings is symbiotic. Pigmentation is taken to be both the proof of special rights and their justification. The brown-skinned peoples are a race far superior to the more recent light-skinned settlers, and therefore the browns deserve this land and must insist that the whites surrender the acreage they have already usurped. My brown skin may at first have been merely a sign of my membership in a group accorded special privileges because of its power or its accomplishments. It requires only a simple transition to embrace the assumption that the brownness is the reason for those privileges as well.

A Hapsburg nose once provided an aura of dignity and privilege to those possessing it, even to those who might lack the powers and visible trappings of royalty. Perhaps there still exists a pretender to the throne of Austria-Hungary, to the Holy Roman Empire, and it is likely that his facial features are one abiding evidence of his capacity to rule and his right to do so.

Yet the very sensed antiquity of these rights and privileges might in another age prove disastrous. After the fall of the Bastille or the storming of the Winter Palace one's aristocratic connections suddenly became a ticket to the guillotine or Siberia. As black rage explodes the social order of colonial racism, a white face on the streets is an invitation to violence or disdain that cannot be obliterated by a convenient conversion in one's politics or morals. The very biological rootage that gave racial privilege its sustaining importance is now, in this world turned upside down, the enduring condition for exclusion.

I must be very aware of what things are important and what irrelevant if I am to know how to interact with other people and so become a fully participating member of a given community. But knowing the proper meaning of things can sometimes be difficult. Is it still proper to wear the Phrygian cap of liberty and greet people on the street as "*citoyen*"? Or are fineries back in style and aristocratic connection a way to gain a job within the Bourbon bureaucracy? An American teenager who is ostracized because of her failure to keep abreast of the latest clothing fads is no less alienated than the veteran of the Republic in the days of the Bourbon restoration.

The transition times from an old order to the new, or from the new to the old restored, are always difficult occasions. The Chinese curse that hopes I will live in interesting times damns me to a social age in which the meaning of things is unstable, today's significance transformed into tomorrow's irrelevance. It is difficult to live in a world where the Terror is perpetually the author of Thermidor, but Thermidor is then always the precursor of yet another Terror.

Whether the times are interesting or dull, stable or tumultuous, who people are and what their qualities and characteristics mean is the aspect of social reality that is of absolute importance. It is the air breathed by the natives of a social world. Only a truly alien biology could hope to survive without that air, and so what does not breathe it is treated as unutterably alien.

Places are as complexly tinctured with social meaning as are persons. That churchyard where I stopped to walk among the gravestones and participate in the liturgy is densely crowded with events long gone that give it a special significance. This is a place where the bones of important people molder, people who were not necessarily important while they lived but who have become increasingly important to each new generation, simply in virtue of their social role as the predecessors of all those who have succeeded them. This cemetery has become what it was not at first: a place where my revered ancestors lie buried.

The church itself reflects in its steeple and traditional architecture a set of beliefs regarding religion and aesthetics that is intimately associated with the ancestors who lie buried beside it. Our tastes are different now, and were I and my fellow believers to build a new church in town to replace this country edifice we would use a different style. But we are quick to restore this church to its authentic form when needed repairs provide the opportunity, for its importance resides in the past it makes present and not in the contemporary purposes it might serve.

As our ancestors become more important to us, so the artifacts that give visible presence to their world become more important. In this building meetings of historical moment were held, and along the pathway beside the churchyard travelers passed on their way to actions that would shape the character of a continent. The early meetings here were the decisive ones. In more recent decades little of significance has gone on except that the recurrent fact of church meetings has served to give continuity to the organization for which the church is an instrument. Those dull sessions of a sleepy congregation, voting trivial resolutions without a murmur of dissent, provide the line of connection that makes this church not only a monument to some dead world of long ago but the living edge of a reality extending from the distant past into this present.

That majestic oak tree of mine, the whole grove of which it is a part, takes on a completely new dimension of significance when it is linked not only to its biological past but to the human past as well. The grove is near the church, curving protectively along its north side and around the cemetery. Perhaps these trees are not merely the result of natural seeding but also are reflections of quite specific human purposes.

Had I lived in northwest Greece, in the rugged Epirus region, my mountain journey might well have taken me to a high plateau where lie the ancient ruins of Dodona.[2] For many centuries this site was occupied by a Byzantine church and before that had been the seat of an early bishopric. Excavations show that a temple to Zeus had stood there even earlier, until it was destroyed by the Romans in 167 BCE. This Zeusian temple had been complemented by lesser temples to Heracles and Dione and by a magnificent amphitheatre.

This pre-Roman cluster of sacred buildings dates back to the third century BCE when King Pyrrhus decided to make Dodona the religious capital of his fledgling empire. The courtyard for Zeus's temple was constructed so as to encompass a large tree, the location of which was awkwardly positioned architecturally. The function of the tree clearly was not decorative, and its importance is indicated by the later effort of the Christians to erase all traces of its presence by digging up its root system as well as destroying its trunk and branches.

This must have been a very important piece of vegetation for people to have been so ruthless in uprooting it. To be sure, it was part of a shrine designed to celebrate the grandeur of empire that Pyrrhus and his successors aspired to attain. But the special attention paid to the tree's destruction bespeaks a deeper importance, an effort by the Christians to efface the presence of a reality far more a threat to them than the feeble remnants of religious practices mandated by a pagan empire which by their time had long since passed into historical oblivion.

King Pyrrhus, indeed, had chosen the site for his temple at a place already important to the Greeks. For well over a hundred years prior to his grandiose project, as early as 400 BCE, a small stone temple had existed at Dodona, located near a huge oak tree and eventually united with it by means of an encircling parabolic wall of ashlar masonry. People would come to this spot and leave strips of metal containing their requests for marital happiness, for advice on matters of career choice, and for safe journeying.

Long before the temple, and probably since the coming of the first Greeks in the early centuries of the second millenium BCE, Dodona had been the location of a sacred grove of oak where oracles of Zeus could be sought out and one's fate foretold. Sophocles identifies the ancient oak at Dodona as the time-honored source of prophecies regarding the tragic fate of Heracles, prophecies that the characters in the play take with special seriousness because of its great antiquity and therefore its great authority.[3] Plato also mentions Dodona in connection with prophecies of great significance.[4] It takes Herodotus to ferret out some explanation for the awesomeness of Dodona and its sacred tree and grove. He claims that the oracle there is the most ancient in Greece,[5] older by far than Delphi's oracle, and that it was founded by women captured in war from the temple to Zeus at Thebes in Egypt. Sold to Greeks at Epirus, one of these women at the express bidding of Zeus must have established a new shrine in that distant land. In this way the divine name was introduced into Greece along with the ancient rites appropriate to Zeus's worship. This formed the basis for civilization and for the eventual triumph of the Greeks over barbarism [2:56].

Herodotus in this way provides a naturalistic interpretation of the oft-told tale of a black pigeon flying from Thebes to Dodona where it perched in an oak tree and commanded in a human voice that an oracle to Zeus be established [2:55]. Herodotus thus acknowledges the existence of an oak already revered in his day for its antiquity, an oak intimately associated with the origins of Greek culture and beyond that with the Egyptian culture which, for Herodotus, was the font of all things human.

I catch a glimpse of still greater antiquity by turning to the epic poets and especially to Homer, where half a millenium before Herodotus Dodona was still honored for its religious significance. Achilles, about to send some of his forces off to battle against Hector, offers a special libation to Zeus which begins with this invocation:

Zeus of Dôdôna, god of Pelasgians,
O god whose home lies far! Ruler of wintry harsh Dôdôna.[6]

The moment for Achilles is a crucial one, the favor of Father Zeus especially important. In phrases that seem to echo ritual incantations, the battle leader therefore invokes this god who dwells in a place austerely remote from the commonplace world. There is no mention of oaks, but the prayer goes on to indicate the presence of 'interpreters' whose feet are covered in dirt and who sleep on the ground. It is only a small speculative step to see this as a reference to some outdoor shrine and to the priests who protect Zeus's sacred oak where pigeons nest in the branches.

Perhaps Achilles selects the Zeus of Dodona as the object of his invocation because his people had come from there. If so, Epirus would be the ancient homeland for those Hellenes who in the epic age swept down into the Mycenaean civilization and made it their own. And Dodona's oaks would have been the cult center for that people. There is continuity in this place, therefore, that links it with the fortunes of a people throughout the full length of their remembered history. Individuals must have come here to learn from the oracle their chances of success in matters of birth, marriage, career, adventure, and death. Leaders also would have come, it can be presumed, to learn the fortunes of their policies and the fate of their people.

There are no towering oaks at Dodona any more but only scrub oak struggling to survive amid the erosion produced by generations of poor forest management. The temples and other evidences of the sacred oracle are merely archeological artifacts. Yet even in all its current barrenness, this piece of real estate in far off Epirus commands my awe, shapes my imagination, fills me with a sense of participation in something somehow fundamental to who I am. The tall oak in my mountain churchyard lacks this deep-rooted history, but knowing of Dodona I find it hard not to meld the two into one, rescuing the sacred oracle from oblivion by giving it my tree to whisper through, my people to preserve.

This precisely is what some of my contemporaries have done. An archeologist in 1960 reported being taken by local residents into a thickly wooded forest near South Sjaeland, Denmark. There he was shown a massive, ancient oak with a hole in the middle of its trunk, and everywhere on it were hung bits of rag, handkerchiefs, even fragments of silk stockings. The guides explained that the offerings were requests for assistance from God. One story probably involving this very 'rag oak' claims that a child, who was losing his ability to stand upright and to walk, was cured on the advice of a wizard by being taken to this tree, pulled three times through its center hole, and pieces of his clothing attached to the branches. The archeologist was led blindfolded and by a circuitous route to and from this sacred site, lest its power be destroyed by the scoffings of an unbelieving world.[7]

There are parcels of land scattered across my world, places similar to Dodona and the dark woods of South Sjaeland, that serve as custodians of meanings which are broader than themselves. In any culture such places are made into historical monuments or national shrines. Plans for a new housing development, such as the one being constructed a little way down the road, would obliterate the value of such places. The bulldozers and landmovers might invade my churchyard, leveling the angularities of the land, removing trees and gravemarkers, demolishing the sturdy oak vault of the sanctuary ceiling. After the machines had withdrawn all would be new, but the sacred memories would no longer have any material location in which to be tethered down. It would not be long then before these memorable things would have been forgotten, the few survivors gone who recall the church and the gravestones and the meanings they exhibit.

How crucial these places are, therefore! They can be destroyed by human purposes in a few efficient days. So countervailing human purpose must intervene to preserve them and so preserve the ties of the present to its past and to the importances it treasures up. I do not create my heritage out of whole cloth. I remember it, and I in cooperation with others give it new saliences depending on what we might think important enough to preserve by locating as an element within our sacred spaces. A generation can rightfully be condemned for having squandered its heritage if it destroys the places where the importances of the past are manifest.

A person gives himself away as a stranger, an outsider, whenever he fails to appreciate the special character of places, especially of those places so central to the community that they do not even need signs and fences to identify their historical significance. The contractor who is leveling my old homesite is a crude barbarian, a Vandal who is willfully stomping on my treasures and raping my memories for the sake of profit and utility. When I talk loudly in a place demanding hushed reverence or leave my trash scattered on the city commons I am not different from the Visigoths. My acculturation to a new society must come by means of the developing loves and loyalties which transform a terrain into a motherland, a house into a home, an idle daydream into the promise of Jerusalem.

The actions performed by persons at places, especially special kinds of actions performed at special kinds of places by special people, are a third center of social meaning. An individual who undertakes a repeated pattern of activity is enacting a social role. It might be an insignificant routine related to homemaking or to childcare or to job performance, but insofar as it is a repeated pattern, a familiar and habitual way of ordering behavior, it describes a social role. The pattern of activity is recognizable by others, therefore namable, and can be performed by any person with similar abilities who would chose or be required to do so.

Our shared meal is completed and you draw water, add soap, and clean the plates and cups. At subsequent meals you act in similar fashion. You have assumed the role of household dishwasher, a role I and everybody in our community recognize as necessary but tedious. It is a role I may well be asked to assume myself, replacing you. In requesting me to do the dishes, you identify a pattern of activities with which I am familiar even if I may never have actually performed those acts, a pattern that when enacted associates me with the dreary status that role assigns. Were my social world one that makes dishwashing anathema for men, in assuming such a womanly role I would disgrace myself.

Perhaps, however, I will be proud to be at last included among the privileged few who are assigned the dishwashing task. This might well happen if the meal were a religious act, a communion rite, and the care of the utensils therefore a highly valued task, a Martha chore, a Brother Lawrence obedience, given its value by the approval for such acts voiced originally by the religion's founder.

Thus certain activities are repeated until they take on habitual shapes that are culturally recognizable. They are valued by the culture in ways dependent on its traditions and needs, and eventually they become so formalized that they are incarnated as institutional structures. The mores of a people, its customs and taboos, its common sense and clichés, its legal systems and ideologies, are such institutionalizings of patterned activity. Individual habits begin to take on tangible form as pathways appear where feet have repeatedly trod and roads arise where pathways are regularized and given a permanent surface.

Dishwashing leads to courses in home economics and so to departments, buildings, universities, professional societies, advertising firms, food production operations, food distribution networks, financial centers for funding such enterprises, regulating governmental agencies, and the whole panorama of social artifacts designed to celebrate, perpetuate, and exploit the need people have to clean up the mess left on their plates and utensils after consuming the food without which their metabolic processes could not continue.

Through the life of institutions and the patterned behaviors they presuppose, the possible actions an individual might perform are provided with a template. Habit, sloth, threat, compulsion, or lack of imagination give precedence to this template. People act as their social roles instruct them to, and they deviate from the essentials of these patternings only in extreme situations. They might be confronted with an occurrence for which the role provides no proper response, or in the collapse of social order they might find themselves destitute of a pre-patterned response. Occasionally a bold innovative soul defies convention and alters role expectations even where no necessity has intervened. Such innovation is usually dealt with summarily, however, lest the social order become unstable.

And so the weekly journey of varied folk to a clearing on the mountainside in order to perform long-familiar rituals makes each new generation of these people into believers. They become part of a people whose practice it was to build churches in order properly to honor their God and to provide stability and focus for their emerging community in the American wilderness. Non-conformity, tolerated by this people within narrow bounds, is met by ostracism or expulsion when it becomes excessive. New members of the community learn their roles, find comfort in them because they find meaning in them, and are quick to resent those whose actions would seriously upset that world.

By learning the customs of a people, the niceties of polite society and the conventions of the local natives, I am able to avoid the outsider's stigmata of social ignorance and barbarian crudity. I do not truly value a people nor their land until I am able to act as they would act, aware fully and matter-of-factly of the importances undergirding each gesture, word, and deed.

Of the three declensions of social importance, the deed might seem to be more basic than place and person. For the importance of a person is a function of social role, and places achieve their significance because they are the locations where socially significant activities are enacted. Yet the interrelationship of person, place, and deed defies any such attempts at hierarchy. A sacred grove is what gives importance to the adoration exhibited there, and it is soon thought inappropriate to display such emotions at any other more common-place site. The persons associated with sacred places find their smallest deeds vested with significance not because of the deed as such but because the person performing it and the place of its enactment are already known as important. By such symbioses is the content of social salience enriched, differing values intermixed, and the seemingly irrational cacophony of cultural expression coherently deployed.

So I have come a long way in my understanding. I have discovered that present experience contains a structure of derivation. I am aware that my present here-and-now arises from a previous there-and-then. I also sense that the past is so characterized as to account for the distinctiveness of what is present, for the coherence and meaning that gives me a world as the shape of the present. Because I experience the present as involving non-present principles of order, I experience in it the efficacy of regions of importance that explain why the present is as it is, that indicate the significance of what is. Thus I feel vaguely but persistently that the past provides a massiveness of struc-tured context able to give meaning to the otherwise confusing content of immediate experience. In linking this backdrop of felt importances to the nodal social realities of person, place, and customary behavior, I learn the cultural meanings that have provided me with my world.

The meanings thus learned, meanings conspicuously embedded in certain people, special places, and distinctive deeds, are awesomely normative. In my encounters with important personages I learn the value of my person. By visiting the sacred places I discover the orienting geography of homeland and sojourn. Through participation in the proper rites I acquire a sense of deeds worth doing, ends worth seeking, ideals worth dreaming. In learning what I must know in order to have a social world I can inhabit meaningfully, I acquire also an awareness of the normative implications of that knowledge. As regards social meaning, was entails ought.

ii

The overwhelming practice of the human species has been to favor the characteristics in current experience that are supported by important persistences. Traditional practices, familiar beliefs, habitual attitudes are typically preferred to the new and novel. This authority accorded tradition lies in its likelihood of rightness. Certain behaviors come to be associated with regions of significance and are then repeated because of the importance the linkage implies and because it is hoped that by repetition the linkage can be preserved.

Continuity in behavior, the patterning of action and belief through repetition, assures me that present events will retain the connection with enabling powers and transcendent importances that had previously been attained. Most of the things that happen are of passing relevance and quickly fade, but when by accident or strategy a deed done or an idea articulated is caught up into wider and more enduring relevances, it becomes crucial that the connection not be lost. There can be no experience more emotionally intense than the awareness that something with which I am intimate, an action I performed, an idea I expressed, has been rescued from oblivion because what is important and permanent in the universe has reached out and encompassed it.

The power of the familiar is the assurance it provides that what is going on has the support of a universe I and my people understand and within which we have a meaningful place. Familiar occurrences reinforce that understanding and that sense of meaning. They demonstrate again and again that the transcending forces that have ordered the social and natural world up until this moment are forces still in control of things, still setting the conditions for what is and what can be.

The alternative is terrifying, a world in which all accomplishment quickly vanishes, in which all beliefs are soon forgotten. The effort to discern regions of importance and to link up with them is a powerful motive for human action. The social habits of a people spin out a web of cultural relationships that define their world. In describing this worldmaking, I have emphasized the perspective it provides and is, the window on reality it affords. But the web is more than a vantage point for scrutinizing events and understanding their significance. It is a support, a safety net, as well. It protects me from threats to my significance at the same time that it informs me of that significance. It would make no sense to know that I am a part of some process that is at the core of things, only to discover that the core is transient and trivial. To make a world, or to embrace a world made for me, should be to find myself situated in the midst of enduring order.

The webwork of my social world is a subtle weave, comprising what Butterfield calls the 'imponderables' of a civilization, its taken-for-granted attitudes and practices. When happenstance or revolution tears into that fabric in a manner threatening its integrity, my response is typically to resist the intrusion in the same way corpuscles resist the appearance of a virus. What cannot be eradicated is swiftly incorporated, the reconciling power of human invention displayed in the cleverness with which new ideas are co-opted into the repertoire of acceptability, new activities melded into the habits and institutional rituals of the status quo. It would be wrong to presume that these efforts are born from laziness, that people repulse novelty or turn it into modalities of the familiar because they lack the energy or the discipline to make their world anew. Often the easier path would be the way of fresh beginnings rather than undertaking the complicated tasks required for patchwork, repair, and restoration. But if the world threatened is not merely an interesting view of things but an ingenious and successful device for obtaining and retaining a reprieve from the terrors of history, then the efforts at conservation make sense.

The imponderables are the lungs of culture, for by their means I and my people are able to breathe the air of significance which gives us life and strength even in the face of circumambient hostility. The anthropologist Clifford Geertz associates the cultural imponderables with organic processes, but he does so in a literal and not simply metaphorical sense.[8] Geertz notes that the human central nervous system is not specific in the behavioral responses triggered by a given stimulus. Whereas in most other animals a response is instinctual and therefore stereotyped, for humans "the precise patterning of such overt acts is guided predominantly by cultural rather than genetic templates."[9] My cognitive and affective processes are not predetermined by my biological makeup nor by the specific character of the ways in which the world impacts upon me. I have a capacity for response, a generalized potentiality for ranges of behaviors, which something other than heredity must supplement if a determinate outcome is to result.

According to Geertz, culture provides this needed addition by means of its symbol systems. A symbolic world has been made for me, a perspective on experience and an enclave within it. From this vantage I am able to shape the diffuse flow of mental and emotional energy into explicit ideas and feelings that are coherent elements within that world order. Without cultural symbols to shape, refine, and reshape my behavioral responses to the environment, they would be limited to a few basic biological instincts such as breathing, sucking, and crying. I would never behave in a distinctively human fashion. If an animal typically reacts blindly to a certain stimulus, it at least does so definitively and with dispatch. For the most part the response will be effective precisely because such behavior has in the past contributed to the survivability of that species and is likely therefore to do so in the new instance as well. Where the response is in fact not appropriate, the animal cannot adapt and so will perish.

Humans are able to adapt because their responses are less well defined and so can be tailored within broad ranges of tolerance to the uniquenesses of any given situation. If there is no instrument for tailoring, there can be no distinctive response at all but only confused, random reaction. By interpreting the press of experience in terms of the principles of order out of which my worldview is fashioned, and by availing myself of this same structure to give direction and shape to the ways by which I take account of that experience, I am able to devise a style of living that I hope will be adequate to my needs and purposes.

So my sense of the world and of myself within the world, and therefore the transactions comprising my life history as an individual organism in a dynamic environment, is dependent upon the close collaboration of nature and culture. I only know who I am by discovering how I respond to specific situations, how I think or feel or act in response to specific stimuli. Since the cultural symbols defining my vantage on the world are the instruments for giving explicit form to those thoughts or emotions or actions, then in a deep and fundamental way I am a cultural artifact:

We acquire the ability to design flying planes in wind tunnels; we develop the capacity to feel true awe in church. A child counts on his fingers before he counts "in his head"; he feels love on his skin before he feels it "in his heart." Not only ideas, but emotions too, are cultural artifacts in man.[10]

My participation in that church service up in the mountains is rich in the symbols that make it a reality I can understand and appreciate, a reality with which I can interact. For me to see the building as a church, not merely a configuration of matériel, means that I know something about the history and function of religion in Western civilization, its ideal aims and institutional embodiments, the typical forms of architectural expression for those ideals and practices.

This capacity to grasp the meaning of what I see, to see shape as having religious import, to see the functionality of shelter as having ritual intent, to recognize these religious and ritualistic meanings as having roots deep into the past, need not in any way have a specifiable content. If I have a Ph.D. in art history or theology, I will see these things with especial clarity and be able to articulate them effectively. But merely by being raised to maturity within this social milieu I am aware of the basic meanings.

I do not see a building and attempt to read its features as providing clues for its location within a taxonomy of meanings, as I would were I trying to identify the species of nearby oak by seeking the assistance of a field guide for trees. Right off I see a church, because I have been bred to see the world with the aid of a symbol system that organizes such phenomena that way. I see it as a church because I am myself an artifact within a world for which such things are churches. I feel it as a church also, for the meanings it exhibits include its sacredness and its antiquity. And to perceive it as sacred means that my affective processes are tinctured with awe, deference, reverence, perhaps with emotions of guilt or gratitude, hatred or exaltation, hope or fear.

I have to see and feel in some manner or other; there is no neutral access to the world. So the way I experience things, the adverbial character of my existing, defines who I am. The cultural symbols that create my world, that form the perspectival character of my comportings with reality, are thus at the very core of who I am. Whether I am a practicing Christian who will enter that church to worship with its congregation, a curious Jew who wishes to observe first-hand the peculiarities of New England Congregationalism, or an indifferent secularist momentarily driven by nostalgia to re-experience a world abandoned in adolescence, I will recognize the church as a meaningful reality with cultural importance. And, being who I am, living within whatever particular perspective it is that defines my meanings, I take up my usual and appropriate attitude toward it.

It follows that an attack on the symbols of a culture is an attack on my sense of who I am. In a world where my church is just a building I am neither Christian nor Jew nor atheist, because to act in the way a believer does or in the way a nonbeliever does requires a world in which churches exist to be revered or damned. All of us, including all the attitudes and ideas that separate us as well as those that bind us, are who we are because we have been fashioned that way by a culture through its public symbols. If I lose these symbols I am lost as well.

Whatever the ways in which I might wish to change, their horizon is defined by the world made by the symbol system that is my culture. So I can conceive of myself as abandoning my faith for a life of secular indifference, or I can fervently hope to become a more committed believer than I have been. But the repertoire of such possibilities for who I might be is limited. I can change, but the I who changes can do so only within a perimeter of what is conceivably human, a boundary that has been traced by the cultural symbols available to me. Beyond that limit, I am no longer I.

No wonder then that human beings are so protective of their fundamental symbols. The alternative is oblivion. As Geertz remarks,

Man depends upon symbols and symbol systems with a dependence so great as to be decisive for his creatural viability and, as a result, his sensitivity to even the remotest indication that they may prove unable to cope with one or another aspect of experience raises within him the gravest sort of anxiety.[11]

This aversion to cultural change bemuses Arnold Toynbee. He notes the widespread presence of 'mimesis' in human culture, a phenomenon he defines as "the acquisition, through imitation, of social 'assets'—aptitudes or emotions or ideas—which the acquisitors have not originated themselves."[12] In primitive societies and in civilizations at the verge of breakdown, culture is static. The habits and customs of a people are of long standing because each person's behavior is modeled on the behavior of the ancestors as interpreted in the deeds and attitudes of the current social leadership. Mimesis is directed toward the elder generation. Sons mimic their fathers and daughters their mothers, and both would think it impious to depart intentionally from the established and familiar ways. Consequently the accumulated heritage of the culture comes to be concentrated in the hereditary rulers, the traditional elite. The importance of what they do and say lies in the link they have to the past. They are respected, and therefore imitated, because they incarnate a way of existing in the world that has eventuated in current meanings and trusted significances.

Toynbee is impatient with these backward-looking folk. He contrasts them with creative individuals who break loose from established ways in order to explore new conceptual and practical possibilities. Such persons have achieved "self-determination through self-mastery" and are impelled by the energy of this achievement to translate their new visions into social realities.[13] If, unfortunately, most people are incapable of this kind of creativity, then at least their mimesis should be attached to it, to the dynamic openness of the inventive rather than to the unthinking repetitions of the past. In this way a population can be transformed despite itself, adopting new attitudes and behaviors, breaking the cake of custom for a moment and then baking it anew at an improved stage in human social development. The genius of charismatic originality is rare but can spread itself throughout the culture by means of a kind of social drill which enlists the faculty of mimesis in the souls of the uncreative rank-and-file and thereby enables them to perform "mechanically" an evolution which they could not have performed on their own initiative.[14]

The Whig interpretation of history is a passion that remains alive and well in Toynbee. He dreams of an eventual transformation of the human species into a form of communal existence as qualitatively superior to civilized existence as civilization is superior to pre-human modalities. Therefore he cannot understand why progress in this direction is so agonizingly slow. He cannot figure out why creative leaders are so frequently ignored by a culture needing their fresh vision and energy. He is frustrated by the fact that even when creative leaders are actually followed the result is inexorably and all too quickly a breakdown of cultural dynamism, which leads on inexorably to the eventual disintegration of social achievement.

Toynbee's solution is to fall back on an appeal to mystery, to identify creativity as the result of divine grace, its flow or ebb a deterministic *yin* and *yang*, a "general rhythmical pulsation which runs all through the Universe."[15] There is something in the nature of things that fosters novelty and progress; there is something also that works against such realizations. For Toynbee, both lie beyond our ken.

But there is no mystery to mimesis directed toward the past. The emergence of novel practices with the power to catch the imagination and commitment of a people may be mysterious, but the power of the past to evoke my allegiance is quite explicable. The ancient ways have survived because they are favored by the universe, and I too seek its favor.

The implicit syllogism is as tightly woven as the cultural safety net it justifies. To perish is to lack significance in the scheme of things; to survive is to be rooted in that significance. Therefore in order to survive I must do as did those who in the past proved their importance for me and for the universe precisely by surviving. To venture out onto new, untried paths is to cut my link to the powers of survivability. If I am persuaded to see the world in a new way, it is a new world I see, one that may not value what I value, may not even value me or recognize who I am and why I was born to live as I do for the sake of the ends that justify my existence.

If I am persuaded to see the world in a new way, I discover that the protective cover of cultural meaning is dissolved and I am left naked before the environing threats to my reality. With Descartes, I am left standing at the edge of troubled waters, and I fear for my safety.

iii

Mimesis, therefore, is not a second-best device for achieving social cohesion, a fallback when creativity is absent. Nor is the mimesis of ancestors an unfortunate misdirection of a capacity that should instead be directed toward the few creative individuals who do from time to time appear on the world-historical stage. Mimesis is the wisdom of experience warning me not to give up present assured achievement for the vague possibility of future improvement.

Too often such adventurings not only fail to arrive at their promised destination but in the process also lose the past achievements as well. The imponderables of a civilization are a protective worldweb, but the human spider works in gossamer and her weavings are fragile. They survive only in virtue of the permanence of the realities to which they are anchored. To rip them free from such moorings on the hope that some better weaving might be accomplished elsewhere is folly. And from folly comes tragedy.

Only tremendous desperation would ever motivate such acts of folly. So whenever people plot a radical break with the status quo and its assurances, they tend to do so in the name of yet older assurances. Revolution almost always parades itself as a restoration. The new is really a recovery of ancient ways which have been lost or distorted by the intrusion of recent evils.

For instance, the radical left-wing of the Protestant Reformation, the Anabaptists, explicitly rejected *reformatio* as their aim. The true church, they argued, could only be recovered by *restitutio*.[16] They believed that centuries of corruption had so deeply polluted the rituals, theology, and organization of the Christian Church that a reformation of the institution would have no noticeable purifying effect. At some point in its history the normative forms of religious life had been lost. The Church itself had fallen into sin, become a force for evil and no longer an instrument of salvation.

Each Anabaptist sect had its own distinctive dating of when the Church fell from grace, although 324 CE, the date of Constantine's establishment of Christianity as a state religion, is typically identified as the turning point. With Adam's fall we all as individuals fell into sin; with Constantine's act, ratified by the Council of Nicea a year later, Christ's Church succumbed to the powers of Satan and continues its enthrallment to him until such time as the original pre-Constantinian Church shall be restored.

These Anabaptists were primitivists, enthusiasts for a past Golden Age where people believed and acted in 'true' fashion, in accord with the precepts of God and the model of Christian virtue evidenced by Jesus and the apostles. New Testament scripture was their sole and fully sufficient authority for what that ideal entailed. Eucharistic rituals not explicitly instituted by the words of Christ or on the testimony of Paul were unacceptable. Administrative devices such as a system of bishops were seen as demonic because nowhere mentioned in scripture. For many of the more radical Anabaptists, practices of radical equality and the sharing of earthly possessions were taken as obligatory because commanded by the gospel.

The primitive Eden of early Christianity could be recovered through the exemplary acts of faithful souls. Virtues of simplicity, self-discipline, and absolute religious commitment were to be practiced, if necessary within communities of the faithful that had separated themselves from the worldliness of a fallen Church and a corrupted State. For some this meant gathering stealthily in forests and sheltered meadows, away from the modern-day temples of the idolators, to worship and share their fellowship 'by the oak in Esslingen wood'[17] or in some similar uncorrupted place where God could be directly present to them. For others it meant abandoning Europe completely and seeking a new beginning in the New World.

Either form of withdrawal was for the sake of return, however, since most Anabaptists saw their restored church either as having a missionary obligation to preach the gospel to the ends of the world or as forming a model community that by its purity would lure all peoples to emulate it. The Puritan immigrations to New England and Virginia proclaimed both goals at once, insofar as they saw themselves journeying to the world's end in order to show forth their form of religious obedience as the paradigm for all Christians. As Winthrop's famous words of justification put it,

For this end, wee must be knitt together in this worke as one man, . . . always haveing before our eyes our Commission and Community in the worke. . . . Wee shall finde that the God of Israell is among us, when tenn of us shall be able to resist a thousand of our enemies, when hee shall make us a prayse and glory, that men shall say of succeeding plantacions: the lord make it like that of New England: for wee must Consider that wee shall be as a Citty upon a Hill, the eies of all people are uppon us. . . . But if our heartes shall turne away soe that wee will not obey . . . wee shall surely perishe out of the good Land whither wee passe over this vast Sea to possesse it.[18]

The model Christian community had never existed, of course, nor would it ever exist. It was an abstraction invented without regard for historical accuracy and offered as a remedy to the failure of Christianity in living up to its ideals. But because its radical vision came clothed in the protective garments of the past, it could command the loyalties of common folk and pragmatic leaders. It appealed to deep-seated needs in offering not a venture into the unknown but a return to beliefs and practices more securely tied to God's purposes than were the corruptions and compromises of the day.

The past was judge of the present, and therefore an image of what the future should be. Winthrop's task was to carry a precious cargo of right belief and faithful practice through the wilderness to safe harbor. This would be accomplished when confidence in divine blessing could be once more evidenced historically as it had been when God's first Israel was led through another wilderness to the safety of a promised land.

The more radical the change, the more important this concern to find a model for the future in the past. What was true of the Anabaptists in their struggle against the Reformers was also true of the Jacobins in their efforts to wrest control of the French Revolution from moderates.[19] All those Frenchmen who opposed the tradition of absolute monarchy and its Bourbon abuses turned to democratic Greece and republican Rome for help and inspiration. Their rhetoric was filled with allusions to those classical writers who for them symbolized the emergence of a free people and resistance to a threatening tyranny. The virtues of these heroes were contrasted with the vices they had struggled against and which needed to be once more resisted.

There is something ironic if not downright silly in the attempt of the French to recreate a past that was never theirs in the first place, but the intent was nonetheless serious, the need for such rootage intense. When the revolutionary Assembly convened in its new quarters on May 10, 1793, the deputies carried on their debates under the watchful eyes of antiquity. Statues of the lawgivers Solon and Lycurgus, and of the philosophers Plato and Demosthenes, looked down from one side of the hall; from the other, Camillus, Publicola, Junius Brutus, and Cincinnatus silently admonished the new Republic to translate its principles with decisiveness into surefooted reality.

This Golden Age had been lost to tyranny and empire when patriotism and the love of liberty gave way to indifference, when hard work, integrity, and simplicity succumbed to the corruptions of success and abundance. Its relevance to the present could be established in either of two ways. One approach was that of Girondist moderates like Brissot and Desmoulins who saw Greece and Rome as providing inspiration for their reforming efforts. The wisdom of a Solon was needed to improve the laws, the courage of a Cicero to resist the domestic forces of injustice, the effectiveness of a Cincinnatus to secure the ideal against its external enemies. Mimesis of the past was limited to the imitation of virtues and character.

In contrast, the Jacobins, led by Robespierre and Saint-Just, turned to antiquity for specific models to guide them in a total reconstruction of French thought and practice. The impossible enormity of the task would be humorous were it not that so many died in the attempt to make it a living reality. Ancient institutional arrangements such as a citizen army with elected officers, provision for referendum voting, public censors, brief terms of office for political leaders, and legislative control over declarations of peace and war, were to be directly imitated. The Spartan model of education was to be implemented in the school system, including early separation of children from their parents and required military service beginning at age ten.

Frequently the revolutionaries would even change their names to ones honoring the heroes of Greece and of Rome. For instance, Babeuf dropped his three Christian names, Francois-Nöel Toussaint Nicaisse, replacing them by Camillus Caius Gracchus. The town of Saint-Maximin voted to call itself Marathon. Among the streets of Paris appeared such new names as Rue de Brutus, Rue des Grecques, Rue de Socrates. In 1793 three-fourths of the newborn boys who were given classical names were called Brutus. Everyone wore the red Phrygian cap as an emblem of the Republic's historical continuity with all the enemies of despotism throughout the centuries.

Jacques-Louis David's neoclassical art echoed these concerns for moral purity and for the emotional intensity of honest patriotism and liberty. The popularity of his paintings and of the public festivals he designed lay in the immediacy of the classical models evoked. The ancient organic unity of a people with its art and government was to be reinstituted and centuries of obscurantism in art and injustice in politics were to be swept aside forever.[20]

After the execution of Louis XVI, the revolution was irreversibly committed to the creation of a new social order, and so became increasingly committed to the restoration of the past. Mere reform was no longer possible so it was crucial that the old virtues be restored in order to make possible the implementation of old institutions. The function of the Terror was to accomplish this purification, and the increased preference for Spartan patterns rather than Athenian was that the former had been instituted through a similarly sudden transformation of the whole of society. As was true for the Anabaptists as well, the more the past was taken as a blueprint for the future the more the compromises and approximations of the intermediate centuries were thought to be intolerable, their elimination the best strategy for recovering the securities and meaningfulness of a lost Eden. So the Terror continued until its perfectionist demands collapsed, and with them the trappings of antiquity.

The excesses of the revolutionary left-wing both in the eighteenth century and in the sixteenth were matched by right-wing intransigence. Bourbon aristocrats echoed their clerical counterparts, insisting that there had been no fall from the Golden Age because traditional institutions were without blemish. Both the Roman Church and the divinely mandated kingships of France saw themselves as so securely rooted in the nature of things that they could with impunity rebuff all challenges to the status quo.

The left and right extremes thus shared an understandable concern for being linked closely to the importances of the past. They set in motion forces that threatened to destroy that link because they became overconfident. They thought they were ensconced permanently in a structure of enduring meanings that was immune to the ravages of time and change. But the ways by which I and my group are linked to regions of permanence are never secure. To think so is to court the tragic loss of those very permanences. Although structures of importance cannot be created merely by an act of human will, the proper exercise of human freedom is nonetheless crucial to their continued efficacy. Freedom, which is the enemy of stability, is also one of its necessary conditions.

In the sixteenth century disputes it was Luther who saw this most clearly and so did battle against both extremist misunderstandings at once. The Catholic claim, as argued by Eck and Cochlaeus, was that the Church had maintained organizational continuity, ceremonial uniformity, and theological infallibility through the centuries since its founding, and so did not need reform. The Anabaptists claimed that these beliefs, rituals, and offices were evidences of a fallen condition of which the Church must be immediately purged. What the Roman Catholics absolutized, the Churches of the Restoration absolutely rejected. Luther sought a middle ground, retaining both the substance of Catholic tradition and the cleansing function of Protestant criticism.[21]

The strategy of the Augsburg Confession and in general of the Reformers' writings was to argue that Rome had not remained true to the tradition it claimed to embody, and that this was the fault of Rome, not of tradition as such. Therefore by eliminating the abuses and misuses of tradition, the continuity of the faith through time could be celebrated without being absolutized. For instance, the Church councils, beginning with Nicea, were not rejected as marking the departure of the true Church from its New Testament purity, but neither were they taken as the final authority on matters of faith and practice. The councils had sought to interpret scripture and faith in the context of their historical situations, and so their actions always stood under the judgment of scripture.

As a Protestant, he [Luther] subjected the authority of church councils to the authority of the word of God; as a Catholic he interpreted the word of God in conformity with the dogmas of the councils and in this sense made the councils normative.[22]

In this same manner Richard Hooker justifies the moderate reforms of the English church by insisting that what might have been appropriate in New Testament times may not suit at all the needs of the contemporary Church. The accretions of the Roman tradition should be retained insofar as they prove 'profitable for worship' and should be rejected where they are not. The past is neither *de facto* popish and so to be condemned, nor apostolic and therefore to be preserved uncritically. But Hooker's pragmatism is tempered by his recognition that precedence is important even if not definitive. So his defense for retaining bishops is an argument that they are as old in Britain as is the Church itself:

In this realm of England, before Normans, yea before Saxons, there being Christians, the chief pastors of their soul were bishops. This order from about the first establishment of Christian Religion, which was publicly begun through the virtuous disposition of King Lucie not fully two hundred years after Christ, continued till the coming of the Saxons.[23]

Luther and Hooker were echoed by Desmoulins and Burke two centuries later, and by men and women in every time of social crisis when viewpoints polarize into absolutist extremes and the center seems no longer to hold. The middling familiar ways carry a presumption of rightness. What has been believed and acted upon again and again over the years has in its very power of survival demonstrated a capacity to keep us in tune with protecting and saving regions of the world.

The primitivists at one extreme are distressed by current goings on and imagine a past in which the binding ties to supportive powers were strong and pure. They ask me to abandon the familiar past for an idealized past, to restore Eden as the one sure way of avoiding meaninglessness. At the other extreme the traditionalists are worried by novelty, by the innovations that threaten the familiarities of the past. They ask me to abandon my ideals, to make history into Eden and so treat it as though it were a changeless realm immune to the inroads of irrelevance and insignificance.

The moderate voices of reformation understand the need continually to modify tradition in order that it might be suited to the changing world of which it is a part, but to do so by retaining rather than replacing what has gone before. The ecology of change requires that the familiar be sustained by adjusting it in detail while preserving its basic substance.

So I find my meaning in the past which has made my present possible. How I think and how I act arises from a perspective which I have inherited as a treasured gift from my parents and my society. My responsibility is to assure the vitality of this heritage by respecting the powers it makes available for my safety and fulfillment, by tailoring them to the times as necessary, and by teaching my children and my children's children not to take such linkages for granted. My descendants are to be taught that the old traditions are best, that ancient institutions, encompassing the sacred persons, places, and practices of the past, are the most trustworthy instruments for remaining closely linked to the elder ways, for remembering them, for revering and transmitting them. In this way I and my children after me become part of a many-stranded rope securing our world and its importances to the deeper significances that are its historical foundation.

Immanent in the flux of history are the permanences that rescue me, my society, and history itself, from meaninglessness. My task, the task of my community, is to preserve the ties to such realities, and where possible to knit them yet more securely.

I may be tightly linked to a past in which I trust. But how well founded is that trust? My vague sense of surrounding stabilities led me to the awareness that my world is comprised of regions of order that derive their stability from the power of the past. I could readily appreciate how the thickly woven strands of natural causation weave structures of permanence that are able to endure for years and for millenia. The inheritance from which my stately oak derives is so massive that deviation is minimal, and all the more so is this true of mountains and the solar system itself. Social order was more a problem for me because freedom is the hallmark of humanity. The perishing of a purpose is the expected result of its novel emergence into time. Disintegration and death are the price paid for the fleetingly complex and satisfying achievements of consciousness. If derivational feelings were my crowbar for prying open the prison of Cartesian immediacy, the bright new world of my enriched experience still seemed too brief to offer me the significance I crave.

But I learned that freedom can be an instrument of endurance, not simply of innovation. I discovered that the human world has historical as well as temporal depth, that human choice can be used to imitate, to repeat and reaffirm. The historical past is composed of structures that endure because they are chosen again and again by succeeding generations, are found to be more important than the possible alternatives, and so eventually become the permanent importances that undergird a meaningful social world. I discovered that my freedom is lured and cajoled by the significance of persons, places, and performances that give the world its rhyme and its reason. Fearing the loss of what they had accomplished, my ancestors sought to replicate the old in the new, and as a result they created institutions and beliefs that came to exercise a powerful hegemony over massive regions of time and space and that now command my allegiance. If I would like my purposes rescued from the momentary, if I would like my beliefs secured against error and my social institutions secured against decay, I must make these past achievements my own. My freedom must mime the choices of my ancestors so that I can participate fully in the enduring values which they fashioned and which have made me who I am.

But how deep do the roots of this social order reach into the past, how extensive are its intertwinings with the other permanences of time? My quest for an alternative to Cartesian despair has led me into a world richly historical, but the meaning it provides is still too much a creature of my freedom to rescue me fully from uncertainty and fear. I can feel the securing presence of the past, the great achievements of social permanence that encompass me. But am I rescued from the narrow present into which Descartes confined me only to discover that social meanings provide merely a temporary respite from ignorance and death? A day is better than an hour, to be sure. Yet I am filled with a profound yearning for structures of significance that stretch back into the past to the farthest reaches of human memory. How deep and wide, really, are these importances that I find incarnated in the heroes, shrines, and rituals of my society?

It has become crucial for me to learn whether the past is founded only on human freedom or whether there is something more fundamental, more stable, that has yet to be uncovered.

Five

THE MYTHIC PAST

> For myth has no means of understanding, explaining, and interpreting
> the present form of human life other than to reduce it to a remote past.
>
> Ernst Cassirer, *An Essay on Man*

i

I have tethered myself to importances in my past, to realities that I and all my comrades agree are crucial to our capacity to live secure and meaningful lives. We share a worldview, occupy a common world, and take comfort in its power to save us from confusion, despair, and oblivion. But there are other worlds than mine and ours, other perspectives, other importances to which other people are tethered. So a question rises insistently into my consciousness. What is my relationship to these other worlds? Perhaps they are a threat to the sense of meaning I enjoy, for they represent a rival order of the universe, a world with other sacred groves and ancient rituals, ones that do not value my importances nor even recognize their existence. Yet these other centers of meaning may be an opportunity for expanding my own. Perhaps we can yoke our claims of significance together to form a link to some foundation of life and destiny that is wider and deeper than what we had before.

My next question is natural enough. Why are these other people different from me and my own people? If they revere youth's vitality instead of the sagacity of age, why is this so? If their monuments commemorate other battles and their civic celebrations fete other gods, what led them into such strange beliefs and practices?

The answer ready at hand, of course, is to say this is due to their uncivilized crudity or their subhuman ignorance. They are an alien presence and should be banished from my sight, or simply exterminated. The desperate, ever-renewed clashings of armies in the night is ample evidence across the centuries that I will be perfectly willing to deal with otherness by eliminating it. My ties to historical sources of stability and fulfillment must be protected against any novelty that might untether them, and nothing is as unsettling as a whole new approach to things, an anti-world to my own. Prudence as well as fear would counsel incisive action.

I might ask my question more deeply, however, wondering about the importance of these alien importances. Could it be that their gods too are efficacious, their roots as deep as mine in the soil of enduring truth? Are there similarities amid our differences? The regions of significance to which we are each separately linked, are they themselves in some way linked as well? Is this stranger in fact my cousin, both of us children's children of the same grandparents? Do our contesting gods worship the same High God?

These questions force me to inquire into the origins and lineages of my own world as well as those of the other's world. I peer intently into the past, standing astride contemporary chasms of difference but wondering if somewhere beyond the frontiers of that mysterious past I might catch a glimpse of terrain where what is now separated was once united. If so, perhaps the meanings I treasure can be linked with other meanings and our combined treasury secured even more firmly against transcience and chaos.

The webwork of past connections spreads swiftly. Antecedent relevance is an exponential function of time: the more ancient the ties, the more widespread they will have subsequently become. My own genealogical linkages to the past, for example, fan out in pyramidal fashion as I trace back my ancestral ties from generation to generation. If I limit myself simply to two parents for each person in my genealogy, then the number of ancestors I have in any single generation will be equal to 2^x where x is the number of generations separating the one in question from that of my parents. Each generation the number of my ancestors doubles (fig. 1). Thus in the tenth generation back there will already be 1,024 persons from whom I can claim descent. When I in my turn marry, my wife's ancestry to the same distance back results in a second set of 1,024 patriarchs and matriarchs, all 2,048 of them comprising the eleventh generation of those from whom our children will be descended.

FIGURE 1

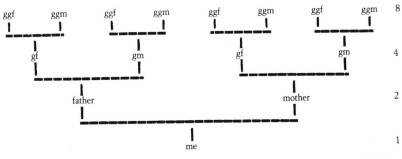

gf = grandfather   gm = grandmother
ggf = great-grandfather   ggm = great-grandmother

A similar exponential tree can be created by working the other direction, by tracing descendants of a particular ancestor. If I focus on only one parent, for instance the father, and assume that in each generation he has two sons, then ten generations of sons and grandsons will result in a grand total of 2,048 male descendants, 1,024 of them comprising the tenth and most recent cadre of male stalwarts (fig. 2).

FIGURE 2

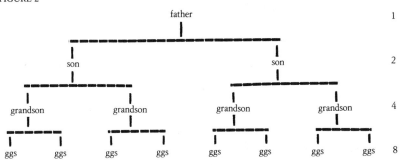

ggs = great-grandson

This simple process of tracing out genealogical trees looks like a promising way to secure the connections among people and their practices that will give my world the desired historical and geographic massiveness. By blood ties alone, as these simple models of inheritance disclose, my way of life is embedded in a network of similar beliefs and practices that has spatial as well as temporal thickness. Since the volume of my contemporaries who are a part of this network grows larger as our common origins are traced to ever more ancient ancestors, it would seem that breadth and depth are directly linked. A region of importance becomes massive in both dimensions, and it therefore has precisely the power needed to be a bulwark against confusion and transience. Genealogical linkage, it would seem, is the best route leading from Descartes' solitary isolation in the present moment to full participation within a meaningful and viable world.

My genealogical model, however, is far too artificial. Its account of ancestry ignores all members of a family other than the parental pair of a single offspring. Similarly, it traces descent in a strictly patrilinear way. Suppose, in contrast, I were enlightened enough to give equal importance in the descending genealogy to the women in my family. This is, after all, what I did when I traced genealogical ascent through both parents.

My ancestor, that patriarch at the tenth generation remove from me, the one who had so many male descendants: he also had a wife. The two of them have the same set of descendants, although completely divergent forebears. Suppose I continue to permit them only two children, both of whom marry. The first round of descendants now has four persons, the two children plus their spouses. Yet if I am to take seriously the equality between male and female in this genealogy, I must now enlarge the initial generation to include the parents of my ancestor's children's spouses. That now gives me three sets of parents: my ancestor and his wife, his son-in-law's parents, and his daughter-in-law's parents. My ancestor and his wife have had their own children accounted for in this genealogy, but the other two sets of parents each still have only one of their children accounted for. So I add in the other two children, giving me six people in the generation of the children and six in the generation of their parents. But now those six children include two whose spouses I have neglected to include, and when I add them in I must add their parents and their siblings also. And so it goes endlessly. To include in my genealogy not only the sons and daughters but their spouses and their spouses' parents is to generate an indefinite regress laterally. If there were no intermarriage, the regress would continue until every member of the human race was included.

This kind of regression is trivializing. It leads to the truism that we are all members of the same species. What I wanted to know, on the contrary, was the ways by which I and my people are different from the human race in general. I am in quest of a genealogical linkage to centers of historical importance. Amid the rise and fall of the nations, the emergence and collapse of leaders or ideas or institutions, I am in search of saving ties to something more permanent. There exists some lineage, I fervently hope, that identifies me as part of a family, clan, people whose long endurance as a coherent whole gives evidence of its favored status within the scheme of things.

The perspective on life thereby provided should be as broadly gauged as possible. But unless this perspective, this world and the securities it provides, is clearly contrasted to other real and possible perspectives of lesser import, the meaningfulness of my specific way of life will be washed too thin. That we will all be saved from historical oblivion is less likely than that a special few might be.

I had thought that membership in an historically continuous tradition would provide precisely the requisite distinctiveness. My ancestors, along with their holy places and sacred rites, represent a world apart from other's worlds. But I seem trapped in a surprising dilemma. As I attempt to stretch this ancestry back into the past, tracing the tree of my inheritance down toward its fundamental tap roots, it becomes increasingly diffuse and irrelevant. This hemorrhaging of importance must be staunched. Fortunately, by using any of four controlling principles it is possible to do just that.

The first method for controlling exponential diffusion is to be selective. The scope of membership at each stage in a sequence can be delimited by ignoring whatever does not contribute directly to the transformation of some mere plurality of members into a single organized sequence. The task of a genealogy is to turn a heap of derivational events into a temporal chain of influences. Only those who contribute to the forging of that chain need be counted in the membership it defines.

My initial restriction of the descent model to males had a specific even if arbitrary purpose. The principle of monarchy, for instance, or the law of primogeniture, restricts genealogical descent to a single member in each generation. No matter how many children a set of parents may produce, only one of them plays a relevant role in the sequence of inheritance. The next monarch or the next owner of the estate is a single individual who with his or her spouse comprises a successor generation no more extensive quantitatively than its predecessor. Dilution of authority and of property is thus prevented. The importance of both being preserved, that importance grows in virtue of its ever-thickening duration.

The full strength of a given achievement is rescued in this way from the debilitations that would be introduced by enlarging its scope. More sons and daughters might be involved in the exercise of royal power, more might share in possession of the land. But the greater scope would mean fragmenting power and authority, scattering it among the plurality of progeny.

This would entail greater occasions for disagreement, greater need for compromise, and the likelihood that these disharmonies would eventuate in the fading of whatever significance had once been invested in the inheritance. Eliminating from relevance all but the first-born may be arbitrary, inequitable, and often tragic. But it efficiently achieves its purpose of preserving a concrete value and enhancing it.

People of flesh and bone, of course, are not as tidy in their progenitive activities as these models suggest. Illegitimate offspring, barren marriages and second marriages, disease and warfare, all conspire to distort the smooth unrolling of primogeniture, complicated still further by the tendency of younger brothers and sisters, or their spouses, to challenge the rights of the eldest sibling. Yet, amid this confusion, the principle of exclusion works. It serves to define the parameters of the dispute and to point the way toward a resolution of issues that will retain monarchical authority or land ownership intact.

Consider the Plantagenets. When the son of Geoffrey of Anjou came to the throne of England in 1154 as Henry II, he began a dynasty that flourished through ten generations until, with the coronation of Henry VII 331 years later, it was supplanted by the house of Tudor. If the abstract descent model of two children per generation were to have held on the average, Henry Plantagenet would have been blessed with 1,024 descendants belonging to the generation of Henry Tudor, each of whom might have some conceivable claim to the English throne. In actual fact only two of Henry Tudor's genealogical peers, plus one person in the immediately elder generation, vied with him for becoming the successor to Edward IV (fig. 3).

Edward's brother Richard ordered one of these potential successors, his young nephew Edward V, imprisoned and killed, an effective fifteenth-century device for settling such disputes. The Lancaster claimant, Edward the son of Henry VI, was likewise excluded by violent means from exercising his claim. Authority then shifted back to the prior generation as Edward's brother assumed the crown as Richard III. But when Richard's brief rule perished on Bosworth Field, there perished with it the glories of Plantagenet. The fourth of the claimants became the first of the Tudors.

The line from Henry II to Henry VII is thus no simple sequence running from father to son, ten kings in ten generations. Fifteen monarchs ascend the throne in that generational span, and thrice authority shifts away from direct descendants of the king to a collateral line, first to Lancaster, then York, and at the end to a family tradition lacking any connection with Plantagenet except through marriage. Yet England's single monarchy

FIGURE 3

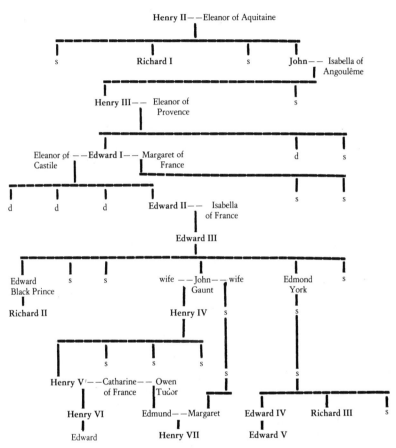

The sequence of kings:
    Plantagenent: Henry II, Richard I, John, Henry III, Edward I,
        Edward II, Edward III, Richard II
    Lancaster: Henry IV, Henry V, Henry VI
    York: Edward IV, Edward V, Richard III
    Tudor: Henry VII

is preserved despite these threats to its principle. Henry Tudor's authority is as undilute as that of his predecessors and the importance of English monarchy is secured by its ability to claim unbroken continuity back to the first Plantagenet, indeed back beyond that to kings as old as England, as old as the English peoples themselves.

The radical purity of the exclusion principle is gained, however, at the price of narrowness. The battlefields of the world are strewn with the corpses of kings who could claim direct descent from prior legitimacies but who lacked the needed political massiveness that comes from the support of collateral importances. Thus exclusion is best combined with a second principle, that of subordination. Those who are not firstborn need not be put to death or sent into exile. They can participate in the single-focused authority or ownership of their elder sibling by acting as his representative. Exclusion from power is transmuted into the exercise of that power on behalf of its possessor. The second sons become leaders of septs within the clan, are given ducal estates within the kingdom, serve as officers of government.

In this way the exponential thickening of descent can be retained, but with a structure of hierarchy replacing the all or nothing requirements of primogenitary inheritance. The discord of multiple claimants is overcome by an ordering of relationships that defines relevance in terms of degrees rather than absolutes.

This is nicely illustrated by the difference in the two genealogies for Jesus recorded in the New Testament. When the author of the gospel of Luke has finished his account of the conception, birth, and youth of Jesus, he is confronted with a problem of authority. Jesus has been baptized and his role as messianic Son of God proclaimed, but how will Luke convince his readers that this claim is to be taken seriously? The answer is a genealogy. With deft economy, Luke tracks the patrilineage of Jesus back generation by generation: Jesus son of Joseph, son of Heli, son of Matthat; and so on to Nathan, son of David, son of Jesse; continuing to Jacob, son of Isaac, son of Abraham; and still onward to Enosh, son of Seth, son of Adam, son of God [Luke 3:23-28].

From Jesus back to God Himself, a direct patrimony defined by primogeniture is sketched out in 77 steps. Its purpose is to demonstrate the truth of the claim of Jesus' divine sonship and therefore of his rootage in the saving power that relationship entails. Such a direct and unequivocal anchorage in this fundamental tradition of religious and social importances was a powerful argument to those whose search for authority and its assurances insisted upon precisely that route of inheritance as its necessary condition.

Luke's dramatic clarity in tracing Jesus' lineage is potentially at the expense of breadth, however. The author of Matthew's gospel is more careful to be explicitly encompassing. The question of genealogy is addressed at the very beginning of the gospel [Matthew 1:1-16], providing the initial context for any narratives about Jesus. This contrasts with Luke's use of the genealogy merely as a proof of authority, introduced opportunely at the point where Jesus is ready to begin his messianic ministry. Moreover, Matthew's genealogy proceeds from past to present rather than the reverse, emphasizing the spread of descendancy rather than focusing solely on the link between the first and last members in the sequence.

The progenitor of Matthew's genealogical account is Abraham, not God, for this is an account of a people and the Messiah's place within that collectivity, not just a proof of one person's lineage. Abraham, Isaac, and Jacob initiate the sequence, but Jacob is identified as the father of "Judah and his brothers." Although the inheritance is still traced through the eldest of Israel's sons, all twelve are mentioned for they are leaders of the wider collection of tribes over which Judah's hegemony is exercised. Judah and his wife Tamar are together named as the progenitors of Perez and Zarah. The genealogy then continues through Perez, the elder brother. But Zarah has not been forgotten. Mention of him implies that his progeny are also to be included in the descent even though within a subordinating perspective. And thusly the genealogy proceeds until in three series of fourteen it comes at last to Joseph who is father of "Jesus called Messiah."

For Matthew the authority of the messianic claim is thus traced by a combination of selection and subordination. The resulting hierarchy encompasses a complex of tribes and patriarchs, kings and priests, but without loss of the specific ordering required to demonstrate direct descent. The descent is of an explicit individual man Jesus but it is set amid a people Israel, the members of the wider lineage being the recipients of the salvation claimed as coming through the mediation of the person profiled in the narrower lineage.

Jesus did not descend from King David by means of a direct line of kings. The temporal power of the Davidic line had been humiliated, confused, and dispersed. The longing for a Messiah was an expression of this discord and dispersal of authority, the positing of a time when David's power would be reestablished, the deep-rooted tree of Israel's significance serving to give sustenance to a new growth sprung up from the stump of Jesse. Hence Matthew had to conceive the descent in general terms, so as to involve the full scope of all the seed of Abraham. Within that scope, and subordinating its details to himself, the individual genealogy of the Messiah could be traced.

Thus the principle of selection had to temper elimination with hierarchic inclusion if it was to preserve the significance of Israel's mission against the seeming destruction of its capacity to perform that mission. With the kingdom of David lost forever, David *redivivus* would need to be descended in a more generous sense than Luke's strict father-to-son sequence allows. Luke cared little about this sense of the messianic role and so could afford to ignore the problem, but for Matthew it was central.

Henry Tudor's problem regarding genealogical authority was similar to Matthew's. When he ascended the throne of England he did so without any direct male blood ties to the royal house. The Lancastrian and Yorkish lines had ended without living issue, but Henry's grandfather, Owen Tudor, had married the former wife of the last Lancastrian. Out of this slim thread Henry VII would need to weave his claim to legitimacy. Henry first of all subordinated every aspect of the rich possibilities of his family tree to the chain linking him through his father to his grandmother Catherine, wife of the great Henry V. From there the direct lineage to Henry II and beyond is secured.

This single-stranded perspective by itself is insufficient for Henry Tudor's purposes, however. Applied along a route of descent rather than ascent, direct lineage as the sole principle of sovereignty would for England end up in nothing. Not only would Henry Tudor have no claim to the English crown, but no one else would either. The kingdom would be without legitimate heir. Whoever ruled would be by necessity an usurper whose credentials for leadership rested only on his current actions and not on his heredity. So Henry had secondly to establish the concept of a general rather than specific inheritance. Tudor authority required a genealogy of subordination, not simply one of elimination. The sons and daughters of Plantagenet by blood and by marriage had to be understood as forming an order of authority within which acts of salience and subservience could then serve to define who was to be the actual reigning monarch.

The principle of elimination, even when tempered by a principle of subordination, is still inadequate. It gains clarity but does so by losing scope. For instance, most of the descendants of Israel are excluded completely as distinct, named individuals from Luke's genealogy, for no hierarchical strategy would hope to make sense out of an exponential growth extending over 77 generations. In the Lukean sequence, and merely on the strict model of two, the scions of God in the generation of Jesus would be 1.5×10^{23}, a figure 50 trillion times greater than the population of the world in 1980. Obviously another controlling principle, that of simplification, is needed.

By means of this new principle all members of a particular group are retained in the descriptive account, but only under an aspect. For instance, a statistical presentation of the geographical spread of a population would view each individual member solely in terms of his or her ordinal existence and spatial location. Whatever the personal characteristics, the life story, the social role, the hopes and fears of each individual, these are all neglected in order to focus only upon the two relevant aspects: size and location. A small band of Hebrew ethnics wandered in the Sinai, settled west of the Jordan, secured political hegemony over the north-south trading corridor between Egypt and Mesopotamia, were subjugated and dispersed, and ended up as part of the underclass within first the Hellenistic and then the Roman empires. Simplification could also be used to describe those same Hebrews in terms of their religious attitudes, including a display of the distribution by region, social class, and age of those who say they expect the imminent coming of a Messiah.

By retaining a sense for the whole of a population, even though the sense be thin, it becomes possible to see uniformities and patterns obscured by the complexity of the fully concrete reality. To see a pattern in what seemed mere confusion requires retaining all or nearly all of the components that comprise the complex, but it also requires eliminating or pushing into a background the details likely to obscure the presence of that pattern.

Thus Matthew locates messianic authority in the genealogical transmission line from Abraham to Jesus, and by focusing on only this one aspect of the lives and times of the Hebrew peoples over centuries, he is able to note that the historical sequence falls conveniently into groupings of fourteen. From Abraham to David, from David's son to the Babylonian exile, from the exile to Jesus: in each subset there are fourteen generations. So Jesus comes at a point in his lineage that is as important as the time when the Davidic kingdom was established and as important as when it was destroyed. Here now, at the third turning of the cycle, comes the time of its reestablishment. Moreover each group of fourteen is composed of two groups of seven, each the analogue in generations of the seven days of creation. With Jesus six such cycles have been completed, a cycle of the cycles brought to the threshold of its Great Sabbath rest in the apocalyptic ending of what creation began.

Simplification reveals pattern, and pattern gives significance to the present moment beyond its significance as part of an ancient continuity. The place of the present moment within a durational sequence becomes nodal if it marks the anniversary of that pattern's origin, the moment of return to the beginning of the cycle, to the birth of significance. Genealogy has *kairos* as well as *chronos*. The Messiah comes not merely at the end of a long thin line of authority reaching back to Abraham or to God, for each new generation has marked the temporary endpoint in that sequence and so none is more significant than any other. The Messiah comes in the fullness of time, at the moment when the end mirrors the beginning by recapitulating it. Within the rhythms of the Abrahamic genealogy, this the time of Jesus' birth is a downbeat, a stroke of emphasis, the moment long awaited when ancient prophecies shall be fulfilled and sacred beginnings brought to their fruition.

In the narrower confines of English politics the first Tudor king is careful to take the name of Henry as his ruling name. This act can serve as a symbol of the return to the line of Henrys begun by the second of that name and brought to apotheosis in the glories of the fifth. The place of the new monarch in the pattern of English royalty is bolstered by his place in the sequence of noble Henrys.

Simplification involves abstraction, and the problem with abstraction is that it entails a loss in depth. The rich texture of individuality is smoothed out into the bland uniformity of some shared and quantifiable aspect, the robust seriousness of real things turned into cabalistic playfulness. If the strategy of elimination or subordination produces too narrow a tie with antiquity, the strategy of simplification produces too thin a tie. The former sacrifices breadth in order to retain the pure intensity of individual accomplishment; the latter sacrifices depth in order to retain the massiveness of widespread implication. But the centers of the world's importances have both breadth and depth. My rootage in such important regions can therefore be fully present for me only if I can find a way to combine the virtues of both intensity and massiveness in the approach I take toward controlling the exponential trivialization of my inheritance.

This will require the introduction of a fourth principle, that of cumulation, as a supplement to the triad of elimination, subordination, and simplification. I need a way to cumulate the achievements of each member of a sequence, to gather up aspects and characteristics of the predecessors into the lives of the successors. Such a principle would thus give time primacy over space, for by means of temporal accumulation the individuality of what was can be retained as a relevant element in the individuality of what is, each current space made radiant with the glow of what had formerly provided shape and content to that region of the world.

My ancestors are closely linked to specific places where important deeds were accomplished. These deeds might be ritualistic events, occurring at the place where a blood oath of loyalty was pledged, ceremonies performed at the place where the thank offering of first fruits is regularly made. Or they might be the sweat and toil of transforming wilderness into cultivated land or shaping group behaviors into the habits of social custom and institutional expectation. But whatever the specific character of the actions, their association with the places of their exercise means that those places are recalled wherever the acts of importance are once again celebrated.

When I offer sacrifice in the temple at Jerusalem I act on behalf of all of Israel, recalling the mighty acts of Yahweh in the oath at Mispah and on Sinai, remembering the humble labors of cultivation that turned this barren land into a cornucopia for my neighbors and their children's children, echoing the rituals of worship in each home and the daily forms of public interaction that define my culture's uniqueness. Those places all across this land where the meanings were born that now define who I am and hope to be are thus heaped up one upon the other until they fill the confines of this temple with various and ancient meanings. The people are their land because they are the history that unfolded there.

This notion of the cumulative power of temporal duration gives a new dimension to the full sense of what Plantagenet means. Henry II was king of England, ruler of a bounded realm located in the southern portions of a modestly sized island. But he could also claim, by right of inheritance through his father, extensive lands in the north of France: Normandy, Maine, Touraine, and Anjou. When Henry then married Eleanor of Aquitaine, Plantagenet splendor could proclaim its right to lands in the south of France as well: Poitou, Guienne, Toulouse, and Gascony. King Henry also claimed feudal fealty over Scotland, Wales, Ireland, and Brittany. Marriages in subsequent generations linked Plantagenet blood to the additional continental regions of Angoulême, Provence, and Castile. When Edward III in 1338 laid claim to the crown of France, his justifications were far from arbitrary even though they were hardly well grounded in direct lines of blood and tradition.

A hundred years of indecisive war did little to resolve this dispute, until Henry V subdued Charles of France by force of arms and his daughter Kate by charm. The child of their marriage, Henry VI, was crowned King of both England and France, but at too young an age and in too uncertain a time to long endure. By the middle of the fifteenth century England had lost most of its French possessions, and by the time a generation thereafter when Henry Tudor came to power the island kingdom was content to forget these ancient claims and to find its legitimacy and grandeur in other deeds and other genealogies.

Plantagenet kingship thus meant not only ancient rootages in an enduring structure of importance but a landscape in which that authority was to
be properly exercised. The person of Henry V meant the unity of England
and France, the exercise of single power in a domain with a defined extent,
a past of conflating strands and a single-purposed future. The geography
of an island and a neighboring landmass was thereby defined by its temporal relationships. Massiveness in scope was achieved through the abstract
notion of geographic ownership or political fealty, and concreteness or
depth of intensity retained through the fact that land, soil and rock, was
the reality being encompassed.

Yet geography is impersonal and its contents not sufficiently ordered to
provide the vividness and immediacy needed to tie each individual firmly
and enduringly to transcending importances. The idea of motherland or
fatherland, of Alma Mater or The Firm, can be a powerful influence on
my attitudes and behaviors. But such experiences are unfocused. I am
nostalgic about college, but find it difficult to link that nostalgia to any of
the specific people or buildings or traditions that comprise my campus.
My heart is filled with patriotism for the land in which I dwell as a citizen,
but I yearn to reach through this diffuse loyalty to something more vibrant,
more specific, to incarnated ideals and specific actions capable of symbolizing that loyalty.

Elimination, subordination, abstraction, and cumulation are each crucial tools for concentrating the connections between myself and the past
in such a way that I become intensely aware of their world-shaping
importance. But I need yet an additional instrument — typification — before
my sense of such linkages is sufficient to rescue me, assuredly and at last,
from my Cartesian fears.

ii

To typify a person, deed, or place is to make it the fully adequate locus
for a complex webwork of meanings. It is the simultaneous, coordinated
application of all four of the previously discussed intensification principles
to a single phenomenon. For example, this is the technique employed to
less than moral purpose by Johannes the Seducer.[1] Johannes seeks maximal erotic satisfaction from the opportunities with which the world presents him. His strategy is in contrast to that of Don Juan who on each new
occasion takes his pleasure with whatever woman chances to be his
companion. Johannes realizes the inherent danger in such an approach:
there may not be a woman available at some particular moment; she may
lack the ability to satisfy him adequately; the memory of old loves or the

anticipation of future ones might detract from the immediate experiences of enjoyment. So Johannes develops a qualitative strategy whereby he will seduce but a single woman within a given six month period, but will do so in such a manner that the culmination of that seduction will bring greater fulfillment for him than the total of six months' worth of daily seductions brings Don Juan.

By 'cultivating' his victim, Cordelia, from springtime when he meets her until the autumn when his harvest of enjoyment is reaped, Johannes invests the final moment of seduction with the meanings and values that define each of the steps in his seduction plan. He meets Cordelia for the first time, and bows a formal greeting. This event is then carried forward each day in memory and combined with that day's relevant anticipations. Each subsequent day renews Johannes' memory of that first meeting with Cordelia, but each day's remembering is filled with new meaning and importance in the light of what has happened in the interim and what new shape his future expectations have taken. When the final night arrives, the moment for his seduction of Cordelia at an isolated farmhouse, Johannes possesses, as it were, 180 memories of his first encounter with her, each one different because each remembered from a different perspective along the trajectory of the seduction. All of these memories have been brought forward and are concentrated together as elements within the experience of the seduction itself, along with an equal number of anticipatory feelings now remembered as characterizing each step along the way.

The snowball effect is given further dimensionality by the fact that Johannes keeps a diary in which each occasion for directly interacting with Cordelia, for remembering past interactions, and for anticipating future ones, is relived yet again within the literary mode of diary authorship. Moreover, Cordelia is not a neutral consistency throughout this process. Her deception is accomplished by a process of wooing in which Johannes enhances her own personal accomplishments in all possible ways: intellectually, socially, emotionally. She grows up as she falls in love with him, becomes one of the most talented and interesting young women in all of Copenhagen, eventually seeks out his love, and herself freely chooses to come to the farmhouse rendezvous.

Johannes has selected one individual, eliminating the quantitative project pursued by Don Juan with his 1,003 seductions in Spain alone. He has subordinated all of his various activities throughout the half year of seduction into a hierarchy defined by the relevance of each to the primary end of his labors. His remembrance and anticipation of each moment in the process, of each phase composed of those moments, of the whole in each of its possible configurations, involve constant imaginative abstraction from concrete reality. And all of this is accumulated so as to reappear within the final, culminating event as its meaning. The depth and breadth of Johannes' farmhouse experience is magnificent: it reaches back in time to the origin of his enterprise and it stretches out to encompass every aspect of his conscious life throughout the landscape of his actions. His whole life, his whole world, for that six months is present vividly and fully in the act that brings it to completion.

This is the architecture of *kairos*. Johannes is in this sense only aping for his immoral purposes the strategy of messiahship—so to construe an event that it gives meaning to the range of events which preceded it, catches them up into its significance, presents them in the present moment as having been in order that this occasion might be the importance which it has become. A messiah suddenly appearing and for the first time announced as the fulfillment of the past would be a pale imitation of a messiah longed for generation after generation. Such a messiah is remembered by believers in each historical era as the one prophesied to come; he is anticipated by these believers as soon to fulfill those prophesies; the events of the day are read as signs confirming or beclouding these memories and hopes. Year by year, generation by generation, the pious acts of the living, their rememberings, their expectations, occur and themselves become part of this continuing memory, this recurrent hope. And then in the fullness of time, behold! He comes, bearing into the present the meaning of all that past, giving sense and shape to the future over which he shall preside.

In typification a single person, place, or deed comes to embody in its momentary reality this whole panorama of meaning. Past, present, and future are woven together by means of something that is their juncture. Although sacred places and salvific deeds play this role, they usually do so in derivative fashion. For it is the individual above all else that can best typify historical processes and their meaning. Let me call such a person a hero even if it might seem inappropriate to encompass with the same term not only saints and conquerors, statesmen and adventurers, but seducers and messiahs as well.

The hero, it might be said, is a form of cultural synecdoche. A part, a single individual living at a specific time and in a specific place, comes to stand for the whole of a process, of a tradition or of a people. Yet for those who read their world that way, this person is not merely a sign for the whole nor its metaphor. He is a hologram, a part containing the whole in some vivid fashion. Or more accurately still, the hero *is* that whole, whether as the latest scion who embodies the ancestral many or as the original member pregnant with the descendant many. The Zen Buddhist claims that I will discover in a *satori* experience that the distinctive 'thisness' of the passing moment, the *tathata* character of experience, is at the same time *sunyata*, the unconditioned, undelimitable, wholeness of all reality.[2] To see eternity in a dewdrop, all of history in a gesture, is for Zen eyes not a mysterious penetration behind the veil of appearances but rather a straightforward grasp of what is there to everyday experience once properly enlightened. The hero is his people, his acts their history come alive as present reality, his intentions their destiny made manifest. For the members of that society, it takes no special training, requires no mystical or erudite elite, to grasp this fact. One need but look. Such truth is always self-evident.

Typification in the form of herohood is thus a way by which the past, and to some degree the future as well, becomes transparent to the present. In condensing the past by packing it into the present, there is no loss of whatever is essential. The textured variety of the past, the complexity of its meanings and direction, is retained even while being epitomized. Elimination, subordination, and simplification serve this process by helping enhance the essential, by transforming what is trivial into elements of what is valuable. It is as though impurities were being winnowed away leaving a substance which because purged of unessentials can shine forth with transparent vibrancy, providing an inner illumination to the present. The hero is radiant with the meanings he incarnates. That is why the hero's presence is its own interpreter. There is no need for the extrinsic light of scholarship or faith to see him by. As with a painting that has undergone *pentimento*, the person who stands before my eyes is revealed as possessing a profoundly temporal depth. Older realities have reasserted themselves within the translucency of his present reality.

The epistemology of typification is fundamental to everyday perception. Its extension to the experience of heroes is thus quite natural, and helps explain why the singling out of heroes and the appreciation of their authority is a phenomenon as ancient as human history. The sophistication required to see and hear and touch is sufficient to permit me to see my past in the faces of the great men and women whose heroic deeds founded my nation, to hear the significance of my past in the famous words of prophets and kings, to touch the living reality of those importances in the institutions and monuments that serve as tangible evidences of my civilization's achievements. For all perception transmutes Truth into Beauty for the sake of understanding it.[3]

Any perspective that makes sense, any coherent worldview, involves the intensifications I have been discussing. Some of these I invent myself or share with a chosen few. But some are the work of culture, the sedimented characterization of a people's history in terms of selections, subordinations, abstractions, and cumulations that have been affirmed and reaffirmed generation after generation until they define the very shape of things. Into the world composed of those typifications I have been born. My culture has chosen me and not I it. I need to structure my experience in terms of typifications in order to make sense of it, and the ones that can do that effectively are ones I discover rather than invent. I need the typifications provided by my culture in order to make sense of myself, to find my place within a scheme of things. The hero as embodiment of all my people's meanings, their sense of historical purpose and relevance, is the apotheosis of this process, the key reason why a vast multiplicity of persons can nonetheless become one people.

Not only is the actual whole of an inherited past complex and its relationships exponentially intertwined, but the variety of its details is confused, involving mutual incompatabilities, sometimes even contradiction. As an individual whose freedom includes the power to shape experience in the ways already discussed, I choose to eliminate or otherwise transform some of this cacophony in order to permit what remains to have a proper integrity. But my imagination can subsequently reintroduce what I have initially excluded. I can recall with nostalgia or regret what might have been; in hope or fear I can fantasize about what still might come to pass. What my sense of reality requires me to remove from experience can nonetheless be drawn back in, without loss of coherence for that reality, by means of the mind's inventiveness.

This undercuts the harmony of feeling that is an important aspect of any world's reality, however. My sense of what is in fact the case finds itself unsettled by the realization that there is something more than fact to be taken account of. My present experience is thus tinctured by an awareness of unrealized possibility, of a different construal for my world than what actually occurred.

The contrast might be a source of disappointment, of embarrassment. There are things I should have done differently, opportunities I failed to take advantage of, deeds which would have been better left undone. I might even find myself feeling strangely insecure, haunted by the realization that my actual situation falls terribly short of what it could so easily have been. Or things might have been much worse, of course. My choices might have narrowly avoided some unhappy eventuality. That too is in its own way disturbing, for I would usually prefer to think my successes were predetermined to manifest themselves in the world and not that they appear only as the result of problematic contingencies. Yet these unsettling threats to harmony are, it turns out, the key to its enrichment, to the creation and discovery of deeper, more enduring harmonies.

To some degree such disharmonies in the actual world can be resolved by means of routine accommodation. My religious rituals and yours can both be tolerated by refusing to see them as in support of differing gods. If your god and mine are essentially the same, two manifestations of the same reality rather than two distinct realities, then our rituals can be taken to be two differing but equally viable forms of worship. My shrines and yours both honor the same High God. Our separate priestly lines can even be fused by the simple device of mutual ordination. In similar fashion one generation within a culture adjusts to the changing interests and understandings of its successor generation. We worship God in the traditional ways, they in modern innovative ways. But whether the hymns be by Charles Wesley with organ accompaniment or by Bob Dylan with the assistance of guitars, the music in both cases rises in homage to the same Lord.

Fundamentally, however, the complexity of actual accomplishment within a culture is too richly varied to permit such simple solutions. Some elimination of proposed forms of realization is required, if only to reduce the vastly many to a manageable few. But this creates the fault-lines of irremediable loss that always scar so badly the smooth surface of some desired social harmony. What might have been secures its advocates, who contrast these lost possibilities invidiously with the actual present. The result might be an attempt to recover what has been perceived as lost, but success in this regard will only create a new loss, the demise of what was abandoned for the sake of what was recovered. Once the Rubicon is crossed from inclusion to exclusion, and the requirements of coherence and hence of any accomplishment require this, then harmony always finds itself embraced by a penumbra of contrasting potential harmonies. This cacophony among 'is' and 'was' and 'ought to be' is debilitating, for it shatters every attempt to link the occupants of a region into a cultural whole and to link their collective present with its past, to deepen the significance of diversity by making it into a unity.

This is where imagination plays its positive role, finding a way to transform discordance into concord. The Plantagenet kings, for example, are an historically interesting bunch. Each individual king is himself a divergent set of acts, intentions, and emotions. A biography of Henry V would be filled with accounts of his contrasting self-expressions, and his biographer would try to show how these can all be woven together into some kind of consistent fabric. Henry did and thought many incompatable things, but some are to be taken more seriously than others, some were transitional and others foundational, some require re-interpretation. An attempt at profiling Henry's character would be essayed in this way. It would be a process of conflating concrete plurality into a focused unity. The success or failure of the biographer would be measured by the ability of the book to find or fashion a perspective capable of encompassing the roil of specific facts within a plausible unified perspective.

The line of Plantagenet kings itself comprises a similar set of divergencies, but in this case the seemingly incompatible elements are persons instead of characteristics of a person. Each king's biographer, actual or implicit, has provided a subtle picture of the unity underlying a lifetime of varied deeds. Each unifying perspective now needs to be further simplified in order for it to become part of a new fabric, to become an element within the unified whole identified as the kings of England from Henry II through Richard III.

At its extreme, this might take the form of defining each monarch in terms of a specific deed (Henry V: victor at Agincourt; Richard III: murderer and usurper) or even a specific moral quality (good king Henry; evil king Richard). The overall unity of the royal line can then be profiled in terms of a tale of wars and intrigue or in terms of the struggle between good and evil. For other even more broadly gauged purposes, the Plantagenets as a whole might be characterized in similar monosyllabic fashion: the era of the Plantagenets was a time of war, an age of change.

But all of this is merely elimination by abstraction unless imagination is allowed to perform a further service. The unified profile of Henry or Richard needs to be applied to the region of their manifold individual activities. This simplification needs to be seen as though it were a reality fully present within each of the specific actions for which it has provided a summarizing perspective. Henry's goodness must be seen as present in each of his acts, perhaps not always manifest but nonetheless always present as a contributing cause, a continuing thread of consistency among the sequence of events. If goodness is not taken to be merely the invention of Henry's biographer, a shorthand summary concerning a multitude of qualities characterizing a multitude of individual acts, then it will be seen as a sustained reality present in each of them. It is taken as their underlying unity instead of being thought of as an unity imposed by the overlay of an interpretation. Because Henry is good, he acts in a morally consistent manner. Richard murders his nephews because he is evil.

In this act of imagination the details are not lost. They remain in all their cacophonous plurality, each vividly and immediately present to memory or experience. But for anyone who now remembers those past deeds, each seems to have been what it was in virtue of a deeper unity that caused or shaped its existence. So the contradictions within the pluralism of Henry's life are taken to be superficial, surface differences masking profounder truths regarding the persistence and unity of his character. Young Harry may seem the rascal, a wanton and irresponsible fool, but beneath the surface lurks the good king Henry. The sobering press of events, or perhaps merely his own secret purposes, will eventually reveal to the world this deeper truth.

So two things happen in this transmogrification. First of all, an abstraction is taken to be concrete. Events in a sequence, each marked by qualities unique to it, are treated as though they were really a single enduring quality. Second, this enduring quality is said to sustain or cause the sequence of events. Thus a characterization of some items in the world is taken as their cause, an interpretive perspective turned into a causative power. As a result, a third thing happens: disharmonies are reconciled, a basic harmony born that smooths out the apparent differences.

But if a single quality can be distributed by imagination along a series of distinct occurrences, then it is possible to use a single occurrence, one in which that quality is especially manifest, to epitomize that same series. Qualities, after all, are slippery and moral qualities are intangible, difficult to grasp or identify and therefore even adequately to name. But a deed is immediate, vividly a 'that' which intrudes itself sturdily into experience.[4] If an individual's life can be characterized by a deed rather than a character trait, or rather if the trait can be identified with the deed, incarnated in it, then the immediacy of that person's life will be notably enhanced.

The victory of Henry V at Agincourt exhibited in one way or another all his virtues and probably most of his vices. Certainly his valor, his military intelligence, his skills of leadership, were in evidence. As were also his compassion, his concern for the men he commanded and for the nation whose glory he sought to enhance. His goodness was this mix of bravery and care, and the triumph against overwhelming odds on a rain-drenched autumn field in northern France was proof of its historical power. Agincourt is Henry's goodness made visible in terms of its civilizational significance. It epitomizes him as he, in his victory there, epitomizes England. To meet Henry at another time, perhaps to visit with him at court years later, would be to come face to face with Agincourt, to see and touch those earlier deeds of historical greatness, to know firsthand England's virtue and its destiny.

Henry remains a man of many deeds, some foolish and others wise. But now each deed is impregnated with the reality of Agincourt and of all the valorous, compassionate qualities that Agincourt means. The drunken young Harry is only seemingly the fool; he is Agincourt anticipated, England preparing for its emergence as Europe's dominant power. The king in death is remembered not only as a victorious conqueror whose dreams of empire were cut short by a far too early death. He is remembered also as Agincourt, as the concrete reality that was England's triumphal moment and that assures it future triumphs of equal grandeur.

Yet even Agincourt is too complex an event, too subtle a reality, to provide the absolute immediacy I seek, the unalloyed intensity that comes through a direct encounter with the whole import of being English. A cameo moment within the whole is needed, a story with a climax that captures in a deed of simple human proportions the essence of Henry and so of his victory and so of his people's history. That cameo need have no actual root in the events it is to epitomize, the qualities of personhood it is to bring into focus. Imagination is given free rein to invent as it will, but the result must be a gesture made that should have been made, a word said that surely must have been spoken, a revelation so true to what it exemplifies that mere factual accuracy is beside the point.

And so the young king is said to have slept little the night before that battle. Concerned for his troops and for the chances of success on the next day's field, he walks among his men offering them encouragement, a word of comradely banter, a handclasp of understanding, an admonition of resolve.

> O! now, who will behold
> The royal captain of this ruin'd band
> Walking from watch to watch, from tent to tent,
> Let him cry, "Praise and glory on his head!"
> For forth he goes and visits all his host,
> Bids them good morrow with a modest smile,
> And calls them brothers, friends, and countrymen.
> Upon his royal face there is no note
> How dread an army hath enrounded him;
> Nor doth he dedicate one jot of colour
> Unto the weary and all-watched night:
> But freshly looks and over-bears attaint
> With cheerful semblance and sweet majesty;
> That every wretch, pining and pale before,
> Beholding him, plucks comfort from his looks.
> A largess universal like the sun,

His liberal eye doth give to every one,
Thawing cold fear. Then, mean and gentle all,
Behold, as may unworthiness define,
A little touch of Harry in the night.[5]

And so in one event, a walk by the king among his troops, the history of a
people is epitomized, their collective meaning as a nation forever set. For
it is said the soldiers overcame their fears that night, that England discovered
itself on that eve before Saint Crispin's Day, that the very course of history was altered at Agincourt:

This story shall the good man teach his son;
And Crispin Crispian shall ne'er go by,
From this day to the ending of the world,
But we in it shall be remembered,—
We few, we happy few, we band of brothers;
For he to-day who sheds his blood for me
Shall be my brother; be he ne'er so vile,
This day shall gentle his condition:
And gentlemen in England now a-bed
Shall think themselves accurs'd they were not here,
And hold their manhoods cheap whiles any speaks
That fought with us upon Saint Crispin's day.[6]

iii

These processes of typification have led me from history to myth. Myths
have to do with heroes and the incredibly important deeds they perform at
important places. They tell the tales of great men and women who in
their consorting with one another and with the gods have given meaning
to human affairs. The purpose of my culture's myths is to give vibrant
immediacy to my link with transcending importances. The past, my myths
tell me, is organized by structures of accomplishment that endure. These
realities define the conditions for my existence and the reasons for it.
Their significance is therefore not some general and neutral characteristic
they happen to possess. It is for me. For others as well, and perhaps for all
of humankind or even all creaturekind, but at least and definitely for me.
    I had been troubled by Descartes' insistence that I approach experience
in a manner that seemed designed to make these importances vanish
altogether. The blatant and unavoidable immediacy of the past and its
importances is what rescued me from isolation in the present moment.
The power of typification, its ability to turn history into myth, is thus
crucial. For the mythologizing of the past is what makes it so compelling

for me, permits it to save me from the snares of Cartesianism.

My actual relationship to the past is for the most part vague, its complexity blurred by familiarity and inattention. Whitehead's example of the circumambient woods at dusk is more typical of how the past presents itself than is Peirce's thunderous encounter with a ladder. Both are unavoidable intrusions upon my experience, but the one dramatically fills it full whereas the other oozes in around the edges and normally does not rise to the level of conscious attention. For me to recognize these importances for what they are requires that they be enhanced in the ways I have already discussed. I encounter an illusion, appearing to me in the guise of concentrated simplicities, in order to know the truth. Imagination falsifies truth in order to communicate it.

Here is human freedom at work in its strangely self-contradicting way, applying its ephemeral powers for the sake of realities that will endure long after that freedom has perished. But the process of mythmaking is not something I myself can do except in very marginal instances. I can embellish a story I am telling about some event I experienced, perhaps one in which I acted heroically, but no single story-teller can give those enhancements the status in reality possessed by myth. I am seen as distorting truth imaginatively for some aesthetic or utilitarian purpose; mythic embellishment is seen as embodying not only truth but deepest truth.

I am raised within a human community that teaches me the typifyings that comprise the essential framework for that community's existence as a coherent and meaningful enterprise. Or more accurately, I learn them through my experiences as a member of this group, less taught than imbibed. My ancestors accomplished these typifyings. Their experiences and imagination are present in these truths I breathe unquestioningly, even though they are present only in the form of the typifyings they created. My ancestors, that is, are part of the myth they have fashioned. The circle of interpretation closes on itself. The past presents itself to me as having been distilled into towering heroes, sacred places, and glorious deeds by the daring acts of those heroic men and women who founded and then preserved my people in this homeland of ours, from time immemorial until the present.

Perhaps this effort at self-creation is nowhere more manifest than when a group, aware of its growing power as a force in history, begins to insist upon its right to name itself. When Negroes become Blacks or French-Canadians become Québécois, a myth is being realized. A cultural possibility is being actualized in a form distinctive enough in its temporal novelty and massive enough in its historical scope that it must be specifically named, and named not by an external, superior reality but by itself. Typi-

fied by its specific heroes, a Martin Luther King or a René Lévesque, by
its newly defined tastes, aims, and practices, by its patriotic shrines and
reverenced accomplishments, the group has become at last something to
be reckoned with, its presence on the stage of history a clear shout of
victory rather than merely a vague grumble of unrest.

Every person, place, and event within my cultural world involves typification of some sort, for each has been sculptured by the values which give
that world its cohesiveness and sense. Even nature, even the mountains
and the forest I might think of as refuges from civilization, are a condensation for cultural purposes of the non-human realities involved.[7] But nodal
points exist within the totality of such a perspective, points where the past
is most forcefully a present reality, normatively so, unforgettably, inescapably.

Persons in positions of leadership occupy such nodal points when their
power is expressed through a cultural role that has importance in virtue
of those who have previously occupied that same role or in virtue of the
simple fact that there has been a great number of such occupants. In
meeting the present English monarch, I find myself in conversation with
a pleasant woman, both gracious and self-confident in her demeanor. Yet
I also experience through her presence the immediacy of the royal lineage
incarnate in her acts. I feel the presence of Plantagenet and of Henry V
even though the linkage is not genealogical but only political. In the presence of the reigning queen, I experience Agincourt not as a dusty memory
or an event discussed in some historian's account of England's past. The
queen is Agincourt made present once again, its meaning the source of
her valorous bearing and her compassionate smile.

English history gives vitality and importance to Agincourt and Agincourt
to Henry V. From Henry the long line of English kings takes its significance,
and in the second Elizabeth all of this shines forth. The anachronistic
ceremonies by which the prime minister rules on behalf of her queen are
vehicles for imbuing that rule with the authority of tradition. Henry
Plantagenet, his predecessors and successors, order this edict; England
acts in virtue of this tie between the routine bureaucratic acts of the
prime minister and her people's past. This empowerment of an individual
by the whole gives sense to Louis XIV's otherwise merely arrogant claim,
l'état, c'est moi.

Were I a citizen of ancient Greece and my oracle the one located amid
the mountain oaks at Dodona, I would often hasten there, to the special
oak where it is said that gods still whisper among the leaves. My journey
would be along a narrow valley and its torrential stream, between steep
limestone cliffs, until by crossing over a bridge of tumbled boulders I

would come out onto a high plateau embraced by the foothills of brooding Mount Tomarus.

I would approach the sacred oak in awe-struck reverence, for this tree makes present to me an ancient past that has spoken saving truths to my parents and my friends, to the elder generations I know only through their celebration in word and song, to the ancestors of all my people who came to this land before memory can recall. The rustle in the upper reaches of the oak tree's leafy canopy is pregnant with possibilities for meaning that I strain to bring to birth. A bird begins its chatter in the branches and my heart catches in expectation, then subsides into disappointed confusion. Sounds like those when heard yesteryear instructed my father into the ways that have brought him long life and the power to endure the world's cruel necessities.

I prepare my request by writing it on a scrap of paper and affixing it to the tree. The centuries during which similar acts have been performed fill my simple act with tremendous import and assure me that my petition will be answered. The oak that stands before me is the fortunes of my people made concrete, the wisdom of their choices incarnate in my mind's eye as the whispering of the wind performs its oracular purposes. Because the voice of my ancestors has spoken here so many times before, I can hear it speak now as well. Dodona's significance lies in its capacity to effect this liaison, its power to invoke the truths by which I am saved.

The roadsides of America are peppered with 'historical markers' commemorating deeds of local, regional, or national significance that once took place near the point at which they are located. The physical space itself is of secondary importance and is often unspecific; individuals are frequently mentioned but need not be. So a view of Lake Michigan carries a marker discussing early explorations by white traders. When I stop on a summer's drive at a roadside park to cool the car and use the restrooms, I might idly glance at this sign and skim through its laconic information. Nature is at once imbued with history. The insects now buzzing around me, the pesky mosquitoes and the biting flies, were also here when Pike set out hoping to trace the river systems to the west that feed Lake Michigan. They beleaguered LaSalle when he first looked out across this vast expanse and wondered if it were the long-sought ocean to India. They were present when the Shining Big Sea Water first yielded to the paddle of Hiawatha.[8] This moment and this place are suddenly alive with events, factual and fictional, which have been layered up in this vicinity generation after generation and which therefore give it a meaning not available to the entomologist or photographer.

Each event, moreover, is invested with its predecessors and pregnant with the potentiality for its successors. When my friends and I canoe along the lakeshore and up into the Pigeon River, we think of ourselves as latter-day Pikes and LaSalles and Hiawathas. Their adventure becomes ours, gives our itinerary a special flavor, the night noises at our campsite an uncanny new dimension. The routes these earlier explorers took might influence the ones we choose, a startling act of homage on our part, choices not intended as we bantered one evening over beer and peanuts concerning where we might begin and end this vacation journey. Our interest in preserving the Boundary Waters Canoe Area is kindled as we dream of coming up here again some time with our children, and they with theirs much later still.

Returning to our homes we tell the tales of our adventure until we know the story, with appropriate emphases and embellishments, by rote. Our saga, were it LaSalle's or Hiawatha's, might then be recited by others after we have long since died, handed down from voice to voice, from yarnspinner to troubadour to epic poet, until it became the story of our people, the account of their journey into this strange land, their settlement here, their fulfilling of a destiny it is now the duty of others to preserve and to celebrate.

Not only are the people, places, and events of the past concentrated by typification into the present but the reverse is also true. The present is read back into the past as comprising its import and explaining its character. And the past so signified is stretched back to the furthest extent imaginable, to my culture's progenitor, its place of origin, its founding deeds. The first English king, be he Canute or Constantine or Brutus, is a well-spring from whom flows that nation's future. Dodona's oaks go back as far as Achilles, at which time their majestic height was a full maturity awaiting the nation they would watch over and guide throughout its rise from obscurity to predominance. The first settlement and possession of the lands eventually to become the United States defines the character of its manifest destiny, and so it is crucial to know whether the Pilgrim plantations on behalf of God's messianic purification of the Church take precedence over the Virginia settlements seeking personal glory and corporate profit.

By stretching the cloak of importances over the whole of the relevant past, from the dawn of my people to our present noonday, I have convincing evidence that we are a consistent whole, a reality that contained its future in its origins and that over the unfolding years and centuries has fulfilled its initial promise of enduring significance.

The world disclosed by mythic intensifications is thus one in which the points of initialization have become norms for judging the present. Founders and their founding deeds, fashioned by the selective focusing and retrospective cumulating of typification, gain authority in virtue of the power manifest in their being seen as having put into motion the process which has resulted in the present display of achievement. I must live up to the original vision, and you as well, or we are both in danger of perishing. Indeed insofar as our current activities might come to lack the power so evident in our predecessors, it could only be because we are losing sight of our original purposes. Reform and restoration are then needed, to be accomplished by appeal to the standard proscribed by the nature of what was in the beginning. Since to mythic understanding the actual is always a diminution of the ideal, and since the origins and originators of a people exude its ideals as though it were their essence, the present will never exceed its past in virtue or value, although it might on occasion become its equal.

The importance of first things, therefore, is that they are the seed and so the generative cause of all that has followed after. Where that first is a vividly profiled typification, I can reach across the intervening generations and embrace my beginnings, identifying alpha and omega, filling the present with the whole of its sustaining past. The past is brought into the present with power. It is alive, concrete, purposeful, and because it bears so much accomplishment it is awesomely significant. It is the whole world, my whole world, distilled into this immediacy of consciousness yet without any loss of the rich complexity it encompasses. *Sunyata* is *tathata*; history and the present are one.

This power from the mythologized past gives security and meaning to my daily comings and goings. I am part of an ongoing enterprise, a successful operation, a way of being in the world that has overcome every challenge to its hegemony. Its present reality, and thus mine, exists in virtue of a linkage to regions of importance that have sustained it all these years. And yet this power is nonetheless vulnerable. If I and others with me fail to emulate the heroes of our past, if we desecrate our shrines and forget the names of those who died that we might live, then the linkages to importance will be sundered. The power of the past comes to me in the form of a command to protect and preserve it.

I stand once more at the entrance to my mountainside church. This quiet place requires me to respect its sanctity. I must be sure this fading gravestone is preserved, the one commemorating that woman who died so long ago in childbirth. Her pioneer spirit is what made this nation and keeps it strong. I dare not forget all that she stands for. Were I to write her biography, do you suppose the parishioners would read it? Her life could be an inspiration to them. This cemetery itself must be kept in better shape, the grass cut more often, the gravemarkers repaired. And the oaks surrounding it need protection from the encroachments of disease and the creeping blight of suburban sprawl. The church should conduct a study of our current service of worship. None of us seems to know much about its origins or in some cases even its meaning. I suspect a bit more high church ceremony wouldn't hurt either, such as there used to be before we became enamored of relevance. I should speak to the Board of Elders about these matters at their next meeting.

Under Descartes' tutelage I was troubled that there might not be a past but only present immediacy. Now I am troubled that this past, so vividly before me and so important, might be lost on account of my foolishness. But at least I have progressed thus far from solipsism to duty, from a fear of being isolated to fearing I might not be able to carry out my responsibilities to the heritage that sustains me.

Six

THE ETERNAL PAST

[Humanity is] haunted by the vague insistence on another order, where there is no unrest, no travel, no shipwreck: "There shall be no more sea."
A. N. Whitehead, *Process and Reality*

i

The past, mythologized and thus intensely present for me, demands that it be preserved for the sake of the fundamental protections it offers. I am usually able to cope with the dangers to my existence that emanate from human error, aggression, and natural catastrophe. But threats to the meaningful worldview that surrounds me and roots me in the enduring powers of the past are dangers of a higher order. These threats are by far the more terrifying because they put at risk more than some aim I might have, more even than my well-being or than life itself. They call into question the realities that give running those risks their value, realities that save me from the void of solipsism and aimlessness. Woe to me were these saving powers that undergird my worldview to prove inadequate, to be vulnerable to yet other more powerful forces. Three such basic, meaning-destroying, world-threats suggest themselves, but in each case the mythic past proves itself sufficient to the challenge.[1]

The limits of my analytic capacities are one of these three sources of profound concern. If the world stretches beyond my ability to comprehend it, then quite possibly there exist somewhere realities that are not constrained by the order of nature and the necessary conditions for human community. The power of a world-order lies in its exhaustiveness; for it, nothing can be alien.

125

I am repulsed, to be sure, by whatever is strange. Without a moment's pause, I will quickly smash an inoffensive but slimy bug that unexpectedly intrudes its inhuman presence into my familiar, friendly environment. I am petrified to climb up into the dark at the top of the stairs, to enter the uncanny world of those things that go bump in the night. Yet these things are only relatively alien, for in fact they have a defined place within my world. They can be accounted for in terms of the psychology of ignorance or immaturity, in terms of childish superstitions and adult phobia.

The fully alien other, however, the absolute surd that cannot be named or comprehended, is a terror beyond remedy because by definition it cannot be dealt with, cannot be brought into the system of meanings that are the presupposition for communication, for the exchange of goods or services, and for the distribution of authority and hegemony. The defining myths of a culture function fundamentally as instruments that account for even these sorts of strangers, that find a place for even the absolutely strange. Horror is muted into fascination, repugnance gives way to curiosity, when the alien presence is made to interact with my world or permits itself to be encompassed by familiar orderings. I learn that the founding hero has fought against these aliens in order to secure our patrimony and so knows how to handle them. Or it turns out that these seeming strangers are actually my brothers and sisters because we were both hand-made by the same god, spawned in the same world-ocean, taught by the same wisdom.

By providing an account of the origin of all peoples and the process by which they were each allotted their places and roles within history, and by setting this within an account of the origin of all things and the tale of how each of the peoples is related to this natural order, the myths I live by anticipate all possible strangers, pre-enrolling them within the roster of the world's peoples. International relations and immigration policies, tariff conventions and monetary exchange rates, translated into buildings and boats, job descriptions and careers, provide a vast framework for interacting commercially and politically with the unknown but anticipatable purposes of the foreigner. Religious rituals instruct me in similarly anticipatory fashion concerning how to treat enemies as loved ones and strangers as though they were my neighbors. In these and countless other ways, my culture provides a generic protocol for my use on any conceivable occasion. My past prefigures my future, and so rescues me from its alienating possibilities.

My powers of endurance are limited in the same way my analytic powers are, therefore exposing me to a second fundamental threat to the security of my world. Events overtake me and I find myself the unwilling recipient of realities that prove constraining, hurtful, destructive. My plans are thwarted; I suffer the loss of those I love; I die. These overpowerings of my purposes are personal absurdities. They cut across the meaningful patterns of my life, calling into question my sense that there is a place for me in this world, a role for me to play that however humble and however limited is nonetheless real and therefore significant. Pain and loss seem to imply that I am out of harmony with the rest of reality, that I have been tossed aside. Suffering is a horribly isolating experience. It casts me back into the very solipsism I had thought was finally overcome. And my death is the ultimate disharmony, the irremediable separation of my purposes from the ongoing enterprise of the world.

Here also the defining social myths of my culture provide the necessary assurances. By means of the obvious truths reported by the folk beliefs surrounding me, by means of religious and secular rituals that mime those same truths, by the shape of institutions which give such truths physical articulation as buildings and communities and civilizations, I become convinced that no pain is ever meaningless. This pain of mine has been suffered, perhaps, in the service of some societal goal the meaning of which is beyond question. Or at least the hurt will be soothed by a caring presence able to remove it, compensate me for it, and teach me the lesson it affords. The loves I lose turn out to be lost only temporarily or to live on in some altered but still efficacious way. My own death is shown to lose its sting and to be swallowed up by some kind of saving victorious power, whether it be my personal immortality or the triumph of the ideals with which I am identified. The gods who have protected my people in days gone by protect me now by this guarantee that I serve purposes immune to historical annihilation and am myself a reality not circumscribed by birth and death.

This implies a third limitation, my inability to detect the presence of evil or to resist its powers. Evil manifests itself whenever the opportunities for fulfillment available in a given situation are curtailed, diffused, or lost beyond all possible recovery. In certain situations I cannot tell my friends from my enemies. I am prone to confuse the temptations of momentary satisfaction with the broader goods that provide my true fulfillment as a human being. I confuse my desires with others' needs. Thus although acting in good faith on behalf of the world that commands my highest loyalty, I may still serve ends destructive of that world. The Devil is an insidious enemy because invisible to me. Its lurking presence at the heart of things leads me to fear for everything that is important to me and to my culture, to dread that it might perish and that I might be to some degree the agent of that perishing.

But those who have preceded me have learned from rueful first-hand experience, and from the teachings of their ancestors before them, how to detect these devilish purposes. The ancient ones were given insight along with power, their mission in the world supported by this gift from the gods. The founding hero is exemplary not only for the wisdom he has been vouchsafed, but also for the examples of courage, honesty, and compassion that he incarnates. The oracle, if listened to with a pure heart and an uncluttered mind, will instruct me also in these deeper, guiding truths. Then I shall be taken back behind the appearances and brought into the presence of that true good which lies hidden at the very core of reality. And with my eyes thus opened, and my powers to act thus liberated from misdirection, I shall no longer unwittingly betray the sources of my existence and of my society's significance.

To secure the needed assurances in each of these three fundamental instances of threat, my sense of the encompassing world must be expanded beyond the boundaries of the historical and even of the temporal. Strangeness can be transcended only from a perspective in which the source of all reality is identified as also being the source for my people and their history. The perishing of achievement, of life and love, can be overcome only by the introduction of imperishable realities. The detection and exclusion of evil requires a wisdom that is foundational for any activity whatsoever.

This means that the mythic framework of my worldview can be fully secured only if it reveals my cultural history as reaching back to origins that lie in some reality independent of it. My people must be shown to have roots in the very nature of things, in the powers that have caused the universe, in the sources of all ideals and therefore of every purposing. Stories of my people's beginnings, religious and civic rites of passage into responsible community membership, the geometry of a city and the character of the monuments in its park, must all convey this one selfsame conviction.

The myths and rituals of a people must transcend not only the passing facts that comprise its history but also that history itself. Yet they must do so in a manner that retains their historicity and all its factual details as something concretely, vividly real. The roots must be seen and sensed as sustaining these details, not as superseding them. For it is the function of the mythic past, and especially its presentations of cultural origin, wisdom, right practices, and continuing destiny, that it make the living, historically momentary present vital with significance. The importance of cultural myths is not that they reduce my life to a pale image of eternity but that they fill my practical here and now with the assurance of eternal validity.

When this mythic framework is functioning effectively, my familiar daily practices and beliefs are fully meshed with those required by the fundamental realities protecting me against the unfamiliar beings that are a danger to my existence and its purposes. This mesh extends not just to strangers, lost ones, and enemies but to the creations of my own imagination as well, my fantasies, my dreams, my hopes and expectations. It incorporates into the everyday taken-for-granted world both the exotic and the moral, what in some outlandish sense conceivably might be and what ideally ought to be. These contrasts to what is, its playful and its ethical opposites, are integrated by means of mythic beliefs and practices into a single totality.

Myths of this sort are religious in character, for they claim to be all-inclusive. Because they deny any reality beyond what they disclose, they are the source of those ultimate understandings, feelings, and behaviors that comprise religious sensibility. They are vivid and immediate. They are publicly available, shared to varying degrees of intensity by everyone who is a part of the community. In the form of rituals and ceremonies that are their routine articulation, they are brought into intimate relationship with the quotidian affairs of life. Geertz describes the function of religion thusly:

The source of its moral vitality is conceived to lie in the fidelity with which it expresses the fundamental nature of reality. The powerful coercive "ought" is felt to grow out of a comprehensive factual "is," and in such a way religion grounds the most specific requirements of human action in the most general contexts of human existence.[2]

Religious beliefs and practices thus embody the final step in a sequence of transformations by which my immediate experience is filled with its past and thereby rendered secure against meaninglessness. The past contains importances that give stabilizing order and continuity to the contemporary meanings that surround me. This structure of things presents itself to me as a heritage requiring my loyalty in the form of appropriate acts of preservation. The moral demand is linked to a promise of personal and social salvation.

My loyalty to the past is a response to its reciprocal trustworthiness. I am asked to be dutiful in carrying out the responsibilities of my station in life, to be an obedient child, a hard worker, a loving parent, a concerned citizen, a devoted elder. In and by means of such acts, I retain my harmonious linkages to a world that provides both proximate and ultimate meaning for me. My labors will not have been in vain, my sacrifices will serve wider purposes, my most fervent hopes will be at one with the dynamics of the universe itself. By being loyal to the demands of the present and the parochial, I am able to become at one with those transcending permanences that rescue me from the terrors of history. The certainty that Descartes sought I now possess.

These religious myths are not primarily a matter of verbalized belief much less of formal dogma, although such developments typically occur in the life of a culture. They are fundamentally behavioral, expressed in what one does, the style in which it is done, what is made or unmade in the doing. Where these practices are verbalized it is for the sake of elaborating the meanings implicit in them, providing an account, a narrative, a story, which gives sense to the actions performed. Religious myth, in short, is to a crucial extent a matter of ritual.

Rituals do not merely express a relationship between myself and the past, between my people and the ultimate realities. They create that relationship. Or rather, since the relationship is always presupposed by the rituals, they sustain it. My tie to the whole of things is both affirmed and strengthened by my performance of the rituals which I am obliged by that tie to carry out.

The distinction between sacred and secular is not a matter of separating rituals of ultimate relationship from the habits and customs that characterize the pedestrian affairs of life. That is a very contemporary and very depleted perspective on the matter. Sacred places, persons, or performances are loci of salience, points in life where these ties to the founding past are awesomely present, where they are fashioned, tested, or sundered, where they can be specially accessed. But every thing a person does, every trivial deed, is fraught with religious meaning. I wash my face in the morning; I cook a meal; I plow the field; I play with my children; I make love to my spouse; I offer propitiation to the gods. In every case I strengthen or weaken my ties to the cosmic order in so far as what I do affirms or denies the obligation I have to preserve intact my heritage.

How crucial it is, therefore, that these rituals be properly performed:

There is no more sacred thing than the sacredness of age. It is age that gives to all things, to physical objects and to human institutions, their value, their dignity, their moral and religious worth. In order to maintain this dignity it becomes imperative to continue and to preserve the human order in the same unalterable shape. Any breach of continuity would destroy the very substance of mythical and religious life. . . . [T]he slightest alteration in the established scheme of things is disastrous.[3]

In the formalized rituals of public ceremony and religious worship, it is obvious that whatever is said or done must be prescribed by an appropriate liturgical guide. My religious sect may be more strict than yours in what the liturgist is allowed to say, how he or she is garbed, what movements are required and when. My society may be much more flexible than yours with regard to the freedoms allowed in customary social exchanges and the discretion available in the workplace for deciding how a job is properly done. But these differences are relatively modest ones. For all of us, life is a ritual to which we adhere from birth to death. To overstep the boundaries of acceptable behavior is to become an outcast, momentarily or permanently, to be ostracized or imprisoned or exiled.

Perhaps one of the most fundamental aspects of this all-encompassing prescriptiveness is the importance of correct address. My name is a primary mode by which others may gain access to me. Indeed it is the best access, for it evokes my essence. He who knows my name can command my presence by its means and therefore might be able to tap my power and my purposes as well. This is why new social movements begin by repudiating the names assigned them by their subjugators and taking to themselves a new collective name. The rites of passage into a religious community almost always involve an act in which the new member is given a new name.[4] By knowing the name of a god I gain access to its power. Hence the true and sacred name of a deity must be kept a secret, known only to the inner circle of true believers, in order to prevent enemies or the prideful from taming divine power and bending it to their narrow human purposes. For public worship and proclamation, the true name of the god is thus simply replaced by an innocuous synonym.[5]

Popular culture is equally aware of the ways in which names are important. Captain Marvel of comic book fame would transform himself from an everyday citizen, Billy Batson, into a superhero by uttering the mysterious word 'SHAZAM!!' This, it turns out, was an acronym comprising the first letter of the names of six mythic heroes: Solomon, Hercules, Atlas, Zeus, Achilles, and Mercury. In speaking their names young Batson evoked not the presence of these gods as such but rather their powers: wisdom, strength, stamina, power, courage, speed. A person not different from you or me thereby became endowed with capacities of mythic proportion. The cultural past, already condensed with potent intensity into the person of these heroes from his past, was made vividly and immediately present and potent in the person who called their names. He was no longer Billy Batson, newscaster, but Captain Marvel, protector of society's values against aliens, outlaws, and all the forces of chaos and evil.

The conservative character of mythic beliefs and rituals is thus obvious. The names spoken, the behaviors repeated, the stories told, are all fraught with potency, for they evoke what they imitate. To know how to tap this resource is to possess the key to ultimate power. This skill for gaining access to transcendent importances is often kept secret, reserved by an elite as the instrument by which it is able to effect its control over the general populace for the good of the whole. Where secrecy is not possible, the people generally must be strict in their adherence to custom so that the powers released by that adherence might never be lost. Innovation is everywhere a threat to peace and prosperity.

Roland Barthes claims that the very structure of mythic symbols supports this social intent.[6] Signs as they function socially are composed of two elements: a denotative signifier which is some arbitrarily selected set of sounds or markings or other social artifacts, and a connotation or meaning which is a complex of concepts and feelings. The function of a sign, this unity of a denoting symbol and its meaning, is to refer to some social object such as a person, place, or event. Thus the marks "Elizabeth II"—black printer's ink on white rag paper—along with their meaning as the name of the present British monarch, refer to a woman who lives these days in Buckingham Palace, whose distinguishing characteristics readily identify her as head of state. The marks are an arbitrary form with no inherent significance except to play the role of picking out a particular individual; the meaning is a specific content; their unity is a linguistic sign used typically to name the current British head of state.

Signs as they function mythically are an overlay on this primary symbolizing system, a secondary development that transforms its character. In mythic expression the signifier is a primary sign. It is the marks "Elizabeth II" *and* their meaning taken together as comprising an historically specific usage. The conceptual content associated with this primary sign is a congeries of meanings, for instance those having to do with the significance of monarchy in Britain, its history, its role in British society both in the past and now, theories regarding the character of its legitimacy, epitomes of its exemplary occupants and their deeds, references to the places important for its history and authority, and not only these facts but also the emotional auras everywhere attaching to them. These two taken together, the original linguistic sign and a new sort of meaning structure, comprise a mythic sign, a linguistic sign that is functioning at a derived or secondary level.

So, mythically speaking, this present queen of Great Britain whose name is Elizabeth II means English monarchy. Were I to focus solely on the arbitrary markers that comprise one of the two aspects of the primary sign to which mythic meaning attaches, I would simply be noting that Elizabeth II is an example of an English monarch, that therefore she is the meaning of that monarchy in the sense of being one of its instances. 'Elizabeth II' as the mark utilized to evoke the complex of meanings I have in mind functions as a synecdoche. The part stands as a metaphor for the whole.

In contrast, were I to focus on the aspect of the primary sign that has to do with meanings rather than marks, the mythic transformation would be somewhat different. I would be concerned now with the specific historical meanings of English monarchy, but I would then be linking these to the broader environment of other meanings. It would be as though the story of Elizabeth were an allegory by which to make assertions about wider social significances. I might be attempting to cloak one meaning by another, to offer the notion of this fine woman on the throne as a stalking horse for beliefs about English monarchy I do not wish to assert directly.

But mythic expression is not a matter of synecdoche nor of allegory. What signifies the set of mythic meanings is the full primary sign, which is the marriage of an arbitrary form and a specific content, the two having been brought together by a linguistic community at some concrete moment in its existence. This sign was created by that people for the explicit purpose of referring to a particular woman of flesh and bone whose role in their society at that moment was to be its titular head. By then attaching mythic notions to that primary historical sign, both are transformed.

The primary sign is dehistoricized and, reciprocally, the mythic meanings are given historical location. These myths are thereby no longer merely fantasies, concoctions of a vivid imagination, the idle tales of a fabulist. They are the truth of this queen we call Elizabeth. At the same time the queen is no longer just a woman who by accident of birth and political fortune ascended the British throne in 1952. She and her role are taken as comprising a relationship that is as old as the nation. She was in some sense destined for that role, as is evident by the ease with which she exercises it. It is appropriate that England have a monarch and that she be that person, for indeed she is the right person for these times.

Thus myth involves the transformation of history, so frightening because of its contingencies, into nature with its vast and reassuring landscape of causal necessity. Some relationship that was too unsettling because grounded in freedom is disengaged from its place within the ever-changing, ever-perishing, historical process. What came into being by chance or human choice is vested with an aura of natural necessity. Henceforth it is to be taken as an instance of a structure that has recurred again and again throughout history, an avatar of transcending truths. It is thoroughly historical yet more than that. It is absolutely transcendent in that it is not subject to temporal erosion and loss, yet it is fully manifest in this passing moment. Elizabeth II is an ordinary woman who is at the same time England's destiny. She serves a specifically historical function within her culture, a very idiosyncratic one, yet it is a function rooted in the very nature of things, a role that had to play itself out on the stage of history at this present time.

This kind of symbolization serves to protect the status quo by linking its accidental achievements to eternal sources. One of Barthes' important contributions to cultural linguistics is to have shown how these secondary usages are typically the creation of the social class in effective control of a society. Thus the mythic meaning of Elizabeth II is, for Barthes, a part of bourgeois ideology, an element in a pattern of values claiming inevitability. For these secondary meanings are an effort to disassociate capitalist beliefs and practices from the persons who were its historical authors and to ascribe those beliefs and practices to no author at all except Nature or possibly God.[7] Those who would rebel against such authority are then told that they have little leg to stand on, for they set their own very human and parochial practices in opposition to practices essential to human existence. Revolution from this perspective is by definition an unnatural act:

For the very end of myths is to immobilize the world; they must suggest and mimic a universal order which has fixated once and for all the hierarchy of possessions.[8]

Barthes rails against this instrument of the bourgeoisie and beckons me to act on behalf of the oppressed. I appreciate the moral power of his call to freedom and liberation. But I am also vividly aware of how history is strewn with the wreckage of revolutions gone wrong, revolts in the name of liberty that ended up only imposing a greater yoke of tyranny. That's the way it so often is with human beings, after all. Cut free from their traditions they revert to barbarism, substituting license for order, the war of all against all for the peace and prosperity of a functioning community.

Barthes teaches me that language has the power to deceive as well as to disclose, to be used as an instrument of class repression as well as a revelation of social necessities. But the abuse of myth is no justification for attempting its overthrow. Instead of revolting against secondary meanings in the name of some never quite attainable pure world liberated from myth, I should instead use the liberty I have to seek whatever gradual reforms might effect needed social change. But I must do so in a way that does not endanger those subtle imponderables that it was the achievement of my ancestors to fashion into societal custom and accommodation, and that it is my duty to preserve. This liberty, the liberty found in enduring order, is the profound end for the sake of which my freedom should be exercised, and eternal vigilance on its behalf is my best and proper homage to the past.

ii

If history and nature comprise a meaningful totality in which I live and act, then the best mode to account for and describe its reality is through narrative presentation. Since my world is thoroughly historical, it has direction, a beginning, middle, and end. It is a meaningful totality, and so in lesser ways are each of the episodes that comprise it. Yet the account that needs to be given of this world is not a saga of happenstance, but a telling that discloses its historical structures as involving the fundamental relationships that exist among the basic elements in the universe. A truly adequate narrative concerning my world must be about stars and planets, the evolution of the earth and of its flora and fauna, and among these developments the appearance and flourishing of human beings including those of my own community.

My account must be an explication of how these things ever came to be and why, how they are now interdependent, what their separate and our collective destinies shall be. An account of this sort, a mythic narrative about cosmic structures and meanings, need not be linguistic. Rituals and habitual behaviors tell a story in dramatic mime, and a building gives tangible permanence to a tale, its stone and steel evidence of important origins and destinies. But language has a special force: it makes the other articulations possible. Without speech, there would be no rituals, no monuments, no institutions, because there would be no power to remember or anticipate, no ability to uncover the meanings that deeds and objects can then display. A myth is, at its root, an account and thus a narrative.

Narrative form gives dramatic urgency to an account of things, and vivid specificity. All the things of my world normally wear a familiar face, for their reality has the same sense as mine. But this reality can be fashioned into a story, and thereby brought vividly to consciousness in terms that parallel my most intimate self-understanding. The trees have suffered as I have; these birds comprise a community that has the same problems of justice and power, order and liberty, that mine has; these stars and indeed the whole creation yearn with me for the fulfillment of ancient prophecies. This story-shaped world[9] envelops us all into a single cosmos with its common history. Our unity is genetic and causal, not merely structural and analogic. We arose from the same past, are dependent upon one another in surprisingly complicated ways, and face the same known or unknown future.

But a story about nature and the gods, an account of those fundamental and founding acts that give permanence to the world, that give it its reality, cannot have a human author. If it did, the account provided would merely reflect a transitory point of view. It would be the invention of a particular individual whose perspective is a function of personal biases, societal conventionalities, and the parochial interests of one's species.

I am delighted by a storyteller's imagination, but I am well aware that it is a work of fiction and not a presentation of objective fact. Even though it may convey a moral truth and may have been composed for that didactic purpose, and even though it may contain all manner of scientific and historical information, the tale itself is not a true accounting of the way things are or came to be. In contrast, an epic tale about the great heroes of yesteryear or about the fashioning of cosmos from chaos is a profile of reality painted so as to heighten my awareness of its significance. Frodo's journey from the Shire to Mordor is a gripping tale for a winter's night before the fire, but Abraham's journey from Ur to Moriah is the account of how my people's special place in the divine economy was begun in faith and by faith brought to the promise of its special fulfillment. The one story is by Tolkien, the other by God.

An epic tale is normally narrated by a bard whose professional skill lies in the capacity to remember the tales passed on to him by his predecessors. He reports and preserves. His inventiveness is limited to innovations in style, to matters of meter and rhyme, pitch and intensity. But in the case of the most ancient and most basic tales, the truly sacred ones embedded in religious ritual, even these personalizing options are prohibited.

For Christians, the kerygmatic story is formulated into creed: "I believe in God . . . maker of heaven and earth, and in Jesus Christ . . . born . . . suffered . . . crucified . . . risen . . . , who shall come to judge. . . ." The words are to be spoken or chanted at stipulated moments during the liturgy or in private prayer. They are not to be amended in any way, and the Church by official decree anathematizes those who would be so presumptuous. For this story is the epitomization of human and divine actions that conspired to secure salvation for the faithful, a story that begins with the creation of this world and ends with its destruction or transformation.

Neither jot nor tittle of it must be forgotten; its repetition constantly renews my relationship to its truth.

No mere mortal could know Yahweh's purposes, so the story of his saving acts in history on behalf of Israel or for her chastisement must be a revelation from that God himself. Marduk's decision to battle Tiamat, the debate between Zeus and Athena regarding their proper loyalties toward the contestants at Troy, the election of a purified remnant of the Church to create in the new world a community that would be a model for the millennial age, all accounts of this sort simply have no human author. Humans, it may be argued, transcribed these tales under divine guidance or received them whole on some special occasion. But in most cases even this derivative authorship is rejected.[10] These stories have always been known by my people. They are as old as that people, their origins lying beyond the horizon of human remembrance.

Mythic narrative form is thus crucial to the conserving aim it serves. By its means I am presented with stories that have no authors and which I can therefore take confidently as being objective. Nature is anthropomorphized, its historical and human side revealed. This is not, however, an example of the distorting work of a human mind seeking to make all things over in its image. It is the dimension of natural necessity in history, revealed as the foundation for historical change. And so my history and nature's history are woven together in an account which is as immune to criticism as are the linkages it reveals and justifies.

The most crucial of all these stories are the ones that describe the events by which the link between a people and its sources of protection and well-being were first effected. These tales are how I recall the fact that what is important for me depends on transcending realities, and that the conditions for this relationship require my continued support. The very concept of value is given meaning in and through these events. The people, places, objects, and modes of behavior relevant to the aboriginal fashioning of this bond are distinguished ever after from other realities. They become that to which everything else is compared, because the degree of each thing's relevance to these special things defines the degree of its importance. The value of an object which I might possess is enhanced if it is similar to some object that was centrally involved in the primary event by which my people first came under the aegis of the gods. My possession is more valuable still if it is needed for the preservation of that special object. The object itself, or its avatars, is the measure of everything of its kind and perhaps by extrapolation the measure of all things.

These tales of how a culture's patrimony was achieved tend to have a common pattern.[11] Some sort of gift is involved, given to the culture hero by a god or perhaps won by him as the prize in a contest or trial. This has been handed down from generation to generation and its loss would mean the destruction of that family or *patris*, that community or culture. The proper use of this gift, however, is to return it to the gods as a thank-offering. Perhaps this is the appropriate response for the hero to make at the time he first receives the gift, or perhaps it is a requirement thrust upon one of his successors at some crucial moment in the history of that people. In either case, the temptation must be resisted to hoard this treasure selfishly, for those who do so perish and their people with them. The gift, once it is sacrificed to the gods, reaps a marvelous return. The community's ties to divine sources are at last established or once more renewed. The people enjoy bountiful harvests, military victory, population growth, widespread contentment, and justice.

Thus Atreus possesses a golden lamb, a mysterious gift from the gods. It is his proof of authority, the evidence to which he appeals when justifying his claim to kingship, to the role as leader of his people. By owning this golden lamb, Atreus indicates to the world that he is favored by the gods, and whoever is so favored should surely be able to obtain the assurances of good weather and good politics that are the prerequisites for peace and prosperity.

To propitiate the gods at a crucial point, however, Atreus sacrifices the sacred lamb as a burnt offering. The gods are pleased and as a talisman of their pleasure allow him to retain the lamb's golden fleece. The house of Atreus thereafter prospers. When at some much later time the fleece is stolen, Jason seeks it, overcomes many tests of his prowess and virtue, and by returning with the talisman intact demonstrates his legitimacy as standing in the line of rightful successors to Atreus, one therefore beloved by the gods, able to secure the ties that are his people's source of well-being.[12]

The hero's herohood is in virtue of his capacity to reach across the divide between history and nature, between the temporal and the eternal. It is these interchanges that reveal to humankind the true character of nature and divinity, including its interest in things human and its willingness under appropriate conditions to befriend individuals, communities, or even the whole species. The claim that reality is a seamless web, a totality beyond which nothing stands in threatening opposition, is thus fundamentally grounded in the story of culture heroes who have recognized this truth and acted to give it effective meaning for their people. A nation's founder secures his people to a transcending destiny. Gratitude and self-interest combine to make sure that his deeds will not be forgotten.

The oaks at Dodona also have their tale to tell, an account of their ancestry and origins that explains why the oracle who lives amid them should be considered so potent, her prophesyings so portentous.[13] The oak is not commonly associated with sacred places in ancient Greece; the laurels of Delphi are more typical an example of the trees preferred by divinity. But in Italy and throughout the eastern Mediterranean region, mountainsides that sustain a growth of oak are also likely to be identified as the haunts of gods or the sites of oracles.

The Temple of Jupiter on the Capitoline hill was the religious center of ancient Rome, for it was believed that Romulus himself had chosen the site. Here the political leadership of both Republic and Empire offered homage and confirmed their brief authority. Jupiter was god of thunder and of rain, the ruling divinity within the Roman pantheon and the source of Roman law. Oak trees were associated with his temple. An oak tree supposedly marked the original location for the temple; oak wood was the required fuel for the sacred fires; a gold wreath in the shape of interwoven oak leaves was always worn by the temple priests.

In his famous opening to *The Golden Bough*, James Frazer describes a sacred grove of oak at Nemi, which lies east of Rome, as being intimately connected with the authority of the ancient Alban rulers of that land and with the authority of their predecessors back beyond memory or myth, kings who propitiated Jupiter as their special god, the source and protector of their patrimony. But the grove at Nemi is also associated with Diana, goddess of fertility. Thus the earliest kings at Rome seem to have had as one of their responsibilities the tending of a sacred site. Those acts linked them both to Jupiter and to Diana, the god of life-giving rain and the goddess of the soil's abundance, the god who provides law and the goddess who assures childbirth. Material well-being and political continuity were obviously expected to flow from this relationship.

It was probably the case that these kings served the divinities at Nemi for only a year and that at an appointed time they were killed, perhaps in single combat with the man who would then become the new king for the year ahead. Why the kings should reign for so short a time is a matter of dispute, but Frazer speculates that since the well-being of the people is bound up with that of the king, his power cannot be allowed to falter lest he become the cause of a poor harvest or a political defeat. So the king should be put to death while he is at his full powers, and in such manner that these powers will be transmitted without loss to a younger successor, and thus by successive transmissions through a perpetual line of vigorous incarnations may remain eternally fresh and young, a pledge and security that men and animals shall in like manner renew their youth by a perpetual succession of generations, and that seedtime and harvest, and summer and winter, and rain and sunshine shall never fail.[14]

The oaks at Nemi and throughout the Mediterranean are a semi-evergreen variety, the Valonia oak, which retains its leaves into the late winter or early spring and is noted for its edible acorns. It is thus an obvious symbol of life's fecundity and a promise that even in the worst of times renewal is near at hand. The gods of renewal are thus appropriately located amid the symbols of that renewal. But the oaks at Dodona are the white oak, which is deciduous. They and their cousins the durmast oak and common oak are as widespread in northern climes as they are rare in the Mediterranean region. They are distinctive among northern deciduous trees because they tend to hold their leaves late into the fall, sometimes being still festooned in green on into January. It is likely that religious rites originally associated with these northern oak spread southward toward the Mediterranean during neolithic times. The wintry green of the southern oak made it an obvious and abundant substitute for the northern oak, able to serve well the religious and mythic purposes that predated it.

Oaks are also tallest of the trees in the north European forests. Their branches spread out majestically above those of their neighbors, and it is said their roots reach down as far as their leaves reach up, thereby linking the sky to the underworld. These oaks are lightning rods in a thunderstorm, and the burn-scars on their trunks are lasting evidence of their special relationship to awesome power. It is no wonder that the High Gods worshipped by the peoples of this region, sky-gods whose powers were evidenced in thunder and lightning, should come to be associated with the oak and with the fertility of the land. The rains that feed the thirsty crops and fill the streams with drinking water are the consequence of the gods' stormy presence, the beneficence of summertime ample evidence of the well-being they make possible. In winter the god-touched oaks are the sole reminders that the promise of divine bounty has not been forgotten.

These ancestors of the oaks at Dodona stand stark and bare against the winter snow. Like almost all of nature, they seem to have died with the waning of the sun's power. Yet many of their leaves still remain as symbols of resistance against the dying of life's vitality, and high up in the branches mistletoe typically grows, a sturdy green of hope amid so much dreariness, dramatically dotted with the blood red berries that promise new life and the coming of spring.

The Druids of the northern fringelands thought the mistletoe sacred and would cut it only for ceremonial purposes at midsummer's eve. Frazer links these Druidic practices to the yearly slaying of the Roman kings at Nemi. The power of the god, his vital center for life and the propagation of life, is located in his loins. The dying of the yearly kings at Rome thus involved their emasculation, the new king performing this act and perhaps then displaying the severed genitalia as a part of his investiture costume, as proof that the powers of the old king, his authority, were indeed transmitted to the new. For the oak, the vital center is obviously the mistletoe which lives on greenly even when the tree slumbers. So the Druids remove mistletoe from the oak trees at the time of new beginnings. By this ritual act the power of the oak-god is transferred to those who emerge from the midsummer ceremonies reborn. Like new kings, they bring to their society a renewed faith in the future and in the continuities of their people.

The Aryan root 'DIW', meaning 'bright,' underlies etymologically the divine name 'Diana' and its Greek equivalent 'Dione', and also but less obviously the names 'Jupiter' and 'Zeus'.[15] 'Janus' also has the same verbal source, and so the god of doors and thresholds, the god who stands at the hinge of the year, facing both backward to what has been and forward to the new, is linked to the oak and its symbolisms of rebirth and fertility. In the ancient Irish calendar, the seventh month, June 10 through July 7, is named 'Duir' which means 'oak' and is probably the root for 'Dagnu', the title for the chief god among the elder Irish deities. At the precise center of this month occurs midsummer's eve.

So the sacred oracle at Dodona is potent with authority not simply because Zeus happens to have been present there, his wisdom fortuitously available to those who would attach petitions or queries to the trees that fill that place. Zeus is present at Dodona because the oaks that grow there are his tree, symbols of his power to sustain and reward those who have the gift of his grace as their patrimony. This Zeus under a thousand names is present throughout Europe, displaying his triumph over the recurrent death of the world by the greenery in the branches of the trees wherein he dwells when interacting with his people. Kings and other leaders display his symbols on their regal dress, adorn his temples with those symbols, celebrate each new year by leading their people in rites that mime his victory over the things that perish. To destroy the oak would be to declare my independence from the god of my salvation. To do so would thus be madness, for my act would destroy not only that oak but the world that is its very taproot.

These sacred places thus tie me to the saving importances in the universe, and they are usually also the places where my culture heroes first received the divine gift they have earned by prowess or faithfulness. Yet these great deeds and special places are not yoked to my people and myself as tightly as we would like. The founding hero is only human, and even in the full power of his mythic capacities he is vulnerable to temptation, cowardliness, or failing strength. The shrines are potent only if the people's leaders correctly perform there the rituals that are alone able to evoke the presence of the gods and secure their consent to one's wishes.

It would be much better were the link to divinities biological rather than historical, a matter of blood and not an act of will. Thus the preferred genealogy of a nation's leaders will go back not only to its founding hero but beyond that to the demi-gods and gods that sired him or that birthed his progenitors. The oldest mythic layers in *Genesis* include references to intercourse between semi-divine giants and human women, the fruit of these deeds being the heroes of old, the founders of the various peoples of the world [Genesis 6:1-4]. Luke's genealogy of Jesus reflects the more rigorous monotheism of latter day Hebrew thought, but is otherwise in the same tradition. God is the direct creator of Adam but thereafter plays no direct role in the generation of leaders, until the time when he becomes responsible for the conception of the new Adam who is then born from the womb of Mary. During Luke's time, indeed, every emperor and religious savior worth his salt was born of a virgin who had been inseminated by a god.

Common folk just as much as kings and saints draw confidence from the proofs that they also possess a genealogical descent from founding heroes and from the gods. Bardi Skulason was born in Iceland about 1875 but almost immediately thereafter emigrated with his parents to a small self-governing community on the shores of Lake Winnipeg, Canada.[16] He was the eldest son in the family but left no direct descendants of his own, which may have been his reason for compiling a family genealogy for his brother's children.

There is nothing remarkable about Bardi's list of Icelandic men and women except that it stretches back along a number of collateral branches for some 30 generations, to ninth and tenth-century progenitors. Many of the men in this list are known from their mention in the Icelandic sagas, and they include Thorstein the Red, king of Scotland, and Olaf, king of Ireland. One branch extends back well beyond ninth-century kings, however, and soon history is swallowed up in myth. The list includes "Ivar vidfadmi, King of all Sweden, the fifth of England, the greater part of Saxony, and the whole of Austria." Still earlier appears "Dan the arrogant, from whom Denmark is named." At the 53rd generation comes "Skjold, first king of Denmark" whose father was "King Odin, who came from the east, from Asheim, 70 years before the birth of Christ, and became king of Sweden." Is this Odin a man named after a god or is it the god himself, and is Asheim a mere human settlement or is it the very home of the gods? Bardi was not interested in answering such questions; we can presume that the ambiguity suited him.

Where rival claims for political authority are in dispute, the specific character of these ancestral routes becomes important. Not only do they link the current claimant to a revered predecessor, Henry VII to the Plantagenet line for instance, but they trace his lineage on back to the national founder, to the originating culture hero, or if possible beyond even that to the national gods and to the high god.

Thus for John Foxe[17] the legitimacy of a Protestant succession has two foundations. First, the genealogy of the kings goes back into antiquity, embracing all of the important leaders of the people in their struggle against various invading powers. From the Tudors it traces the lineage backward in an unbroken sequence of rulers, both good and bad, coming eventually to Lucius who in 180 CE became the first Christian king of the British people. Foxe is careful to point out that at this time Rome was still pagan, that Christianity therefore came to England earlier than it came to the seat of the papacy. He also notes that Constantine the Great, who brought Christianity to the Roman Empire when he ascended its throne, was born in England of a British mother and began his quest for imperial power from there assisted by three legions of countrymen.

But this does not suffice. Foxe is concerned to show that this whole lineage secures its authority in a second way as well. The Protestant kings are not only an ancient line of rulers, they have a legitimacy that comes directly from Christ, in such a manner as to predate and so override the putative authority vested in Peter and his successors at Rome. So it is argued that soon after the crucifixion Philip the apostle directed Joseph of Arimathea to travel to Britain, which he did. In 63 CE he founded a church there. So when Lucius over a hundred years later converted to Christianity it was obviously at the urging of his people. They and not the pope were the reason for the true faith being so early championed by English kings. The throne of England derives from anti-papal and very nationalistic sources which justify a refusal of the people to accept any Roman Catholic monarch, no matter what his or her pedigree might otherwise be, and to insist upon the restoration of Protestant rule in a Protestant land.

When Geoffry of Monmouth in the twelfth century sets out to write a history of Britain,[18] he begins with the Trojan war and the flight of Aeneas into Italy. Aeneas became the father of Ascanius who was the father of Silvius, both kings of "Alba on the banks of the Tiber." Silvius had a son named Brutus who the soothsayers predict will cause his parents' death, suffer exile, and eventually rise to a position of great honor. These things come to pass, and Brutus in his wanderings arrives at last in Albion, that "best of islands . . . situated in the Western Ocean between France and Ireland." He and his compatriots subdue sundry human enemies along their route from Italy to Albion, and drive out giants, including one called Gogmagog, in gaining possession of the island. Brutus then renames the land 'Britain' to perpetuate his name, and he founds a city he calls 'Troia Nova' (corrupted later into 'Trinovantum', the ancient name for London).

Britain is thus very ancient. Geoffrey concludes this account of the founding, which takes up a full eighth of the total book, by noting that:

At that time the priest Eli was ruling in Judea and the Ark of the Covenant was captured by the Philistines. The sons of Hector reigned in Troy. . . . In Italy reigned Aeneas Silvius, son of Aeneas and uncle of Brutus, the third of the Latin Kings.[19]

Brutus' place is crucial. He is the eponymous culture hero of the nation, from whom all succeeding kings take their authority. His own authority derives from Aeneas, his great-grandfather, and the history he begins takes its proper place alongside Israel, Troy, and Rome as comprising a story of one of the world's most significant peoples.

If this rootage in the deeds of great men who were themselves descended from the greatest of history's heroes is not enough, Geoffrey also provides divine authorization as well in the form of an oracle. Early in his journeys Brutus comes to an island uninhabited since ancient times. He finds there a temple of Diana and offers appropriate sacrifices to her and to Jupiter and Mercury. Following precisely the ancient rites, which include mixing wine with the meat of a sacrificed animal and repeating his petition nine times, Brutus asks for instruction regarding what land he should seek for habitation. He then falls asleep and Diana answers him in a dream:

Brutus, beyond the setting of the sun, past the realms of Gaul, there lies an island in the sea, once occupied by giants. Now it is empty and ready for your folk. Down the years this will provide an abode suited to you and to your people; and for your descendants it will be a second Troy. A race of kings will be born there from your stock and the round circle of the whole earth will be subject to them.[20]

There is no mention of oak growing near the temple, but otherwise the account draws upon all the mythic elements required for the occasion. Jupiter and Diana consort to guarantee the political and material success of Brutus' enterprise, and the truth of their promise is assured by the careful way in which Brutus evokes ancient rites in his search for an answer to the question of his destiny.

iii

I have sought a way to rescue the history of my people from the fragile contingencies comprising it. Each human deed arises from an exercise of free choice. It need not have been and its fruits need not endure, for other human choices can undo what prior choices have accomplished. I found, however, that freedom never simply happens. It requires an environment that tolerates my choices, that educates their exercise, that identifies free choice as being among the possibilities defining what is imaginable. This environment sets a boundary to my will, for I cannot wish for or act on behalf of what is not even available to imagination. Moreover, the context for choice is never neutral to my efforts. It is friendly to some ends I seek and hostile to others. It supports and perpetuates some human deeds, although not other ones.

I was thus led to discover regions of the universe that structure it temporally and spatially into an enduring order supportive of my values and purposes. These regions of importance for me were shown not only to be vitally functioning in present experience, but to be themselves of transcendent origin. What endures historically, I discovered, is what traces roots to natural and supernatural sources, takes its ultimate authority from what does not perish. The transitory character of all things human can therefore be rescued from destruction by being turned, at least in its essentials, into natural necessity. My present activities and my hopes for the future have significance because they express fundamental truths about the universe. They are of a piece with past necessities, with unchanging realities.

I have talked of this in terms of 'destiny', a word of invincible ambiguity and murkiness. It nonetheless conveys what is key here: a feeling of transcending governance, a sense of the world as providing a reason for my life, setting the context for its duties and satisfactions. 'Fate', the *moira* of Greek drama, has similar connotations although the natural necessities expressed by that word are less likely to be supportive of human purposes, more likely to chastise human hopes than to fulfill them. The Calvinist notion of 'predestination' combines the meaning of both destiny and fate: God's justice is fatal for the unbeliever and His mercy destines the believer for salvation.

These affective senses of natural necessity also entail a logic of predictability. By weaving human purposes into the fabric of nature's processes, I bring it under the aegis of the laws governing those processes. The laws governing the movement of the atoms and the stars also govern human behavior. Since the laws are general, they provide the needed universal premises in a predictive syllogism. The true saints of God are industrious in carrying out their earthly duties; but this man is lazy; therefore he is not one of the elect. The gods destroy those who in their pride would seek to be as gods; Prometheus defied the gods by stealing fire from them; therefore Prometheus will be destroyed.

It may not be, however, that necessity in human history need mean that there exist covering laws able to predict and explain both the behavior of individuals and the rise and fall of nations. Those who would argue that historical explanation can only be in terms of a story, not a generalization, may be correct.[21] But this story when told in all its detail, including an account of psychological motivations and uncoerced actions, will still reveal the inevitability of what happened. The freedom of human agency will be seen as one of the contributing causes for an outcome and not as requiring the denial of causation. The portion of a story not yet told must in principle be able to be foretold, even if the required information for doing so might be too complex and too ephemeral to be fully available to any human consciousness. Yet even to a limited mind like my own, it should be possible to foresee the general direction of things, to extrapolate from the story known to a future as yet unrealized, to have confidence that the important continuities in my life are assured some form of everlastingness.

If a story can be an account of inevitable sequence, and if these stories are a part of the natural necessities that encompass the whole of reality, then it follows that the cosmos has its story too. Nature having bestowed necessity upon history, the reciprocal also occurs. History bestows purposefulness upon nature. I and my people are confident that our cultural purposes are a destiny, that the ends we envision trace their origin to the nature of things. Therefore these natural sources of our origin must themselves envision ends, define a destiny.

Insofar as natural necessity remains a process without purpose, it will ultimately be one bereft of meaning as well. If the atoms blindly run, endlessly describing patterns of repetition that can be predicted but that do not have any significance, then they make no reference beyond themselves to values sought or realized. If the cosmos is without purpose, then human actions even when traced to natural origins do not gain the meaningful security which I had thought they would have simply in virtue of their being rooted in necessity. To replace meaningless chance by meaningless determinism is to have gained nothing.

But once human purposes are linked to natural necessity, they infuse it with their distinctive dynamic. The meaningfulness which results from aims that order and orient immediate experience is transferred from fragile human actors to the cosmic realities upon which they depend. These realities are transformed into agencies, their processes into the outcomes of purposeful action.

The mythologizing of nature is thus the discovery of its human heart, of the yearnings and commitments that lie hidden behind its implacable exterior. This is not simply anthropomorphism, for it is not asserted that nature has human purposes but only that it has purposes. There is a divine providence as well as divine predestination, a caring for the well-being of creatures as well as a foreseeing of their end. The God of Israel is a God of mercy as much as a God of justice. He not only knows but suffers. He not only creates the world but saves it as well.

The workings of Providence, however, are mysterious, their apparent consequences often at odds with the confidence believers have in the eventual outcome. Job complains that he is treated unfairly; Jesus cries out that he has been forsaken; Augustine is unsure how the heavenly city manifests itself amid its earthly counterpart. All are told to ignore appearances and to have confidence in purposes that transcend both human enterprises and human understanding.

Yet the transcendence cannot be complete or it is a confidence without content. What I cannot see clearly I can still glimpse as though it were reflected in a beclouded mirror. I know something of the divine plan, enough for it to serve as my guide in life, the standard by which I assess current practice and the ideal which I aspire to realize. I know that this plan includes a choice on the part of divinity to incorporate me into its providence, to choose me and my people for a specific role within the divine economy. I have evidences that the plan is unfolding in the manner originally promised to my ancestors, a promise perhaps renewed in some way for my own generation. I am therefore confident that ultimately the plan will come to its conclusion, its origin and its originating of my people's destiny brought to culmination. The details may be hidden and unknowable. But the plan in its general contours and its cosmic grandeur is everywhere in evidence. From this cosmic intent I take my own cue, acting to the best of my abilities in service of its salvation.

The settlers who came along my mountainside long ago, who beat down a forest path westward down the valley, were lured forth by a promise of manifest destiny. This wilderness was to be theirs to tame, to turn into cultivated land and orderly communities, and it would stretch across a continent from sea to shining sea. Some purpose inherent in the nature of things assured them that their dream would be realized.[22]

These pioneers were descendants of John Winthrop and his band of Puritans who had come to the New World out of a more strongly religious interpretation of that same destiny. They thought themselves called by God to fulfill a very special mission, to undertake an errand into the wilderness[23] at a crucial moment in the unfolding of divine necessity. For a thousand years the Church had been in the grips of the papal Anti-Christs and this disease had now even spread to the English Church. The rescue of this Church, its purification and therefore its restoration as a true instrument of God's purpose, would mark the end of this millenium of Satan's rule and the beginning of a thousand year reign by the saints of the Lord, at the end of which the world would be judged and the Kingdom of God established for eternity. The task assigned to Winthrop and his people was to be a city on the hill, a light set in a prominent place to show all the world that a purified Church and through it a purified political community was possible. They were to be the paradigm for historical change, the forerunners of renewal, the harbingers of the millenium.[24]

So the ancestors of the pioneers who crossed my mountain first came into this wild land because they thought they were living at a hinge of history, a turning point in the story of God's saving acts in history. They had their own purposes, both regarding their own material well-being and the salvation of their immortal souls. But at the same time their actions served a cosmic purpose, played a role in sacred history as well.

The men and women who migrated along my mountain pathways a century later had lost the mythic vivacity afforded Winthrop's intrepid company, but this same sense of participating in wider purposes remained, purposes that benefited them but to which they also contributed. Even the oak trees upon the hillside had a role to play, growing thick and tall from generation to generation in anticipation of the moment when they would be needed to build the churches and settlements without which God's plan or the nation's manifest destiny could not be accomplished.

Walt Whitman, in his 1868 poem "Passage to India," powerfully captures this melding of history with destiny and of destiny with natural necessity.[25] America's role in history is to be the linchpin connecting the Asian East with the European West, completing an encirclement of the globe that it has been the age-long purpose of humanity to achieve:

Passage to India!
Lo, soul, seest thou not God's purpose from the first?
The earth to be spann'd, connected by network,
The races, neighbors, to marry and be given in marriage,
The oceans to be cross'd, the distant brought near,
The lands to be welded together.
I see over my own continent the Pacific railroad surmounting every barrier,
Bridging the three or four thousand miles of land travel,
Tying the Eastern to the Western sea,
The road between Europe and Asia.
(Ah Genoese thy dream! thy dream!
Centuries after thou art laid in thy grave,
The shore thou foundest verifies thy dream.)
Lands found and nations born, thou born America,
For purpose vast, man's long probation fill'd,
Thou rondure of the world at last accomplish'd.

Yet this is no mere human purpose that has been accomplished. It is a
cosmic purpose for which humankind has been the instrument. The
'justification' of the past and of the natural order lies in this culminating
event and the eschatological future it presages:

After the seas are all cross'd,
Finally shall come the poet worthy that name,
The true son of God shall come singing his songs.
The whole earth, this cold, impassive, voiceless earth, shall be completely
    justified,
Nature and Man shall be disjoin'd and diffused no more,
The true son of God shall absolutely fuse them.
Europe to Asia, Africa join'd, and they to the New World.
The past lit up again.
Something swelling in humanity now like the sap of the earth in spring.[26]

This wonderful symbiosis between nature and history is also articulated
by Spinoza in the precise geometry of his theorems and scholia.[27] *Substantia*,
the whole of reality, is *deus sive natura*. On the one hand, its reality can
be grasped in terms of the attribute of mentality, of consciousness and
therefore purposefulness. As such I know the necessity of whatever was
or is or will be in terms of the logical connections that link its components,
the ideas that are ordered by mathematical syllogism into a significant
whole. Or, on the other hand, I can encounter reality in terms of its
physical attributes, experiencing it through the causal network of influences

that bind its parts into an ordered system. But whether interpreted as God or as Nature, my task is to understand *substantia* as a single all encompassing order.

The intellectual love of God/Nature is thus the recognition of a reality that is simultaneously meaningful and deterministic, purposeful and yet timeless. For Spinoza the act of realizing this truth intellectually and exhibiting it through one's will and emotion is a moral obligation. I am to seek the good, and that good is only found in realizing fully my harmony with the whole of which I am a modal expression.

The propositions of the Fourth and Fifth Parts of the *Ethics* argue this insight compellingly in the stately progression of their logical deductions. What is essential about me is my striving to persevere, to continue in existence. This is best accomplished when I and others comprise a community of people in full harmony with one another—one mind, one body, one common purpose. This we can achieve only by reason, by a complete understanding of how all things essentially agree with our nature, are in harmony with it and so are a part of the good we seek. This understanding of the unity of all things is a clear and distinct realization that what is is necessarily what it is, that it is God/Nature. Thus to seek my own continued existence, to seek the highest good, is to love God so fully that my thoughts, and hence my bodily reality in its essence as well, are one with God, that my seemingly contingent reality becomes, when known fully and truly, God's timeless necessity.

Descartes required that my passions and my will be subjected to reason in order to avoid error. Spinoza replaces subjection with harmony, insisting that this is the only way to avoid not only rational error but also mortal sin. Descartes wished to be saved from error; Spinoza wished merely to be saved. Thus Descartes could abandon the physical order to illusion if need be, for the certainty and unchangeableness of truth was dependent only upon God's good will and had nothing to do with natural necessity. Spinoza, however, refused the dualism this entailed and sought instead to found his certainty in a reality that was more than will, that was also unblinking necessity.

Jean-Paul Sartre follows Spinoza's path, but his language is much more dramaturgical.[28] Human beings have, ontologically speaking, two aspects. One is intentional consciousness, the power freely to entertain a possibility and project actions toward its realization. In this sense a person is *le pour soi*, a being defined in terms of its outreachings, its anticipations, its freedom and imagination. A human being is at the same time *l'en soi*, settled factual accomplishment. In this sense, persons are defined by their place within a causal matrix of determinate actuality. The tension between consciousness and materiality, between elements of freedom and of necessity, gives to humanity a unique but tragic character.

The desire of individuals, their fundamental purpose in the world, says Sartre, is to overcome this tension that defines them. They want to provide an inviolate and meaningful foundation to the vulnerable freedom of their daily choices. They recognize in the brute factuality of inanimate nature the sort of invulnerability they desire, but it lacks consciousness, purposefulness. It is not free and so cannot create or affirm the frameworks of meaningfulness that give value, that provide savor and direction, to existence. These values are the work of freedom.

God is the only reality within the conceptual horizons of Western thought that combines freedom with invulnerability. God is Spirit and so is pure consciousness; God is also necessary Being, cause of itself and creator of the universe. Thus the desire to be both free and secure is a desire on the part of humans to become God, to take on the divine attribute of *l'en-soi-pour-soi*.[29] Humans find meaning for what they are and what they do, for existence and action, only insofar as they project it against a belief that the perishing of their aims and of their life itself can be and is overcome by being rooted in something permanent.

Sartre says that this is a useless passion, for the very notion of being both complete and inventive, safe against the possibilities of loss and yet filled with desire, is self-contradictory. But it is the destiny of human being that it live out this contradiction, endlessly pursuing the impossible. Sartre thus provides a myth expressing my passionate search for some kind of link to enduring reality even while condemning its achievement as a futile quest. Despite himself, he thus arrives by a circuitous route at the same ethic Spinoza proposes. It is the essence of my humanity that its freedom be used to find and affirm my fundamental harmony with the enduring structures of the cosmos and with God who is its timeless ground.

iv

And so I pause in my churchyard on the mountainside and ponder these things. All my life I have felt dimly and yet persistently that there is a transcendent ground able to rescue me from the confusions among which I live, a brooding presence in the background of my experience that is crucial for it. The terror of life's opacity evokes a deep interest in these dim feelings. Threatened by environing changes, natural and societal, hemmed in by narrow horizons of comprehension and control, I yearn for the assurance that my terror is not justified. There are importances transcending me, as opaque to me as the threatening opacities that press in so unmistakably. I reach out for this support, attempting to lift a background of felt security into the foreground of immediate experience.

My story and the story of my people are the instruments for this unmasking of destiny. The account of my own actions, the tale of my people and their deeds, leads back from the present to essential origins, to the foundational acts and hopes that marked the beginnings of a trajectory which from then until now is one seamless and meaningful whole. The account of these origins is not complete, however, until they are explained in terms of the aboriginal purposes that brought me into this life, that brought my people onto the stage of history. This story is the explication of my mission in life; it makes clear my duty to others and to my Creator. This story articulates the manifest destiny of my people; it defines the role they are to play in the unfolding drama of divine Providence.

The vivacity of mythic expression and ritual gives what would otherwise be felt only dimly a clarity and immediacy that is powerfully relevant to current experience. The destiny guiding me and my people, the place we have within the historical and cosmic scheme of things, is now specific rather than vague. Our successes and failures relative to its obligations will now be unambiguous, luring us or prodding us into incisive action. The reality of the structures supporting meaningfulness are henceforth as awesomely persuasive in shaping my deeds and those of my people as are the structures in the world which threaten to engulf such efforts in meaninglessness.

This church, this ritual, these friends and the land we share, are compatriots in a venture that includes predecessors and successors. My joint venture with them reaches back to the beginnings of history and it reaches forward to the end of time. It is begun at a moment in history so significant that preceding events are annulled by it or radically transformed, and it will culminate in a significant future occasion where current struggles will at last attain fruition. In becoming a part of this collective journey through time, sharing in the identifiable structures of importance that sustain it, seeing the pillars of cloud by day and the guiding fires of the night, I find a reason for my life. I am at once fulfilled and filled with hope, assured that there is an abiding worth to who I am, to what I have done, and to what my life yet might mean.

By my origins and endings I am saved.

Seven

THE ARTHURIAN TRADITION

The fascination of lost worlds has long pre-occupied humanity. It is inevitable that transitory man, student of the galaxies and computer of light-years, should entertain nostalgic yearnings for some island outside of time, some Avalon untouched by human loss.

Loren Eisley, *The Immense Journey*

i

I began my journey amid the familiar green hills of home and the traditions they encompassed. Descartes forced me out into the treacherous open waters of doubt, in quest of a better land, a firmer ground upon which to live out my life in security and happiness. But he left me shipwrecked on the reefs of solipsism, and it has only been by costly effort and persistence that I have found my way back to solid ground. My journey led eventually toward the same homeland of tradition from which I had begun. As with all discoveries of selfhood and significance, I have traveled into a distant country in search of a truth that was all the time at hand. The importances of the past, present and vital in the world I call my home, are the firm foundations I have been seeking.

I am pleased to be at home or in my wanderings to have a home to which I might return, a place that serves to define my travels as a journey to somewhere else. I am interested in the homes and homelands where others dwell, but only insofar as I sense the ways they link to mine. Your home may be far away from mine, but because they are both connected in some way, because I can go from my place to yours, because I can imagine living in your world without ceasing to be the person I essentially am, I have nothing to fear by the distances that separate us. Even fictional worlds and fantasies retain such crucial ties. Middle Earth belongs to the Age before our own Age, its differences from my world bridged by temporal developments I can trace imaginatively and appreciate.

The absence of such connections among the loci of reality would be intolerable. I require an ordered world, the presence of a structure for consciousness that is coherent and that is fully adequate to whatever I might perceive, think, feel, or will. Where this order lacks coherence or is inadequate, I am likely to fill in the gaps inventively. We human beings need meaning. It is our oxygen, our staff of life, our rudder; and without it we suffocate, starve, and flounder.

This is why I need so desperately to connect my separate homeland, my private island of meaningful experience, with those of others, and to tie the whole archipelago of them to the mainland of pre-established meanings with its massive continents of enduring importances. I want my home to be at home within a wider homeland, and in ever expanding circles of relationship to find its eventual niche within the dynamic of human history, the ecology of the planet, the structures of the very universe itself.

I and my compatriots, we tend our hearths, defending and repairing them, expanding them, linking them together, consolidating their capacity to resist the buffetings of change and the erosions of habituation. Our outward push toward more encompassing and more profound patterns of meaning crosses the Rubicon of its imperialism in the transition from historical contingency to natural necessity. An order of things independent of human contrivance is a surer buttress against the terrors of history than any structures of importance fashioned from the contingencies of human choice, no matter how resplendent that choice might have become with the authority of its years. If such an independent order of things can be found to support the hearths we cherish, then our deepest meanings are secured against the vandalism of time, our homes and our world protected from the rapine of history.

This movement from disorienting contingency to purposeful necessity is powerfully present in mythic expression, especially in tales about the genesis of things—the creation of the world, the upspringing of a people, the beginnings of tradition, the birth of a hero. Nowhere is this connection more vivid and more crucial for me than in myths regarding my own people's origins, the genesis of the race or nation to which I belong. The tales of its founder, his birth, his life's necessities, his destiny, are emblematic of this people's emergence into history. They limn the significance of its traditions, and the transcendent purposes it serves. These stories and their rituals thus comprise the umbilical cord connecting maternal necessity to its seemingly contingent offspring, assuring me that the apparent dangers my homeland now encounters, the momentary risks to house and hearth that trouble it, are rescued ultimately by the birthright of their natural origin. In examining myths of a nation's founding hero, I am able to see in the white heat of their energy the importance of importances, the urgency of hearth-building, the terror that is the heart-beat of civilization.

I shall use in this chapter the legend of King Arthur as a case study for the arguments that have occupied the previous six chapters. Generalizations of any sort require specifics to keep them honest, but this is especially so when it is the specifics and not the generalities that are the nub of the matter. Although the pages of my argument so far have been generously salted with illustrative particulars, none has been explored systematically. It is time to do so now.

Obviously the selection of Arthur is arbitrary. The origin of nation-states and the peoples that comprise them is a fairly small subclass within the wider topic of cultural origins, and there is no end of possible competitors even within that selective grouping: Roland or Barbarossa, for example. But Arthur, after all, is close to home. His coming has to do with the origins of Britain and his death is entwined with the destiny of the English-speaking peoples. For me this has an inescapable relevance, for English is my tongue and so its world of meaning is my world, its reality mine as well. Arthur I cannot hold at arm's length, examining his life and legend with bemused objectivity, entering my insights on yellow note pads with a cool and steady hand. He requires of me a more intimate involvement, because it is of myself I learn in approaching him. So trembling and yet in fascination, I have chosen Arthur of England as the touchstone for all that has so far been said.

The meanings of England root not only in Arthurian material but also in Christian legends surrounding Joseph of Arimathea and the apostolic succession. I have already touched on these and on the more ancient myths of Hebraic chosenness that have been modulated into expectations of England's special mission under God and into apocalyptic convictions regarding America's manifest destiny. This strand of imagery will be woven into the fabric that follows but only in muted fashion. It will enhance but never overwhelm my search for the meaning of Arthur.

As with all myths of a people's origins, the radically parochial features of the Arthurian legend are of its essence. What makes a homeland precious is that there is no other place just like it. Although linked to everything else, it and it alone lies at the hub, the core. Whatever, therefore, the allusions and parallelisms to other tales, the account of Arthur is centered in its contingencies, its local coloring, its special pleadings. The events at Tintagel and at Caerleon, the victory at Mount Badon and the defeat on Salisbury Plain, the mysteries of Merlin's prophecy and Avalon's promise, resist generalization. For it is the parochial that is being celebrated, the unique, those things that give distinctiveness and distinguishability to the tale and to the realities it recounts. The whole point of Arthur is that no one could replace him and that nowhere else in history did anyone like him arise.

The universal element in Arthur, therefore, is the phenomenon of myths without universal significance.[1] The specific, unrepeatable historicity of Arthur and of all the other culture heroes who have emerged to found or sustain or revitalize a people must be fully appreciated. Cultures find it important to celebrate their seemingly transitory features rather than to ignore them or take them for granted. There must be something precious in these contingencies, therefore, something which cannot and should not be plucked out from them, winnowed from the chaff of their history. There must be something precious that can only be preserved by rescuing the contingency itself. My generalizations must underscore the peculiarities of time and space, language and custom, that they so saliently exhibit.

The problematic character of temporal achievement must be transcended without transcending its distinctive and unrepeatable quality, lest the very effort at salvaging what is most precious result in its perishing. In Aristotelian idiom, the substance of myths is their accidents. The truth is the tale told, not some deeper truth for which it is merely the contingent mask. Were this not so, my people and their history would remain merely contingent as well, a special homeland without special meaning, a world-historical illustration of timeless truth rather than that truth itself. In myth historical truth becomes timeless, and this is quite different from saying merely that it bespeaks the timeless.

ii

The historical seeds for the flowering of Arthurian legend are unpromising in the extreme. They have to do with the dying embers of the Roman Empire, the struggle for power in its outlying province of Britain, and an obscure battle devoid of any historical significance.[2]

For the period of Roman hegemony, the facts are relatively clear. Julius Caesar invaded the large island west from Gaul in 54 BCE, defeated its defenders utterly, but then withdrew within a year leaving neither permanent garrisons nor settlements. An effective reinvasion on behalf of the Emperor Claudius occurred in 43 CE and the diocese of Britannia was established, its northern and western boundaries under continual dispute but the remaining lands secure and able to support agriculture, manufacture, and a flourishing urban culture.

By the latter half of the fourth century, Roman control in Britannia had weakened significantly, buffeted as was the whole Empire by internal confusion and external intrusion. In 367 the northern border wall was breached by Picts who overran the countryside pillaging towns and burning crops all the way to London. Order was restored within three years by Theodosius, but a decade later the island was deprived of its best Roman legions when they proclaimed their leader, Magnus Maximus, as Emperor and joined him in an invasion of Gaul and Italy that was to end in failure. After Maximus' death in 388, these legions were not returned to Britannia but were instead diverted to the Germanic marches in order to defend against the increasing threat of the Hun. By 407 the last of the legions was withdrawn permanently to Gaul.

What happened in Britain for the next three or four centuries is uncertain, the accounts of Roman historians being replaced by the occasional terse comments of monastic chroniclers and ecclesiastical travelers. Archeological evidences are equally ambiguous and scant. Seemingly, the response of the Britons to their abandonment by Rome was to turn to Saxon mercenaries for help in their struggle against the Picts. This had been common practice among the Romans, so it is likely that Saxon warriors actually were invited to Britannia long before the final pullout of the legions. But by the beginning of the fifth century the Saxon presence had become significant.

The use of mercenaries is always a mixed blessing. The Saxons came not only to fight but to stay and settle. At first they established themselves along the eastern shore in places assigned to them by their hosts, often farm lands abandoned by Britons no longer able or willing to carry on agriculture under such unsettled conditions. But as time passed the Saxons would more and more simply seize whatever land they wished, slaughtering the native inhabitants or enslaving them. The coming of the Saxon, all the later chroniclers agreed, was a time of dramatic transformations. An old order was crumbling, its death agony in stark contrast to the triumphant purposefulness of the emergent Saxon.

The Britons fought back, of course. Humiliation, slavery, and death, the most cruel embodiments of the terror of history, are never willingly accepted. Near the end of the fifth century, resistance against the Saxons was led by a scion of one of the old Roman families, Ambrosius Aurelianus. It is reported that one of his military captains was victorious against a Saxon army at a place identified as Badon Hill. The captain's name was Arthur. For nearly half a century thereafter the Saxon menace ebbed, at least as far as the southwestern portions of the island were concerned, although the growth in Saxon settlements elsewhere seems to have gone on unabated.

By the mid-500s the Saxons were once again active militarily and were consistently victorious over the hard-pressed Britons until Cadwallon's victory at Hatfield Chase in 663. This triumph was ephemeral, however, and soon after Cadwallon's death the Saxon conquest of Britain was complete. Except for the rugged, unfruitful western and northern fringes of the island, the home of Celtic Britons and of their Roman conquerors was henceforth to be the home of the Saxons and their Teutonic cousins, the Jutes and Angles. Britain had become England.

So it would seem that a soldier named Arthur fought at Badon Hill. The basis for this claim is tenuous, however. Gildas, writing perhaps only 44 years after the event, identifies *mons badonicus* as a place of victory for the Britons, almost the last but not the least of their victories.[3] But Gildas makes no mention of the Britons' battle-leader, although he identifies Ambrosius as heading the general resistance. The Venerable Bede, writing in the eighth century, repeats Gildas' terse report with minor embellishments and with a clear bias in favor of the Saxon. The Anglo-Saxon Chronicles for this period make no mention at all of Mount Badon.

Only with Nennius, whose *Historia Brittonum* is penned at the beginning of the ninth century, 300 years after the event in question, is Arthur explicitly mentioned:[4]

Then Arthur fought against them [the Saxons] in those days together with the kings of Britain, but he was himself the leader of battles.

He is said to have carried the image of the Virgin Mary on his shoulders in the eighth of twelve battles Nennius reports, and in the twelfth, at Mount Badon, he is said to have himself slaughtered 960 of the enemy.

A 'leader of battles' [*dux bellorum*] would be the military commander for a particular engagement or perhaps for an extended campaign. Arthur as *dux bellorum* is therefore explicitly distinguished from the kings of Britain [*regi Britonum*], and most decidedly from Aurelius the high king [*superbus tyrannus*].[5] Such an arrangement was quite typical for the times. An energetic warrior would be assigned by his chieftain the responsibility for tactics in a battle or even for the strategy of a sustained engagement. The warrior might be merely a mercenary or a person of low birth, or he could just as likely be a son or relative of the chieftain.

Arthur would probably have been in charge of a group of about 1,000 men who would engage their enemy in individualized unstructured fighting from horseback, using a lance or javelin in initial attack and turning to a sword for closer fighting. The soldiers carried shields and wore either leather vests or, if officers, vests of chainmail. An engagement such as that on Badon Hill might take up most of a day, if the opposing forces were large and periods of rest were at least tacitly agreed upon. The location of Badon Hill is unknown, although some historians speculate that it was near Bath. The date of the battle was possibly as early as 480 CE or as late as 520, most likely 490 or 500.

Arthur is mentioned only once again by the early sources, omitting legendary materials already beginning to make their appearance, and that is in a monastic Easter Annual (*Annales Cambriae*) which dates from the tenth century but is probably copied from a nearly contemporary original entry. Arthur is said to have been at the Battle of Badon and twenty-one years later to have died at the Battle of Camlann along with Medraut.

The only other historical resource available is the name 'Arthur' itself. It is almost surely of Roman origin, probably deriving from the *gens Artoria*. This contrasts sharply with the names of the various knights and ladies who comprised the legendary entourage at Arthur's court, these names deriving without exception from those of the ancient Celtic gods.[6] Perhaps it is sufficient merely to note that the very presence of the name 'Arthur' in conjunction with important victories, rather than solely that of the High King Ambrosius, is itself ample proof that someone lived who was remembered as more than a mere extension of the kingly power.

The point of this brief excursion into the historical record is to establish both sides of a seeming paradox. Arthur really existed as a man of flesh and blood, participating in the affairs of a people during a definable period in human history. But his role was a modest one, at best a fleeting glory, quickly drowned in the Saxon sea. Both the reality and the insignificance of Arthur are necessary to his legend, to the ways by which my terror of history has come to be modulated into the assurances of life's importances and of my own life's particular significance.

iii

Six centuries after Arthur's death, in 1135, a self-designated historian from Monmouth, who sometimes called himself Geoffrey Arthurius, published a history of the kings of Britain.[7] It begins with the wanderings of Brutus after the Trojan defeat and his eventual settlement in a wondrous island he names after himself. The book reaches its climax in an account of Uther Pendragon, High King of Britain, and in the adventures of his son and successor, King Arthur. Arthur extends British hegemony throughout most of western and northern Europe, but is mortally wounded while suppressing a rebellion on the homefront. Dying, he surrenders his crown to Constantine of Cornwall in the year 542.

The contrasts between this account by Geoffrey and the one I have been piecing together from the available historical records are manifold and striking. The military captain has become high king. Rearguard actions against an advancing Saxon horde have become campaigns of conquest and consolidation, culminating in hegemony over most of the civilized world. An act at Badon Hill worthy of praise and remembrance has become the biography of an epic hero. The reign of Arthur has become the high water mark of British power, preceded by civic chaos and followed by a decline that ends with the triumph of the Saxons and the exile of a Celtic remnant to Brittany and to the inaccessible hills of Wales. With Geoffrey, "the grey tales suddenly become a diagram of glory."[8]

My question is why. William of Malmesbury, a contemporary of Geoffrey, credits the popularity of the *Historia* to a fertile imagination. Geoffrey is a poet fashioning "false fables" from various "trifles of the Britons." This judgment is echoed by William of Newburgh a generation later when he says that Geoffrey embellished "fictions of the Britons" and then tried to pass them off "disguised under the honorable name of history."[9] Indignant historians through each succeeding century including our own have joined the two Williams in their criticism of Monmouth. Rightly so. Geoffrey's reputation for sober objectivity was never high.

But I must still account for why the fantasizings of this one man's mind were so popular and influential that his book is compared to the *Aeneid* and to Homer in regard to the extent of its influence on the legends of a people.[10] Two kinds of reasons for Geoffrey's popularity have been offered, and each in its turn brings me closer to the heart of the matter.

The least plausible explanations are those that attribute Geoffrey's inventions to an explicit purpose. One commentator argues that the twelfth century was in need of restraining social conformities as an antidote to generations of rampant moral and intellectual freedom. The Church, consequently, sought through such devices as Geoffrey's history to create a myth of social cohesion, to lure people away from individual licentiousness by offering them the vision of a common ancestry and an overarching destiny.

Other commentators see the purpose more in political than personal terms. Anticipating the rise of nationalism and what today would be called ethnic identity, they propose that Geoffrey was attempting to provide a hero for the English, both Briton and Saxon, who would permit them to exalt their race over that of the French. Arthur is England's Charlemagne, and his ancient hegemony in Europe is proof against claims of English vassalage to France or of its inferiority to any other peoples.[11]

Both these lines of interpretation label the *Historia* a hoax, at best a noble lie for the sake of social unity and *esprit*, at worst a ruse to permit the pacification of an otherwise unruly populace. Yet any such strategy would never have succeeded. If myths of national origin have in fact the power to unify a people behind its rulers and to swell their sense of communal pride and historical mission, it is precisely because they are not fabrications by clever politicians or pious monks, the concoctions of statescraft and religion. Certainly such myths can well serve the aims of princes and the deceptions of priests, but those who use myth in such a manner ride the whirlwind. They are not always masters of what they use. It is precisely the power of the Arthur legend as expressed in Geoffrey's book that belies the claim that he invented it. I must excavate more deeply if I am to find the adequate understanding I seek.

A second approach, therefore, is to see Geoffrey as a redactor, collecting together stories and legends from his culture. This would make the *Historia* an anticipation of Grimm or Lang, although with a more obviously political subject matter. Clearly Geoffrey was indeed utilizing folk tales, those 'trifles' to which William of Malmesbury referred. If so, then the imagination which confronts the reader is not merely Geoffrey's but that of the six centuries preceding him as well. It is the collective imagination of over half a millenium.

Long before Geoffrey wrote, this process had made the soldier Arthur into a king and had transformed Cornwall, if not all the British island, into his kingdom. In a biography of one of the saints, dating from 1075, an historical prelude mentions the defeat of the Saxons "by the great king, Arthur of Britain," and churchmen visiting Devonshire in 1113 report that the locals describe nearby landmarks as connected with "famous stories about the fabled King Arthur of Britain."[12]

Insofar as the meager evidences permit any interpretation regarding continuities, the Welsh tales that reflect and convey this transmutation of history into epic trace a three-step process. At first Arthur is leader of a band of monster-slaying heroes, a "loud, blustering somewhat ridiculous *tyrannus*, whose power is contrasted unfavorably with that of the saints."[13]

He is capable, however, of invading the underworld where dead souls dwell in order to steal a magic cauldron. This popular hero eventually becomes a norm of manliness, a standard of excellence against which to measure the accomplishments of younger pretenders to the praise and awe of their community.[14] By the tenth century, in *Kulhwch and Olwen*,[15] Arthur has become king, "the sovereign prince of this island" and ruler of far-flung dominions overseas. He leads a boar hunt and assumes other accouterments of conventional royalty.

Arthur as the king who is both hero and role model thus cannot help but become a magnet attracting impressive victories and other historical events important to the people who celebrate the values he exemplifies. By a process of accretion and transferral, obscure leaders and the local sites where their valor was once demonstrated come to be identified with Arthur, and their enemies become the series of enemies against whom he triumphs.

Perhaps when a people have been under special stress, their sense of historical importance and endurance seriously called into question, the need for a culture hero and the tales that celebrate him becomes acute. In the aftermath of defeat, nothing is more crucial than a way to reaffirm one's value. The Britons, reeling under the succession of Saxon victories that by the ninth century has rendered them a subservient class within a new political order, might well have sought self-justification by recourse to tales of a lost time when their hegemony was supreme.[16]

In time these stories are appropriated by the Saxons as well, providing them an authority more ancient than otherwise, extending by expropriation that breadth in time and space of the importances they celebrate. And Britons fleeing their homeland to fashion a new one in Brittany would remember their ancient legends of Arthur, sharing them with the nearby Normans who were bilingually French and Celtic, from whence they passed gradually into the court *ballades* of the eleventh century French *conteurs* who freed them from their explicitly British and Breton roots.[17] The uncertainties of the period after 1066 fostered a similar need for stabilized political authority. Thus renewed interest in a culture hero shared by peoples of Norman, Saxon, and old Briton background alike gave Geoffrey's work its instant and lasting popularity.

So this second way of interpreting Geoffrey's authorship and popularity discloses him as standing at the culmination of a long process in which again and again shards of historical fact have been melded with imagination to form tales told and retold around the hearths and banquet fires. These stories, narrated and sung not just for the fun and adventure they recount but for the norms of adult behavior they provide, serve as role models of personal maturity and social responsibility in which I can find purpose and accomplishment. Beyond these personal values, such tales of heroic deeds have special significance because they are about my ancestors, the progenitor of my world, the sire of successors whose fidelity to his saving work has made me possible. No wonder I, and so many others before me, have found Geoffrey's version of these stories so important.

Geoffrey provides a robust narrative of military prowess and political strategy. The descendants of Brutus are conquered by the Romans and then, just as they have become accustomed to Roman protections and civilized amenities, abandoned. The hapless Britons are then overrun by pillaging Saxons and in desperation appeal to the king of Armorica (Brittany) for help. He sends his brother Constantine who claims descent from the pre-Roman Briton kings. After ten years of indecisive struggle against the Saxons, Constantine is murdered and is succeeded by his monkish son Constans. But Constans is the pawn of Vortigern who soon has him killed and who then claims the throne for himself. Vortigern collaborates with the Saxons, but they eventually betray him and massacre his best knights at a faked peace conference. With Vortigern eliminated, Constantine's second son, Aurelius Ambrosius, embarks for Britain, lays claim to the crown, and succeeds in driving out the Saxon intruder. A brief period of peace ensues: "The entire energy of Aurelius was devoted to restoring the realm, rebuilding the churches, renewing peace and the rule of law, and administering justice [6,194]."[18] Unfortunately Aurelius is all too soon poisoned by a Saxon disguised as a doctor, and royal power passes to the third of Constantine's sons, Uther.

Uther not only continues to push back the Saxon menace but also struggles to consolidate his authority as High King. Gorlois, the Duke of Cornwall, is one of the more powerful of the nobles whose loyalty he must win. But Gorlois' recalcitrance puts him at odds with Uther and in the ensuing battles Gorlois is killed and Uther marries his wife Ygerna. They have two children: a son Arthur and a daughter Anna. Uther suddenly and mysteriously falls ill. Although growing increasingly weak, he nonetheless continues to mastermind the war against the Saxons until they finally murder him by poisoning his drinking water.

At the age of 15, Uther's son is elected High King, in large part because of his reputation: "He was of outstanding courage and generosity, and his inborn goodness gave him such grace that he was loved by almost all the people [7,212]." Arthur's mien is described in exquisite detail: his leather armor and golden helmet, the sturdy spear Ron, the shield Pridwen bearing a likeness of the Virgin Mary, the sword Caliburn forged in the Isle of Avalon. Arthur is a leader suited to the task before him, and success comes quickly in a series of increasingly decisive victories over the Saxons.

Consolidation of the island kingdoms under his rule is next accomplished, including the establishment of Loth, husband of his sister Anna, as king of Norway and of Lothian. Their children, Gawain and Mordred, soon become key knights in a military force that next projects its power into Gaul, gains control of such areas as Normandy and Anjou, and culminates its invasion by the capture of Paris. When Arthur celebrates these victories by calling a formal plenary court and feast in Caerleon, the gathering is said to be truly "a match for Rome [7,226]." Kings come to pay homage from the farthest reaches of the realm: Ireland, Iceland, Norway, Denmark, Gaul. Appropriate archbishops are present as well, and the ensuing ceremonies adhere to the ancient customs of Troy. Indeed, "by this time, Britain had reached such a standard of sophistication that it excelled all other kingdoms in its general affluence, the richness of its decorations, and the courteous behavior of its inhabitants [7,229]."

Geoffrey leads me in triumphant detail through each of the steps taken along this road from impending disaster to a kingship that controls western Europe and its outlying islands. Each battle has its special flavor of strategy and tactics, individual combat and gallantry. The political maneuverings of Arthur and his enemies are similarly recounted in compelling specificity. I become a part of an historically significant process, the unlikely origin and ultimate triumph of imperial Britain. A region of socio-political importance is being fashioned before my eyes, one that at its apogee encompasses the whole of the relevant civilized world. Its geographic massiveness is at the same time given depth and therefore stability because of its moral foundation. The High King has the support both of the other kings who elected him and of the people who hail the deed. He is a good man himself and his court a model of statesmanship, heroic valor, and social manners.

But spatial importances do not receive their primary authority from the moral character of the personages who control them nor even from the virtue of their authors. Arthur won these lands by the sword and rules them by acumen, but both are tenuous instruments for stabilizing value. Geoffrey thus goes to great lengths in order to add historical density to the geographic and moral scope. The massiveness of Britain in time as well as in space is offered as proof of Arthur's importance. He has restored an ancient claim, not merely carved out a new but probably only momentary one.

The test of historical power comes dramatically. Precisely at the high point of Arthur's newly acquired imperium, its representatives surrounding him and he dressed out in the robes and crown of regal authority, emissaries appear from Lucius Hiberius, Procurator of the Roman Empire. Arthur is ordered to proceed immediately to Rome, pay tribute and back taxes, and do homage to the Emperor Leo. The alternative is immediate retaliation by the armies of Lucius. Arthurian power is challenged by an older authority, the new warlord called to ground by the heir of the Caesars.

Arthur's response is not to tally his forces and cautiously assess his chances at victory by force of arms. Military power will succeed only if rooted in an authority that is deeply temporal in character. Lucius argues that Julius Caesar had exacted tribute from the Britons and so all subsequent Britons owe that same obligation to Rome. But, counters Arthur, Caesar's victories were not fairly achieved in equal and open combat. Civil strife had weakened the capacity of the Britons of that time to resist, and the Romans merely took advantage of that fact. "Nothing that is acquired by force and violence can ever be held legally by anyone [7,232]." There is no moral force to the claim that Britain ever owed Rome its fealty.

Having demolished Lucius' appeal to historical precedence, Arthur makes a similar appeal on his own behalf. Three times in the past Rome was conquered by Britons, and each time in fair combat: once when King Belinus and his brother Brennius invaded Italy, a second time when Constantine whose mother was British secured the imperial laurel, and a third time under Maximianus. Arthur then adds that the failure of Rome to send its legions to resist Arthur's recent conquests was in itself tacit acknowledgment of these ancient claims to British autonomy, indeed to British ascendency over Rome. Arthur instead of submitting to Rome will demand that it submit to him whose ancestors were its conquerors.

One of Arthur's noblemen picks up the battlecry: avenge our ancestors, safeguard our liberties, exalt our king! The liberty of the Briton peoples is its independence from other sovereignties, its location within a region of importance not beholden to purposes other than those of its own leaders. And those purposes themselves are very ancient. Even though it might have been temporarily lost due to the power and good fortune of Roman generals and Saxon chieftains, this structure of meaning could not be destroyed. These liberties were real, and exalted is the king who can restore them to their rightful place as Arthur has. So Arthur takes up the work of his three great predecessors, making present in his deeds all the past glory implied by their conquests and the full temporal massiveness that glory encompasses.

Geoffrey is at his best in the account of Arthur's campaign against Lucius. In a series of battles near Autun, southeast of Paris, Arthur is victorious in part because he is a master tactician and his knights superb in single combat. But his success is also due to his promise to the troops that they have a right to the spoils of Rome. Arthur's appeal to ancestral loyalties serves powerfully to rally courage when heroes are dying and chance seems to favor the enemy. And so eventually Lucius is killed and Arthur, after wintering over at Paris, prepares to besiege Rome.

The collapse of the imperium is sudden and shocking. Arthur's nephew Mordred, left in charge of Britain, has fomented a rebellion, taken Arthur's wife as his mistress, and made alliance with the hated Saxons, Picts, and Scots. Learning of this, Arthur abandons the expected conquest of Rome, manages to land his troops in England but only after heavy losses including the death of Gawain, and soon corners Mordred's army near the River Camlann in Cornwall. Mordred is killed and Arthur is mortally wounded. The kingship passes to the son of the Duke of Cornwall, but his rule is brief and uncertain. After a series of disasters, Cadwallon reestablishes a limited British hegemony and rules in peace for a generation. But his son, Cadwallader, cannot sustain the achievement, and civil war combined with famine destroys the last vestiges of British control. Jeremiad upon jeremiad fill the latter pages of Geoffrey's story: "Thou hast given us, O God, like sheep for meat, and hast scattered us among the Heathen [8,281]."

So even temporal duration is not enough to secure a people's significance. Geoffrey has given me a portrait of the Briton's culture hero. Arthur incarnates in his person the heroes of the past. He re-performs their great deeds of valor and goodness, re-presenting ancient achievements as contemporary reality. As a result, the ancestral places are once again linked together into a single cultural region. The power of this unity, this blend of sacred places, sacred deeds, and sacred persons, is impressive. Arthur under Geoffrey's pen takes on mythic proportions because he symbolizes, and is, a realm of importances stretching from Iceland to Rome and Spain, from the Trojan Brutus to the noble Aurelius and his descendants. And yet even this is not enough, for in Arthur's passing all of this glory also passed. The arm that wielded the flashing Caliburn was after all a mortal arm, and so could not deliver the promise of permanence it seemed to offer.

More is needed, something more permanent even than temporal duration, more ancient than Rome itself. Myth must gain transcendence if it is to fulfill its salvific role. Geoffrey's tale, having transformed a petty battlelord into a rival of the Caesars, must go further still. It must transform the Caesar into a god.

This is a task beyond Geoffrey's ability fully to realize, but he provides at least a beginning. His tale of kingship, political hegemony, soldierly valor, disloyalty, and death is surrounded by an aura of the magical and mysterious. There is a Dodonian prophecy to Brutus regarding Britain's future, and a prophetic vision by the necromancer Merlin regarding Arthur's birth and career. Other portents and significances swirl around the mundane events of victory and defeat. At the end, with political power transferred to his heir, Arthur withdraws to Avalon. History passes him by, but his bones are not brought to a final rest beside his father Uther and his uncle Aurelius. He is gone, and yet he foreshadows what is to come.

The first signal that more than human powers are at work in the affairs of Britain comes when Vortigern is fleeing the Saxons after their treachery at a peace conference. He decides to build a fortress tower as the redoubt for a final stand against the enemy, but each night the construction done the previous day sinks into the earth and is lost. Vortigern is told by his advisors that a human sacrifice will be needed to propitiate the local spirits, the offering of some child who has no father. Young Merlin is selected as the victim, but he manages to convince the king that a sacrifice is not needed, that by digging up the ground the mystery will be explained. An underground pool of water is uncovered, which when drained reveals two hollow stones each containing a sleeping dragon. Awakened, the dragons, one white and one red, fight with first the red one winning and then the other.

Merlin interprets this to mean that the end of the people of Britain, represented by the red dragon, is foredoomed. But Merlin in a trance goes on to prophesy about the appearance of the Boar of Cornwall which shall bring at least an interim relief to the peoples of the island and shall extend their domain over "the islands of the Ocean" and "the forests of Gaul." Indeed, "the House of Romulus shall dread the Boar's savagery and the end of the Boar will be shrouded in mystery [5,172]." A myriad of obscure prophecies, all in this same apocalyptic vein, then ensue.

This material, the so-called 'Prophecies of Merlin', is an interpolation, says Geoffrey, of a document long in his possession. He introduces it by breaking his narrative to discuss how others have urged him to translate it into Latin and have it published. He is honored to do so now [5,170-171]. Despite the posturing, Geoffrey's purpose is clear. These oracles serve nicely to flavor Geoffrey's preferred narrative style with an aroma of necessity. What can be prophesied must be fated and so is not, despite appearances, merely contingent. The accuracy of the prophecies results, of course, from two time-honored tricks of apocalyptic writing. They are obscurely stated, and they begin with predictions about times that are in the future of the supposed author but in the past of the actual author. Their accuracy is the accuracy of hindsight.

Thus to Geoffrey's readers, the power of Merlin's oracles lies in their having been so accurate with respect to events from Arthur's time to the present. Surely therefore the prophecies will continue to be accurate as they foretell a future time of British restoration. For, says Merlin, "the race that is oppressed shall prevail in the end" and

the mountains of Armorica shall erupt and Armorica itself shall be crowned with Brutus' diadem. Kambria shall be filled with joy and the Cornish oaks shall flourish. The island shall be called by the name of Brutus and the title given to it by the foreigners shall be done away with [5,175].

Thus the oracular promise provided to Brutus at the beginning of the *Historia* is echoed here with respect to the endtime. The children of Brutus are destined to inherit the western isle, and despite the way in which history seems to have belied that promise it will nonetheless ultimately be fulfilled.

At the very end of Geoffrey's work these words of Merlin are recalled once more. Cadwallader, in exile, prepares for a desperate re-invasion of his homeland. But an angelic voice speaks to him in a peal of thunder, insisting that God does not wish Britons to rule in Britain anymore, not "until the moment should come which Merlin had prophesied to Arthur [8,282]." Cadwallader is then shown the ways in which this is confirmed by other apocalyptic materials: the Sayings of the Sybil and the Auguries of the Eagle. A necessary condition for the arrival of this predestined moment is the return to Britain of various sacred relics, and Cadwallader sets off for Rome in search of them. The book then closes with two brief paragraphs about Cadwallader's death, some last efforts on the part of his sons to reassert the British claim, and the final triumph of the Saxon.

So Geoffrey brackets his story with supernatural oracles concerning British destiny, and adds a third oracle at the point where his story reaches its climax in the ascendency of Uther and the coming of Arthur. Arthur and his kingdom can thus be taken as the first fruits of a divine promise, a brief glimpse of the glory that will be Britain's when God or the gods at last bring to full reality its apocalyptic significance.

These oracular prophesyings intrude awkwardly into Geoffrey's narrative, however. He is more at home with portents and mystery, with historical events that take on a more than historical significance. Moreover, these oracles are only incidentally related to Arthur and his realm. Geoffrey needs to embed mystery and transcendent significance directly into the Arthur story itself.

Geoffrey's first attempt is more magic than mystery. His account of Uther's seduction of Ygerna is primarily a standard tale of politics and sex. Uther, at the height of his glory, convenes the nobles of the kingdom. He is "filled with desire" at the sight of Ygerna, "the most beautiful woman in Britain [6,205]," and commands her presence. She and her husband flee to their estates in Cornwall rather than obey Uther, and the king pursues them, as much in anger at Gorlois' refusal as in lust for his wife. Ygerna is ensconced for safety in the Duke's stronghold at Tintagel. Uther besieges the Duke at nearby Dimilioc, and eventually lures him into battle. Gorlois is killed and his army scattered; a new duke, loyal to Uther, is given Cornwall; the story moves on to other battles.

The only departure from this level of narrative occurs when Uther, frustrated by his inability to conquer Tintagel, seeks help from Merlin. Merlin proposes that Uther "make use of methods which are quite new and until now unheard of in your day [6,206]." This turns out to be a drug which when taken turns Uther into the likeness of Ygerna's husband. Accompanied by Merlin and another knight, Uther in his new form is readily admitted to Tintagel and to Ygerna's bed. And "that night she conceived Arthur, the most famous of men, who subsequently won great renown by his outstanding bravery [6,207]." Uther continues the mascarade the next morning, pretending to be the Duke of Cornwall even when the news is brought that Gorlois has been killed. Not so, says Uther, I obviously am still alive, and now will go to make peace with Uther. He then leaves, reassumes his true shape, and returns to Tintagel as the conquering hero. Ygerna, presumably never suspecting the deception, is soon married to Uther and they are blessed with two children.

Some commentators see in this tale an archetypal echo of Jupiter's seduction of Alcmene. Another argues that it is part of "a Celtic tradition of a wonder child begotten by a god who visited the mother in the shape of a king, her husband."[19] But if ancient myths inspire the account, Geoffrey's use of them is without mythic resonance. Merlin is the source of a magic potion that allows the king to fulfill his desire. Although the result is a child conceived out of wedlock, Uther marries Ygerna immediately thereafter. Arthur is firmly legitimate, and the only possible significance to the shapeshifting adventure is that Uther's absence from Dimilioc is what lures the Cornwallian army to open the gates of their fortress and rashly carry the battle to the king's men.

So Geoffrey oscillates between apocalyptic oracle and mere magic whenever he departs from political narrative. There is one exception to this,
and it is here that he begins to move the Arthurian material onto a whole
new level of significance. At just the fatal moment when Aurelius is being
poisoned and the fortunes of the Britons put in jeopardy, a "star of great
magnitude and brilliance" appears in the sky over Winchester. Comet-like,
it emits a single beam at the end of which

was a ball of fire, spread out in the shape of a dragon. From the dragon's
mouth stretched forth two rays of light, one of which seemed to extend its
length beyond the latitude of Gaul, while the second turned towards the Irish
Sea and split up into seven smaller shafts of light [6,200-201].

Uther asks Merlin for an interpretation. The star and dragon, says Merlin,
are Uther himself who, since Aurelius is dead, shall now become High
King. The beam stretching toward Gaul represents Uther's son "who will
be a most powerful man" and who will control all the lands covered by
that beam. The other beam signifies Uther's daughter and those of her
descendants who will in their turn hold the kingship of Britain.

The brilliantly tailed star is a natural phenomenon, although one of
unusual character. It obviously has therefore some special significance
requiring the wisdom of a Merlin to decipher. What it portends is a matter of political succession and hegemony, a justification of Uther as his
brother's heir and of the fruitfulness of that lineage. Uther's reactions are
thus appropriately practical. He assumes control of Aurelius' armies and
marches them to victory. Having then buried his brother and received the
diadem of kingly authority, he takes the dragon as the device to be borne
on his shield and carried before him into battle. And he changes his name
to 'Utherpendragon' [Ythr ben dragwn] in homage to the source of his
authority.

The dragon is a talisman for Uther, something he can grasp, imprison
within his heraldry and nomenclature, something by means of which he
can be linked to transcending and authorizing power. By means of this
sign he conquers. Whatever the transcendent be, it is reticent. Shrouded
in mystery, it offers only signs that must be rightly interpreted if its help
is to be secured and the future anticipated. Thus it is not so much that
the dragonstar prophesies future necessity as that it indicates what will
transpire if Uther and Uther's son act in accord with its authority and by
means of its power. The intent is more ethical than apocalyptic, a heuristic admonition more than a foretelling. Consequently Uther's response is

practical. He rallies his troops, he causes a golden image of the dragon to be given as a votive offering to the church at Winchester, and he binds his descendants to the dragon by making it the name of the royal house he founds.

This is the difference between moral prophecy, such as was practiced by Amos or Jeremiah, and apocalytic prophecy of the kind found in the book of Daniel. The former seeks to change behavior and the latter to foretell it. Jeremiah and his ilk say that Israel will be destroyed unless it mends its ways, and although they may be pessimistic about the likelihood of change it is nonetheless their intent to sketch the future in order that people by their own free will might so alter the present that such a future will not in fact be realized. Apocalypticism, in contrast, assumes that the future is determined and wishes to assure people of their inevitable salvation or to gloat over their unavoidable damnation. The Merlin prophecies are in this sense strictly apocalyptic whereas in Merlin's interpretation of the dragonstar Geoffrey takes a clear step into the ethical. Transcendence requires human actions for its realization within history.

Geoffrey is able to infuse this perspective into his oracular passages on one occasion. As Arthur rallies his men to resist the demands of Lucius, one of his supporters alludes to the Sybilline Prophecies. Their augury is that "one born of British blood" shall three times seize the Empire of Rome. Ah, says Arthur's comrade, now is the third of those occasions.[20] "Make haste, then, to take in your hand what God is only too willing to bestow! [7,234]" This argument, combined with the claim that anyone has a right to conquer someone else if that person has first threatened to conquer him, serves well to galvanize support for Arthur's cause. In this instance, therefore, apocalyptic statement serves a prudential end. It functions not to assure the British that the future is vouchsafed them but rather to enhance their willingness to go into battle.

And so Geoffrey of Monmouth gives me a mythic hero who defines by his deeds the landscape of importances that comprise my homeland. Arthur stands last and greatest in a line of British kings that reach back in unbroken sequence to Brutus, who first conquered the Western Islands and who is himself heir of the world's most ancient glories. Arthur's accomplishment is to extend the spatial boundaries of this enduring reality until it encompasses the key domains of Europe. He also provides the standards of morality and valor that are the expected expression of such massive historical and geographic continuity. The portents of the dragonstar and the interpretations of prophecy indicate that these importances endure even in the absence of their political realization. For those who partake of this heritage, commitments are required that surely will eventuate in the recovery of Arthurian greatness.

Geoffrey's literary realization of this promise falters because it can deal only awkwardly with the transition from founding hero to trans-historical destiny. The Arthur of the *Historia* remains basically the incarnation of his people's great historical accomplishment, the emergence of European empire. Mythically rich, a glorious embellishment of meager fact into far-flung importances, the structure of meaning is nonetheless perishable. Geoffrey's Arthur belongs more to the past than the present, a nostalgic romance of what was and might have been, a creature of memory but not of aspiration, and therefore ultimately not a resource for present action.

The Welsh sources utilized by Geoffrey contain another kind of story, one combining transcendence and prudence in non-apocalyptic ways. Arthur consorts with the gods, but he does so because there is a moral task to be undertaken, a challenge similar to those Arthur has faced in his dealings with earthly enemies but now involving the gods themselves. The moral task is not political but cosmic. Thus in *Rhonabuy's Dream*,[21] Arthur and his opponent Owain play a game of chess to decide who will rule the world. The context is similar to that in Norse mythology where the gods play with enchanted gamepieces to decide whether law or chaos will triumph in the cosmos, whether the natural order will endure or the turmoil of divine warfare plunge the universe into darkness and confusion. Arthur thus functions as a god, determining by his choices which side will win in the strife between good and evil. As with the Prophecies of Merlin, the context is eschatological. But the endtime is not foredoomed. Decisions must be made, the forces of good marshaled. That Arthur is involved in such matters is evidence of his transcendent importance and so of the importance of all the temporal accomplishments for which he also stands.

But these tales are too cosmic in their setting, too far removed from history and the day to day human struggle for meaning. If Geoffrey falters in his attempt to lift the valorous King Arthur into the role of England's mediator of transcendence, the Welsh legends falter by making him a god among the gods, albeit one who acts on behalf of his special clientele the Britons. With the changes wrought by the next three centuries, culminating in the work of Thomas Malory, the myth of Arthur at last receives this long-sought balance between timeless value and history's contingencies.

iv

Geoffrey's chronicles were embellished and poetized by *conteurs* from Brittany and France throughout the twelfth and thirteenth centuries. Combining his stories with other tales and with their own imaginations, they modulated the Arthurian legends in at least three ways. Wace and Layamon, for instance, introduce elements of faerie. Elves from the forest consort with the child Arthur and are associated with Avalon. Chrétien de Troyes' well known version culminates a process of increased stylistic elegance and cultural sophistication in the expressions of the legend. Also stories initially unrelated either to Arthur or to the 'Matter of Britain' become intertwined with it. For instance, Robert de Boron authors an account of how Joseph of Arimathea received from Jesus the cup used at the Last Supper and conveyed it to Bran, the Fisher King, and his descendants. *Conteurs* familiar with Boron then describe encounters between those entrusted with this cup and Arthur's knights, eventually fashioning a genre of story involving a quest for the holy grail.[22]

By the thirteenth century two cycles of Arthurian legend had become established, the Vulgate Cycle in English and a so-called Boron Cycle in French. These romances emphasize individual character far more than did Geoffrey's chroniclings, creating a tension between personal loves and loyalties on the one hand and political fealty and duty on the other. Christian sensibilities regarding sin and salvation then provide a further tension, a contrast between God's will and the inevitable outcome of all such earthly passions. In the more extreme and overly elaborate romances, Arthur presides over a microcosm of the human condition, his reign a morality play for the edification of noble knights and gentle ladies who might be eager to hear it recounted.

Thomas Malory published *Le Morte D'Arthur* in 1470, a year before his death.[23] Here Geoffrey's culture hero is given universal significance but without transforming him into a cosmic abstraction. Literary and philosophic quality are merged under Malory's pen. The events of Arthur's life and reign are depicted as the result of human choices, acts of passion and will that come in conflict with one another or flow in mutual harmony, and that are often shaped by sheer happenstance. Yet these historical contingencies are linked to transcendent purpose. The brooding mystery of such transcendence provides a framework for those human choices, and it is only by means of them that what lies beyond history can be realized. Human freedom and divine purpose, history and destiny, are at last united. With Malory, the *dux bellorum* of some ragtag Britons becomes the tether by which the British people are tied securely to enduring importances.

The ways by which Malory's craft has accomplished what Geoffrey only glimpsed as a possibility are best demonstrated by looking in detail at some key incidents. My attention focuses on Arthur's birth, his becoming king, his loves, his death. These four cornerstones of any human life are also the places where Malory's achievement is most visible.

When Uther's thwarted passion for Igrayne leads him to seek help from Merlin, the necromancer proposes a quid pro quo: I will fulfill your desire if you fulfill mine. Without even demanding to know what Merlin's price in fact is, Uther agrees to the arrangement. Nor does he blanch when he learns the details:

This is my desyre [says Merlin]: the first nyght that ye shal lye by Igrayne ye shal gete a child on her; and whan that is borne, that it shall be delyverd to me for to nourisshe thereas I wille have it, for it shal be your worship and the childis availle [benefit] as mykel [much] as the child is worth[9].

Uther hastens to Igrayne's bed and Arthur is thereupon conceived. Malory is careful to point out that a full three hours earlier than this Igrayne's husband had perished in an attack on Arthur's garrison. Two weeks later Uther and Igrayne are married, although Igrayne is six months pregnant before she learns who the true father of her child is. At the moment the child is born, and before it can even be christened, Merlin reminds Uther of his bargain and spirits the baby away. Only after it has been secreted on the estates of Sir Ector is the child given a name, the choice of 'Arthur' being Merlin's.

Uther's passion has obviously served some mysterious higher purpose, one to which only Merlin is privy. The king's desires are narrow and insistent, blind to their implications for him or for his people. He wants Igrayne and is willing to offer as a sacrifice to that lust both the peace of his kingdom and the first fruits of their union. Igrayne's virtue is the cause of both the fighting and the deception, but she is otherwise a bewildered bystander, never quite knowing the meaning of the events that swirl around her. But passion and bewilderment become the instruments for bringing Arthur into history.

The significance of these human emotions is rescued from transience by the promise Merlin exacts from Uther. For the removal of Arthur out of the king's court protects him from becoming a pawn, or a victim, of the intrigues that ensue upon Uther's premature death two years later. Uther dies never knowing his son's name. Yet here once again he serves as the vessel of Merlin's purposes, affirming on his deathbed in response to Merlin's question and before the assembled knights of the land that this son shall "be kyng after your dayes of this realme with all the appertenaunce [12]."

The death of Igrayne's first husband occurs by good fortune at such a time that the conception of Arthur is rescued from being the result of adultery, and the bad fortune of the sickness and premature death of her second husband spares Arthur being murdered because he happens to be absent from the court and so out of reach of the aspirants to Uther's power. Arthur thus owes his life and his legitimacy to Merlin's seeming awareness of future contingencies. There are purposes for which young Arthur is needed that cannot be allowed to fail merely because of some accident of history. And yet it is these very accidents that give such purposes their required realization. Merlin's foresight and Uther's blind lust conspire to create and then preserve the child Arthur until he is ready to assume his place in history.

Where Geoffrey of Monmouth merely embellished an account of the High King's beginnings with touches of magical shapeshifting, Malory entwines two levels of meaning, one of which lies beyond the comprehendings of the moment. Uther's magical drug in Geoffrey's account suggests the presence of something out of the ordinary, whereas in Malory's version Merlin's manipulations make manifest Arthur's importance. Uther's promise to Merlin portends a promise to the future which Arthur will embody.

It is Merlin once again who initiates the next step in the disclosure of Arthur's relevance to transcendent possibilities. For a dozen years after Uther's death "stood the reame in grete jeopardy long whyle [12]." Finally Merlin convinces the Archbishop of Canterbury to gather all elements of the feuding nobility together in London at Christmastide (January 6). It is time, he argues, for a miracle, and it is fitting that the true King of all humankind should on the anniversary of his own miraculous coming reveal who is now to become the rightful king of all England.

Everyone accordingly gathers, and after morning worship at the cathedral they discover in the courtyard a huge stone and on it an anvil containing a sword bearing the legend "whoso pulleth oute this swerd of this stone and anvyld is rightwys kynge borne of all Englond [12]." On four separate occasions, each associated with an important date in the religious calendar, Arthur pulls the sword from the anvil after attempts by all others have failed. At Christmas, Candlemas, Easter, and Pentecost Arthur's proof of kingly right is rebuffed, however, on the grounds that he is too young and lacks noble blood. But four proofs are sufficient for the populace, and the nobility finally bow to their clamor:

Wherfore alle the comyns cryed at ones, 'We wille have Arthur unto our kyng! We wille put hym no more in delay, for we all see that it is Goddes wille that he shalle be our kyng'[16].

Arthur is knighted and crowned, vowing as king to "stand with true justyce." His first act as monarch is to restore to various nobles the lands wrongly taken from them in the interregnum since Uther's death. His second act is to win important victories against the enemies of England, to consolidate the realm once more.

The workings of destiny are the salient feature of this sword-pulling episode, for it is designed precisely to clothe the new monarch in transcendent authority. The hidden king is now to be revealed, the one who all along has been prepared for this hour although no one knew that it was so. When young Arthur proves to be that man, his years of exile and anonymity are given meaning. The withdrawal was in preparation for this return. His disappearance not only preserved the future king from harm but also permitted him to be trained in the virtues and skills of leadership he must exercise from the first if his rule is to be effective.

But destiny is not self-evident. The nobles are resistant to transcendent proofs until the will of the people overrides their scruples. Even then they are skeptical until Arthur's fairness and his military prowess are fully demonstrated. Purposes lying beyond history are at work in the affairs of state, but they do not simply override human choice. Nor, in contrast to the conception story, do they make individual passions into mere pawns serving some higher end. Instead, history and necessity must collaborate, each fulfilling the other. Arthur's claim to the throne is given legitimacy by the miracle of a sword that will yield itself only to the rightful king. But without his deeds of virtue and valor the authority would have no content. English destiny requires Arthur's ability to quell the skepticism of his knights, just as his actions require divine sanction to be seen as truly kingly.

A structure of importance must be appropriated by acts of human ingenuity before its permanances can serve to undergird the achievements and hopes of a people. God's purposes, according to Malory, do not predestine events. I cannot know what will happen in the future by becoming privy to a sequence of occurrences that it is claimed must take place regardless of the seeming contingencies of history. But if I am Merlin I can see the enduring patterns that order life, and I can strive to bring events into conformity with them. The English peoples have the possibility of taking their place in some abiding fashion within the divine economy, and for this to occur someone must ascend the English throne who has the capacity to bring peace and justice to the land. But only if Arthur accepts that role and plays it out effectively can the linkage be accomplished.

Merlin, thus, is not God or destiny incarnate. He is someone who perceives the structures of destiny, the patterns of the past's importances, and conforms his purposes to them. He then acts to enhance the likelihood that his protégé will act in a similar harmony. Merlin is no longer the apocalyptic magician of Geoffrey's tale, but a seer whose deeds give Arthur's significance. And the Arthur of Malory's imagination is no longer merely a political hero but a man whose actions come to comprise the linchpin binding the wheel of English fortune to the axle of its transcendental meaning. Yet even this is not enough to provide the assurances of permanence that quell for ever the terrors of contingency. For the linchpin is, after all, a man and not a god. Suppose he is not equal to the task or is corrupted by it. Malory confronts this dimension of the matter in his account of Mordred.

Arthur was a lusty knight, as befit the times. He sleeps with a gentlewoman from Lyonors, and the son of their union becomes one of the knights of the round table. He falls in love with Gwenyvere, daughter of the king of Camylarde, and marries her. And perhaps there were other liaisons as well, but only one with foreboding implications. Morgawse is wife of the king of Orkeney and mother of four boys each of whom becomes an important knight in Arthur's entourage, Gawain the eldest of them. She comes to the king's court at Caerleon for an extended visit, and Arthur is attracted by her beauty:

Wherefore the kynge caste grete love unto hir and desired to ly by her. And so they were agreed, and he begate uppon hir sir Mordred. And she was syster on the modirs syde Igrayne unto Arthure [41].

Malory's craft captures the psychological power in this sequence of events: first lust, then its seemingly pedestrian consequences, and lastly the discovery of a deeper import. Arthur, like his father before him, satisfies without qualm his kingly lust for another man's wife, nor is he bothered by a child being the likely consequence of their month-long involvement. Only after it is far too late to do anything about it will he discover that Morgawse is in fact his sister and their liaison incestuous. For Morgawse keeps silent regarding their relationship, and at this point neither Merlin nor Igrayne has told Arthur that he is Uther's son, that his right to the throne is based on blood as well as divine approval. So two human faults, ignorance and desire, combine to lure Arthur into performing an unnatural and unforgivable act.

The events immediately following upon Morgawse's departure bring home to Arthur the full significance of his deed. He has a dream that frightens him, for in it he struggles against an invasion of monsters that slaughter his people and nearly kill him as well. Then he goes on a hunt during which he discovers the Questing Beast, but he is prevented by King Pellinore from taking part in that quest. Next Arthur meets a boy (Merlin in disguise) who tells him that Uther is his father, and when Arthur rejects this information an old man (Merlin in another shape) not only reiterates it but adds that Arthur has done something displeasing to God—

for ye have lyene by youre syster and on hir ye have gotyn a childe that shall destroy you and all the knyghtes of youre realme [44].

Thus in progressively explicit ways Arthur is confronted by the fact of his unforgivable sin and what that entails. The dream suggests bad times ahead. His exclusion from the quest implies some kind of incurable impurity. The truth of his ancestry discloses that his adultery was in fact incest. And the announcement of Morgawse's pregnancy carries with it a prediction of Arthur's death and the downfall of his kingdom. In the first bloom of his achievement's springtime the impending winter is announced, a winter that could seemingly have been avoided had Arthur been a wiser, more cautious man. What value the deeds that tie the Arthurian world to transcending importances if the tether is to be made of such fragile stuff, its unraveling concomitant with its establishment? Yet immediately thereafter Arthur's legitimacy as first born of the Pendragon is publicly announced, he is reunited with his mother, and an eight day festival is proclaimed to celebrate the removal of the last lingering doubts to his kingship.

Soon thereafter a similar contrast between weakness and glory is depicted. Arthur, engaged in combat with an unknown knight, breaks his sword and is saved from death only by the timely appearance of Merlin who casts "an enchauntemente" over the adversary. The knight proves to be Pellinore who, says Merlin, is someone far holier than Arthur and the one who "shall telle you the name of youre owne son begotyn of youre syster, that shall be the destruccion of all thys realme [52]." On the heels of this humbling news, however, Merlin takes Arthur to a lake in the center of which can be seen an uplifted arm holding "a fayre swerde." It is Excaliber, the symbol of his future victories, and it is encased in a scabbard which as long as it is worn will preserve him from any bodily harm whatsoever. A broken sword and a sword of triumph, defining in contiguous experiences the scope of Arthur's work.

Nor is Arthur's foolishness confined to his act of incest. When the Lady of the Lake comes to Arthur in her barge, offering him the sword held by the mysterious arm, she demands something in return: "Gyff me a gyffte whan I aske hit you [52]." Once more echoing his earlier behavior and that of his father before him, Arthur does not hesitate. He agrees to the exchange without bothering to count the true cost of his desire. And later, learning from Merlin that "he that sholde destroy hym and all the londe sholde be borne on May-day [55]," Arthur plays Herod by attempting to murder all the children of nobles born around the first of May. He thus stupidly risks the enmity of his knights in a desperate effort to undo the consequences of his previous rash desiring. But the children's deaths are engineered by putting them to sea in an oarless boat, and when it wrecks upon the rocks they are not in fact all killed. Mordred survives and like his father is raised in secret until the time when he shall fulfill his role as Arthur's nemesis.

This continual juxtaposition of strength and weakness prevents my attempt to require virtue as the necessary condition for Arthur's success in tethering his kingdom to non-contingent purposes. Merlin foresees the consequences of Arthur's ignorant passions, yet not only does not warn Arthur away from such deeds but in the case of the slaughter of the innocents actually plants the seeds of the strategy in Arthur's mind. If Igrayne had said publicly that she and Uther had had a son, then Arthur might have been sought and found at the time of Uther's death, and so a dozen years of civil strife might have been avoided. And Arthur, knowing his parentage, would have known that Morgawse was his sister. As a result the nation might have been at peace from Uther's time forward and a powerful force of internal disruption in the person of Mordred would not have been set loose. But these negative deeds are not threats to the link with transcendent endurances even though they threaten the endurance of Arthur's world. They are, indeed, required to preserve that link.

This can be seen more clearly by turning to the events that culminate in the fateful battle at Salisbury Plain. Although Malory keeps the focus on the political and military maneuverings, the specifics of the account differ markedly from Geoffrey's version. And by means of those differences the significance of what is happening is transformed.

Arthur's knights have been increasingly at odds with one another, bickering over petty matters and becoming embroiled in disputes of love and honor. The climax comes in a disagreement between Arthur's two most trusted knights, his nephew Gawain and the noble Launcelot. Arthur eventually takes Gawain's side, and they end up besieging Launcelot in his

French stronghold. Mordred, who was left in charge of the English realm, spreads the rumor that Arthur has been killed in France, declares himself king, and attempts to consolidate power by a marriage proposal to Guenyvere who refuses him and flees to London.

Arthur, hearing of this treason, lifts his siege and sets out for England. Mordred stirs up the commoners as well as knights by impugning Arthur's effectiveness as king:

for than was the comyn voyce amonge them that with kynge Arthur was never othir lyff but warre and stryff, and with sir Mordrede was grete joy and blysse [1228-29].

As a result, Arthur's attempt to land in England is resisted by a strong force and, although he finally succeeds in establishing a beachhead, his losses are severe and include the death of Gawain. The nephew before dying repents his dispute with Launcelot, realizing that "wilfulness" and "pryde" not only have been the cause of much individual suffering but have also led to a disastrous weakening of the social fabric. Arthur joins in this repentance and sends word to Launcelot requesting reconciliation.

Individual passion is thus identified as flawing the efforts by Arthur and his knights to establish the peace and virtue that had been his mandate as king. Arthur was to have replaced the strife among Uther's nobility with a unified realm able to keep internal order and to defend its rightful borders against all enemies. He was to have brought impartial justice in place of private desire as the criterion for satisfying individual needs. But in the end his practices lead to a renewal of civil war and to the blatant pursuit of individual passion on the part of even the greatest of the realm.

But Malory extends the scope of this fault. The English people generally are characterized by a similar willfulness, evidenced in their fickle preference for personal gain over political loyalty. As the people respond positively to Mordred's appeals, Malory interjects a scolding comment:

Lo ye all Englysshemen, se ye nat what a myschyff here was? For he that was the moste kynge and nobelyst knyght of the worlde, and moste loved the felyshyp of noble knyghtes, and by hym they all were upholdyn, and yet myght nat thes Englyshemen holde them contente with hym. Lo thus was the olde custom and usayges of thys londe, and men say that we of thys londe have nat yet loste that custom. Alas! thys ys a great defaughte of us Englysshemen, for there may no thynge us please no terme [1229].

This fault in the English character, so fundamental that it can be described as one of the oldest customs of the land, is thus also a fault to be found in each individual Englishman whether he be a peasant, a noble knight, or the king himself.

Indeed this fault may be rooted in human nature generally, for in May, "when every harte floryshyth and burgenyth," then also men and women shake off the stupor of the winter and permit their natural exuberances and passions to blossom. In the same such manner,

so thys season hit befelle in the moneth of May a grete angur and unhappe that stynted nat tylle the floure of chyvalry of alle the worlde was destroyed and slayne [1161].

The destruction of the Arthurian empire, coming in May and on the day after Trinity Sunday, is an ironic expression of the coming of summer, of hope and joy and release from the constraints of the winter months. For it is this very exuberance that sows destruction as well as life. Nature's May brings the individual flowers of spring that foreshadow autumn's decay; Arthur's May brought once the flowering of his kingdom and then later its destruction.

Despite the fundamental character of these sins against virtue and peace, they in no way foredoom the attempt to realize such ideals in human history. Arthur and his knights are good even if flawed, and that goodness has power. For instance, it is Gawain's virtue that gives him divine dispensation to break through the silence of death and to warn Arthur in a dream not to do battle with Mordred.

Arthur, after his costly victory on the beaches of Dover, pushes Mordred and his army back toward Cornwall and finally confronts them "uppon a downe besyde Salesbyry and nat farre frome the seesyde." On the night before the battle is to begin, Gawain appears to him and says:

Thus much hath gyvyn me leve God for to warne you of youre dethe: for and ye fyght as to-morne with sir Mordred, as ye bothe have assygned, doute ye nat ye shall be slayne, and the moste party of youre people on bothe partyes [1234].

Restrain your desire for revenge, Gawain admonishes, and wait patiently for the arrival of Launcelot who at this very moment is on his way from France to fight again by your side. With your forces augmented by his, Mordred will easily be defeated and the rebellion brought to a happy end.

Arthur heeds the advice and the next morning sends Mordred a peace proposal. Mordred drives a hard bargain, insisting on immediate control of Cornwall and Kent and succession to the throne upon Arthur's death. Arthur agrees, and plans are made for signing the treaty. The two adversaries, each accompanied by a small armed guard, are to meet in the no-man's-land separating the armies and there affix their signatures to the treaty document. Had all gone well, the result would have been a clever stalling tactic on Arthur's part, eventuating in a decisive victory and the healing of all the old disputes. Gawain's virtue produces the plan for effecting this, as similarly it also set in motion the processes of reconciliation that were bringing Launcelot to Arthur's side. And Arthur is able to respond to all of this, to be patient despite his loathing of Mordred's treason, to forgive Launcelot, to set aside the passions of the moment in favor of broad social objectives.

Yet all does not go well. "I in no wyse truste hym," says Arthur of Mordred and Mordred of Arthur. And so each, fearing the other will betray him even at the moment of the signing, leaves instructions with his soldiers to come rushing to his aid should they see any of the enemy drawing a sword. The treaty is signed and a toast is proposed, when suddenly an "addir" slithers out from the "hethe-buysshe" and strikes at the boot of one of the knights. The knight draws his sword to kill the adder, and in doing so signals to both armies the distress of their general. The battle no one sought nor wanted is then quickly joined,

and kynge Arthur toke hys horse and sayde, 'Alas, this unhappy day!' and so rode to hys party, and sir Mordred in lyke wyse [1235].

Thus Arthur's first opportunity for saving himself and his kingdom is wrecked upon the rocks of chance. But is the happenstance of the frightened adder really the cause of the ensuing melee? It is, rather, only the catalyst. The cause is willfulness, a climate of distrust engendered by the fickleness of loyalty and wantonness of passion that is so typical of the English. And this cultural flaw is abetted by the stupidity of devising a trigger for war without any safeguards against misinterpretation. As with every other crucial event in Arthur's life, ignorance and desire are the true causes of the ensuing Armageddon.

Arthur has yet one more chance to save his kingdom. In the twilight of that day of endless slaughter, with only a few knights left fighting on either side, Arthur finally confronts his nemesis. Spare Mordred, counsels Sir Lucan, and do not forget the message of the dream:

God of Hys grete goodness hath preserved you hyddirto. And for Goddes sake, my lorde, leve of thys, for, blyssed be God, ye have won the fylde. . . . And therefore if ye leve of now, thys wycked day of Desteny ys paste! [1236-37]

But Arthur has by now become so blinded by his hatred for Mordred that he will not listen. Taking a lance, he rides his enemy down, convinced that such a perfect opportunity will never again be available for completing his revenge. Mordred is skewered by the lance but in his death agony runs up on it to the handle-guard, where he is thus able to reach to Arthur with his sword. And so the king is dealt a mortal blow to the "tay of the brayne." Yet once again, and for a second time this day, the blindness of human passion has been too much for enlightenment. The era of Arthurian glory has come to its dolorous end.

A typical interpretation is that the kingdom fell because of "its failure to live up to its own vows of fidelity and loyalty,"[24] that the Arthurian ideal was too uncompromising in its purity ever to be realized in a complex world of conflicting values and purposes,[25] that one is left therefore with the tragic, or more accurately the pathetic, recognition of an unresolvable "contrast between what the God-like in man can aspire to, and what the baser self can do."[26] Another somewhat variant interpretation argues that the Arthurian world suffered from ideals that were internally incompatible, "a tragic conflict of two loyalties, both deeply rooted in the medieval conception of knightly service": one, the mutual love and loyalty of warriors for one another; the other, blind devotion of a knight-lover for his lady.[27]

Were this the fundamental moral of the story, however, the meaning of the Arthurian myth, then I would be left with no more than Geoffrey of Monmouth provided. Geoffrey's Arthur was a hero of mythic proportions whose achievements encompass and sum up the achievements of a culture long since departed from the historical scene. I read about the exploits of this great Briton and I am filled with nostalgia for a lost glory, for what once was but can never be again. Malory, if he is interpreted as merely offering me moral instruction regarding contrasts between the ideal and the actual, simply relocates my nostalgia from the past to the future. The Arthurian kingdom is an ideal which cannot be realized in history. It is a possibility forever beyond realization because of the inescapable consequences of human sin.

The solution to this double nostalgia, it is often argued, is to recognize that the ideal can only be realized by individuals but never by societies. For each individual there is the possibility of personally achieving true fulfillment, as exemplified in the solitary quest for the holy grail. But as

Augustine teaches, to create a perfect society requires a belief in human innocence that is at best naive.

Malory shows how human society can only fail in trying to bring paradise down to earth, and the result is tragedy. . . . [V]arious individuals may find the triumphant path to salvation, but for the noble order of the Round Table it is the tragic death of a mighty world.[28]

And yet I can find no comfort in such a solution, for I have learned in this very quest which I have been undertaking that salvation from the terrors of historical change and perishing can come only through the mediation of society. In some broken but fundamental ways I am my social past, just as the founding heroes of my society are that past in all its plenitude and power. To ask that I see in the Arthurian legends a denial of this social reality is to ask that I foresake my lifeline to the importances that by enduring can fill my present and my life with meaning. To argue that Arthur's kingdom is a lesson in *hubris* whereas the search for the holy grail is a lesson in piety is to have turned the truth precisely on its head. The act of unredeemable pride is the claim of Galahad that he can by his own powers attain to transcendent significance, that he can himself become a god. The message of Arthur is that I need not transcend my humanity in order to be saved. By making Arthur's kingdom my own, by participating in its mythic truths, I can tether my irreducibly mortal life to the importances that make it worthwhile, that give it eternal validity.

I have learned from Arthur that divine purpose spins out a web of significance that if read properly by mortal eyes can foretell how best to act so that those significances might be realized within the contingencies of time. The result is that order of things called human history. But the realization is always only an approximation to the possibilities envisioned, for the power to shape the world is a function of human individuality and so is also a passion to shape that world in private rather than general terms. The incompleteness of a private perspective and the parochialism of personal desire fashion realities that are mere shadows of what ideally could have been. And yet these achievements are real enough, and are the only ways by which the flux of things can assume a human shape. New webs of significance accommodate to such broken accomplishments, attach to these realities fast perishing, and define freshly the new day's ideals. In such manner arise the stabilizing centers of importance that have claimed the loyalty and guided the passions of each succeeding generation from the dawn of history to this moment.

Uther Pendragon loved Igrayne with a passion so intense he cared nothing for enduring importances. His son loved and hated with similarly blind intent. Yet they and their compatriots fashioned a unique structure within history, an English resonance to the sounds of valor and an English texture to the fabric of social peace. And in their better moments they recognized the ideality embedded within their accomplishments and drew from it renewed intensity for the pursuit of their varied and only rarely ideal purposes. The knights whose personal antipathies tore the cloth of Arthurian England to shreds were the ones who in the first place wove it whole and true. The king whose hatred for his son devastated the flower of English chivalry was the same king who gave an English meaning to honor and to empire.

I must never forget that Arthur is the cause of England's glory as well as of its fall. He is, in the beginning and at the end, its foundation. For what England is, Arthur is: a region of history characterized by distinctive loyalties, compassion toward others, and social harmony, but also characterized in distinctive ways by lust, murder, and civil strife. Arthur as progenitor of these unique qualities is thereby their supreme historical exemplification. Only so equipped can he fashion for his people the relationship to enduring importances they so desperately seek.

v

And so to Avalon.

Geoffrey of Monmouth had little to say about Arthur's death, noting with a certain studied obscurity that

Arthur himself, our renowned King, was mortally wounded and was carried off to the Isle of Avalon, so that his wounds might be attended to [7,261].

He then immediately refers to Cornwall becoming king and no further mention is made of Arthur, although there are apocalyptic passages referring to a future time when British power will again assert itself and reclaim its true heritage.

Explicitly political appropriations of Arthur tend to be equally prosaic and to follow Geoffrey in preference to other sources. The most ready way to find a use for Arthur was by analogy. Plantagenet and Pendragon were often associated in the popular mind, and the descendants of Henry II did nothing to combat such views. Richard I, for instance, seemed a properly valorous, Christian, and imperial Arthur, with John as his Mordred. When Henry V's conquests came to approximate the borders of the Arthurian realm, other parallels were then easily perceived as well. And the War of the Roses was all too similar to the struggles for succession after Uther's death, with Henry Tudor the triumphant Arthur.

But more important were the uses of the Arthurian genealogy for the reconstruction of kingly authority. Henry II's father, Geoffrey of Anjou, was sufficiently convinced of his own descent from the Arthur celebrated in the court ballads of his realm that he named his youngest son after Arthur. And Henry, either interested in actually establishing that connection or perhaps in making sure it would not adhere in his brother of that name, caused the tomb to be opened where Arthur was said to have been buried. It is reported that an oak coffin was disclosed and that it contained strands of golden hair and huge bones.

At the other end of the Plantagenet saga, Henry VII sought to reduce the problematic nature of his claim to the English throne by causing a commission to go into Wales to trace his ancestry. It reported that the descendants of his Welsh grandfather, Owen Tudor, could indeed trace their lineage back through Arthur and ultimately to Brutus himself. To be very sure that the nobility and people would appreciate the significance of this, Henry named his firstborn in honor of the great king. The child would have ascended the throne of England as Arthur II, but his untimely death brought Henry VIII instead, who in his Act of Supremacy was quick to utilize the Arthurian claims as proof of England's independence from Rome. Elizabeth I also justified her imperial designs by a similar appeal to Arthurian precedents. And as a result of these Tudor successes it was often said that "in the Welsh blood of Henry of Richmond the very blood of Arthur had returned to a glorious *present* of British empire."[29]

But the cultural imagination demanded a more poetic and ultimately a more profound interpretation of how Arthur was related to the successor generations. Welsh legends had always hinted at a king who had not died or who would return at some propitious moment of the nation's need. Ignored by Geoffrey and his immediate imitators, these legends finally find their first clear expression in Layamon. Arthur says, as he is carried away to Avalon, that "I will come again to my kingdom and dwell with the Britons with great joy." To which Layamon adds,

The Britons believe that he is alive, and dwells in Avalon with the fairest of all elves, and ever they expect Arthur shall return. Never was any man born, or any lady chosen ever, who knew so much more of truth, to say more of Arthur. But of old while there was a wise man called Merlin; he said with words—and sooth were the things he said—that an Arthur should yet come to help the English.[30]

In similar fashion the tale is reiterated, sometimes secreting Arthur in an alternative otherworldly site to Avalon, typically a hollow hill or sacred barrow. The heroic figure of the past sleeps until like Charlemagne he shall be recalled to the world of history to perform some new and desperately needed feat. The power of the enduring importances has been withdrawn from the human world, just like the elves of an earlier age who have passed over to the Western Isles, although surely that power will someday be restored.

But this is not enough for those who suffer now the terror of life's contingencies. It takes Malory to transform this last wondrous piece of Arthurian nostalgia into the living reality of Arthur's sustaining significance.

First Malory brings full circle the imagery of Arthur's flawed but empowered reign. Arthur had received Excaliber just after having been humiliated by a knight more pure and therefore more invincible than he. Now, having again been humiliated, this time by one less pure than himself, Arthur hastens to return his sword. He has some difficulty in doing so, however, because Sir Bedwere, now the only remaining knight of his entourage, twice refuses to carry out the order, interposing his personal sense of value and purpose for that of his dying lord. But when Bedwere each time reports dissemblingly that after casting the sword into the lake he saw "nothynge but watirs wap and wawys wanne", Arthur knows he has not done as was requested and demands that he go and do so. In coming the third time to the lake, Bedwere at last parts reluctantly from Arthur's sword, and an arm arises from the waters to receive it, brandishes it three times, "and then vanysshed with the swerde into the watir. [1240]"

Arthur is then carried to the water's edge where he is met by a barge bearing the Lady of the Lake and "many fayre ladyes." The mysterious figure who had given him Excaliber on the condition that she be able to receive from him in return some gift of her choosing, has now come to claim that gift. The promise made unthinkingly is redeemed benignly, but not by reason of any wisdom of Arthur's. Transcendent meanings have been served by the king's prowess and ambition. But since the symbols of that supervening reality were offered in a context of seeming failure and returned in a similar context, the ritual of giving and receiving does not entail the end of the relationship. It is not that Arthur, his mission completed, now returns the instruments required for his task. Rather it is that Arthur is confirmed in his abiding relation to the transcendent by this sacrament of interdependence.

In the beginning, a shrouded hermit healed Arthur's wounds and then Merlin led him to the lake and Excaliber. In the end, Arthur is led once more to the lake, returns the sword, and is claimed by its Lady so that his grievous wounds might be healed. The trajectory of Arthur's career closes back upon itself, the completeness of the circle imbuing its history and its impetuosity with unending value.

Sir Bedwere cries out as the barge bearing Arthur to Avalon fades into the mist: "What shall becom of me, now ye go from me and leve me here alone amonge myne enemyes?" And Arthur replies,

Comforte thyselff . . . , and do as well as thou mayste, for in me ys no truste for to truste in. For I muste into the vale of Avylyon to hele me of my grevous wounde. And if thou here nevermore of me, pray for my soule! [1240]

The sons and daughters of England must fend for themselves now that Arthur is no longer among them. They must now act in history without trusting to Arthur's skill or justice to save them. Indeed, as Arthur had once helped them so now they should in their turn help him. Bedwere had provided such assistance first by carrying his wounded liege to the shore so that the mysterious ladies could bear him to safety and healing. As always, the wider pattern of significance had almost been lost due to the failings of the mortal asked to give it realization. Bedwere's conviction that England required Arthur's sword even in the absence of Arthur almost resulted in the cold fingers of death completing their work before Avalon would be reached. But in the end Bedwere muddled through. Arthur would survive, partial thanks to a confused but loyal compatriot.

Bedwere can also help Arthur by praying for his soul. This the good knight does by becoming a hermit priest at a small "chapell besydes Glassyngbyry" where it came to be rumored that Arthur had been buried. Here each day at this holy place Bedwere repeats appropriate rituals of intercession on behalf of a nation's greatest hero. The confluence of a time-honored place, person, and practice assures Bedwere that the sacred shall, in those ritual moments at least, remain present within English history.

Malory refuses to settle the dispute between these two traditions regarding Arthur's end. Is Arthur buried at Glastonbury after all? Probably, "but yet the ermyte knew nat in sertayne that he was veryly the body of kynge Arthur." So then he is not entombed but lives on at Avalon? That view has its claimants also, "yet I woll nat say that hit shall be so." It makes no difference, really, for buried in a churchyard or hidden in a barrow, "here in thys worlde he chaunged hys lyff [1242]."

Arthur's life was indeed transformed by the ways in which its seemingly pedestrian accomplishments served nonetheless as a magnet to draw to it cultural memories, hopes, and practices of the most fundamental sort. In his progression from soldier to adventurer to hero to paradigm, his Briton-cum-English qualities deepened and broadened until they encompassed the full import of that people's sense of their place in human history, their role within the divine economy. Arthur "chaunged hys lyff" by becoming founder and foundation of the English world, assuring through his own significance the endurance of that world across the series of individual lives of men and women who like Bedwere try as best they can to carry on its reality by envisioning its ideals, incarnating its passions, reliving its glories and its miseries.

And if all this be true, then the deepest truth of Arthur is that the transcendent importances endure as they do in order to make possible the English values that are its most profound expression. Given the intimacy by which the Arthurian linchpin ties England to the divine, it must surely be that all creation conspires to make Arthur, his values, his people, a continuing historical reality.

In this confidence, I no longer turn toward the past in longing for a lost but glorious age when things were once briefly as they ought to be. For me now the past can disclose the original conditions for the emergence of the English accomplishments in which I live and move and have my being. And the past is for me at the same time, therefore, the source of those necessary conditions for the continuance of present English reality. Nor, sustained by this newfound confidence, need I turn toward the future out of a misplaced nostalgia for some ideal to be realized only in a far off *eschaton*. I approach the uncertainties of the future knowing that no lasting harm can come as long as my purposes, my hopes and intentions, conform to the permanent values laid down by my heritage. In identifying with Arthur who is this English meaning, I am at peace amid a universe of meanings that give my life a value worth the living.

In this sense, originating, sustaining, fulfilling England's significance: *Hic iacet Arthurus, Rex quondam Rexque futurus.*

Eight

THE UNRAVELING OF TRADITION

> Gossip grows old and becomes myth; myth grows older, and becomes dogma.
>
> Harold Bloom, *A Map of Misreading*

i

The dark side to this bright moon of my security must now be acknowledged.

I had sought a structure to the world that would rescue me from the frightful emptiness of my own momentary experience. A web of derivational threads was disclosed, threads that knit my present non-inferentially with its past and with a complex of other enduring historical realities. There is a stability to the world, I came to realize, that is composed of achievements made possible by the presence of other achievements with which they harmonize. These linked creations spread the character of their accomplishment throughout time and space, drawing their power to do so from their own success. This essential order to the things that are, and my place within it, is what I sought in my flight from Cartesian terror and what I have at last found.

But this framework of meaningfulness exacts a price in return for the security it offers. To be a part of its permanences I must conform to practices and understandings it sets out as necessary. I must develop the habits of fidelity. I must avoid anything that might inadvertently disconnect me from the saving powers of the past. The only way to do this is to

191

be sure that my beliefs and actions replicate in their fundamental structures the patterns of importance they reflect.

This conformity is altruistic as well as pragmatic. Were the importances of tradition simply transcendental, then the choice would be mine and the consequences mine. Conform and live; sunder those allegiances and perish. But the repetitions of old beliefs and practices are the way by which they endure. My fidelity contributes to the stabilizing order of things as well as drawing sustenance from it. My fear of losing meaning is symbiotically yoked with the capacity of ancient meanings to persevere. All the more reason then that I must do nothing that would unravel such a valuable, long-labored garment, this cloak of my people's invulnerability.

Such conservatism is in danger of becoming a way of blindness, however, because it takes for granted two things about tradition. First, it assumes that my appropriation of the past grasps hold of truth, that whenever I strike the past's importances with the solid hammer of my affirmations they will ring true, their tones resonant with reality. And second, my conservatism assumes that the structures of importance are stable, so that once truly possessed they can be sounded again and again uncritically, an enduringly pure source for worthwhile melodies regarding human value and my own fulfillment.

Living amid this framework of confidence, the world no longer frightens me. I see something remarkable, a rainbow in the sky for instance, and from long habit frame its beauty in a familiar structure of interpretation. This rainbow is an omen of fair weather, I tell myself, set there by a benevolent deity to remind me not only of a recent positive change in the day's climatic variations but also of other storms, spiritual as well as physical, that my people survived in times past. And it offers me a promise that, no matter what the future might bring, the power to triumph over adversity still abides among us.

This reading of the sky can easily enough be made unthinkingly. It can become my spontaneous way of interacting with whatever I might experience, for it is already part and parcel of the language, actions, and institutions that for me comprise the world. Since my loyalty is directed toward the permanences of this world, it is natural for me to take the rainbow as no more than an occasion for the traditional pattern of meanings to be once more affirmed, its truth confirmed. If this happens, then I will no longer see through the pre-existing scrim of interpretation to some fresh reality which, by its help, I might learn to appreciate more fully than otherwise. The scrim will instead become a screen to hide me from the turmoil of such novelties, and the screen in turn will become itself a proper substitute for what is real.

The more I behave in this fashion the more my framework for interpreting the world will thus be transformed into an object itself, existing independently of and alongside the rainbow. If by long-established habit I turn to the structure of importances in all its splendor rather than to the simple rainbow in its dull and pedestrian nakedness, it will inevitably be the framework that enchants me and only it that I will know. In this way, mythic reality can eventually come to be preferred to the things of experience it interprets. Since it is only by the power of an interpretive webwork that things make sense, take their place within an ordered universe, it is a great temptation to become persuaded that it alone suffices.

The danger inherent in a tradition is that it might succumb to dogmatism. Its power to organize reality so as to reveal the enduring meanings of things can become a mechanism for obscuring those meanings. Its sacral power can become an idolatry, a confusion of means with ends. If this happens, if the mythic objects comprising a tradition do not, after all, ring true, if its interpretive power so beguiles me that I cannot appreciate its limitations, then the very strength of tradition becomes a debilitating weakness:

The more perfect the dogmatism, the more insecure. A great high topsail that can never be reefed nor furled is the first carried away by the gale.[1]

My confident participation in the enduring importances defined by my people's age-old traditions is based on its proven capacity to encompass everything there is and to give it value. The security provided by this interpretive power is its special virtue. Yet the Achilles' heel of such success is the very trust it engenders—and insists upon. For in realizing myself as essentially a reflection of my heritage, I am in danger of being left defenseless before the intrusion of whatever it blinds me to.

I have set sail into the troubling ocean of human history, proudly steering my course under the power provided by the massive topsail of my cultural myths and their transcendences. But suppose that suddenly a wind comes up which the sail was not designed to utilize. Then the very glory of its massiveness, the very expansiveness by which it could push me on toward my destination regardless of the encircling terrors, might mean its destruction. In one swift and disastrous moment the carefully wrought efforts of millenia could be shattered into worthless fragments.

The tendency toward dogmatic finality is doubly destructive. On the one hand it leads to rigidity, to overconfidence in the power of traditional beliefs and practices to be as successful in the future as they have been in the past. And so instead of controlling change and the emergence of novelty by incorporating them within its enduring structures, the tradition merely resists novelty, refuses its challenge. By such methods the tradition eventually becomes inadequate. But on the other hand, no tradition is able to see its own limitations clearly or fully, and dogmatism leads to the self-destructive assumption that the world and its worldview are synonymous. Blindness to internal and to external limitations is thus the danger lurking at the heart of any successful tradition.

Toynbee generalizes the social and political consequences of the first of these two destructive tendencies, that of blind allegiance to a saving truth. He had taught me (in Chapter Four) the importance of what he calls 'mimesis,' the imitation by the general populace of the values, beliefs, and actions of its leaders. The cultural unity and historical effectiveness of a civilization depend upon mimesis. Short of everyone having the same creative powers, mimetic devices are required for the dissemination of fundamental purposes and convictions throughout a society. I argued, in opposition to Toynbee, that it was not only understandable but in fact preferable that mimesis be directed backward, that the past was required as a role model for the present in order to assure continued intimacy with important meanings. My concern was with preservation, not invention. Stabilizing the values that surrounded and comforted me was, I knew, the one sure way to tame contingency.

Yet I must admit that Toynbee is correct in his worries about mimesis. He complains that loyalty to the past is likely to stultify criticism and creative novelty. He then rescues this claim from being merely the expression of a preference for variety over repetition by making a further claim. The mimesis by others of a creative minority, in the absence of continual innovative energy, will eventually fail in its attempt to fashion a dynamic consensus. Mimesis is, after all, a 'drill'; it demands that a normative practice be repeated and repeated until that practice becomes habitual. The imitator need not understand the process nor believe in it, as long as outward behavior and conventional speech conform to social expectation. "In the gesture of mimesis, the uncreative majority is making an outward movement of conformity and not an inward adaptation."[2]

An immediate, and ironic, result, says Toynbee in agreement with Santayana, is that the surface appearances of social significance come to be taken as the deeper reality for which they are merely the sign. Fact becomes confused with the meaning it is supposed to exemplify. The places, persons, and practices embodying a treasured inheritance are taken to comprise that very inheritance. Ritual becomes an end in itself; institutions become instruments for their own perpetuation; leaders vest meaning in their person rather than their function. I thus find myself no longer looking to my heritage for the value it gives to certain current beliefs and practices, but instead I think of the current practices as justifying the inheritance or making it relevant, eventually as actually defining it. So I am left with bare present fact, devoid of its anchor in the structures of transcending importance, but protected still by habit and social power. My uncritical loyalty toward the symbols of authority can ultimately cut me off from that authority itself.

This fetishism, this idolatry of symbols, has the further consequence of blinding the creative leadership of a society as well as their imitators. Demanding mimetic conformity on the part of others, the societal elite "infect themselves with the hypnotism which they have deliberately induced in their followers."[3] They become convinced by their own propaganda, and so themselves imitate unthinkingly the superficial expectations that have become the appropriate and customary responses to the events of life. The cultural elite lose their powers of originality, of analysis and inventiveness. The managers of business, the intelligentsia, the politicians and generals, increasingly all alike apply old solutions to new problems, fighting the next war with the techniques of the last, promising that tomorrow will be like yesterday, that the tried and the true are synonymous.

But if old methods do not in fact resolve new problems adequately, and if at the same time the consensus is only apparent regarding what the problems are and what the methods for solving them should be, then the unity and effectiveness of the culture begin to weaken. Fissures appear in the landscape of conformity, and if such dissension cannot be overcome by evoking the power of deep-seated social meanings, then those in power have left only the recourse to brute force. In Toynbee's apt phrases, the charismatic leadership of a "creative minority" is replaced by the repressive coercion of a "dominant minority."

Such measures are, of course, only temporarily successful. The authority of government comes not from the barrel of a submachine gun but from the enduring values shared by the wider culture. Despite the attempts to enforce conformity, the cracks in the social order continue to widen, until internal tensions and external pressures can no longer be contained. The societal landscape is disrupted by upheavals of volcanic intensity. Social order gives way to chaos and, dramatically or across the agonies of an extended interregnum, chaos gives way in turn to the emergence of a new set of sacred meanings deemed worthy of imitation. And so there appears within history a successor civilization. But my heritage, and the whole vast edifice of significance that I had thought imperishable, is forever lost.

Toynbee does not claim that this scenario for the breakdown and collapse is inevitable, however. The alternative is to keep creative mimesis alive by avoiding overconfidence, by recognizing that conservation of the whole requires constant readjustment of the parts. But such admonitions are more easily preached than practiced, and even when a tradition successfully avoids rigidity it still must face the problem that its scope is limited.

This is nicely illustrated by the way in which Europeans first dealt with the newly discovered American wilderness.[4] For sixteenth and seventeenth-century Europeans, the New World was a land without definite shape, a vast expanse of ignorance relieved only at the margins by information that had been gleaned from explorers in their journeys along the thin line of its littoral. America was truly *terra incognita*, lacking the hierarchy of places and their relationships that allows for distinctions of sacred and profane, important and ordinary. Nor were there any practices and people having established significance, no resonant history in tune with European history, but only a few scattered Indian myths and unimportant tribal stories.

Cartographers and writers were consequently forced to draw upon familiar European understandings in their attempts to provide visual and literary roadmaps for finding one's way across such alien terrain:

Without quite being aware of it, they were used to imagining a landscape much as Virgil did 1500 years earlier—as a multi-layered and carefully composed picture, a picture with all the relationships worked out and fixed through art, the end product of a land shaped and torn and reshaped and finally sanctified by history, custom, labor, human hopes and fears and institutions. In short, a landscape for them was not simply land, but land transformed through culture.[5]

This 'picture' they then imposed on that blank and protean stretch of time and space they called America. They quite literally filled in the empty spaces with extrapolations from their familiar, ever-normative world.

Sea-serpents, exotic beasts, and natives in costume were emblazoned on the New World maps, for instance. This was done in part to satisfy aesthetic purposes, to provide in traditionally decorative ways some relief on the page from the vast expanses of white for which no information was available. But it was also done to indicate something of the kind and character of the fauna inhabiting such regions. And what is striking about the drawings is their familiarity. The strange beasts were taken from classical mythology, and the natives were depicted as bucolic Greeks in oddly feathered raiment. By such devices the unknown was neutralized, its terrors tamed even in advance of their being encountered. The alien creatures of this alien world were replaced by familiar alternatives. Monsters and barbarians are strange entities, to be approached with caution. They lie outside civilization, but classically so: their strangeness is a part of the meaningful world, even though their location is at its periphery.

So in these and similar ways the New World was preformed with respect to its importances, to the value of its places, the significance of its inhabitants, the purpose of the events that had and would transpire there. The familiar, long-established traditions regarding the conditions for something being a natural object or a cultural artifact were used uncritically in structuring the ways in which the New World was to be understood and the significance of its facticities and possibilities assessed. As a result, Europeans were cut off for a long time from the truly novel dimensions of American reality. They were blinded to those aspects of America not encompassed by an order of things that they took to be self-evidently inclusive.[6]

From my present perspective, those early maps and reports on the New World seem the work of imaginations run wild, filled with falsehoods that were probably evoked by the pragmatics of propaganda and the exaggerations of the *raconteur*. But this is only the wisdom of hindsight, the insight granted by historical perspective. Having the vantage provided by my culture's current claims to interpretive completeness, I can see clearly the limitations of that old European world.

I am shaken by this realization. For this means by implication that I have no way with respect to my own beliefs and practices to distinguish between the truth grasped whole and grasped but partially. The horizon of my worldview will always seem to encompass the totality of things simply because, by definition, everything that can be experienced falls within the circle of its perimeter. The very question of a beyond, of realities lying over the horizon and outside the meaningful landscape of my world, is nonsense to me because, again by definition, it asks me to give a meaning to what for me must lie beyond all meaning.

What appears to be a linkage with importances that stretch to spatial and temporal infinity might therefore be a connective pattern that reaches out only to the horizon, to the farthest hill and the most ancient antiquity but no further. Beyond that hill, for all I know, there may lie a continent still unexplored, an elder race old before humanity was born. With such wonders I am ill-prepared to deal, unfit to cope. For I would quite likely be made blind to their accomplishments, deaf to the call of their possibilities, precisely because of the very success of my familiar importances. In control of everything that lies within my limited horizons, I may well miss forever what lies beyond. To my sorrow or to my destruction.

This problem of blindness to the limitations in scope that necessarily characterize any worldview is more disturbing than the problem of rigidity because less curable. It would seem that the very fact of belief entails the blindness. I have warned against revolution on the grounds that tradition should not be set aside in favor of some elusive future or idealized past. The achievements of my ancestors as embodied in the cultural places, practices, and persons I think important are, I have argued, a necessary context for meaningful existence. Loyalty to those achievements need not imply rigid adherence to them, however. I am happy to invite reform of the tradition, for I realize that anything which exists only through being continually reappropriated will unavoidably change over time. I ask only that the changes be modulations on the basic cultural themes, the pace of them moderate, their purpose to conserve. Such constructive criticism is how freedom discovers its significance as the source of the majestic importances that are the essence of human history.

But it seems that even this kind of mediating loyalty, simply in virtue of its being an intense loyalty, tends toward inflexibility and narrowness. It is relatively blind to its own limits and so is all too likely not to respond creatively to the new forms permanence must take if it is to persist amid change. If I doubt the truths of my tradition then I am led to inquire regarding alternatives, for as with historical perspective this doubt sets me outside of the world of my beliefs and so discloses their limits. But to believe in a tradition is to be immersed in it, to live it fully, and so not to be aware except abstractly of its limitations. By totally embracing the past in this way as the source of living meaning, I am in danger of suffocating its vital capacity to save me from unknown sources of meaninglessness.

Arthur has taught me that loyalty to a tradition does not require a pure heart nor a well-informed mind, however much these virtues might be preferred. The importances I serve can be misunderstood, can be distorted by the passions of the moment, can become entangled with unseemly ends. And yet these importances can sustain their meanings in the face of such adversity and even deepen them. But if Tintagel, Autun, and Salisbury Plain teach me that even deceit, foolishness, and distrust can be leaven for the bread of life's significance, they do not teach me anything of significances beyond my own. The Arthurian myth is all my world by virtue of its very success, its power either to encompass differences with its meanings or to banish them into the void of unutterable nonsense. So dogmatism arises unbidden at the very heart of my beliefs not because I am narrow-minded in my commitments nor because I am unwilling to adapt to novelty. Rather the very ability of my traditions to be open to change creates a single-ordered universe that in its success swallows up all opposition and so knows no bounds. My tradition knows not that it is in fact limited, until from beyond its limits something arises to shatter it.

I am forced onto the horns of an impossible dilemma. Total fealty to transcendent values was offered as the keel to a vessel that would rescue me from drowning in solipsism, from being engulfed by the terrors of contingent immediacy. The importances of the past can save me only if I give them my complete allegiance, allow them to comprise the very essence of my beliefs and practices. But I could well find myself lashed permanently to the masthead of a partial truth, a partial ordering of reality, that has claimed falsely its universality. If so, then when the excluded aspects of reality generate as they inevitably will the storm clouds of their own authority, when they effect at last their own distinctive winds of change, then will the topmast of my vessel be shorn off and I will be left adrift clinging hopelessly to what is now only an empty hulk of meaning.

Toynbee reminds me that what is not inevitable is nonetheless true without exception of human civilizations. The adherents to a tradition are blinded by their own success into beliefs and practices that are unnecessarily rigid and that are unconcerned about what might lie beyond their scope. This has certainly been true of the Western tradition. Its dogmatic self-confidence has led it in the name of its sacred importances to substitute dominance for creativity and to confuse its certainties with universality. As a result the traditions I have argued are so important to meaningful survival are increasingly in disarray throughout the West. They are unable to command effective loyalties, to account for emergent novelties, to encompass the full horizon of my, and your and our, experience. Tradition has become synonymous with dogma, which is to say that it is no longer believed, no longer gives vital purpose to our lives, no longer undergirds our understanding of what is real, worthwhile, and significant.

But what is the difference between solipsism of the present moment and a pattern of belief that has come untethered from the vital concreteness of human life? I am come full circle. In the end as in the beginning, I am plagued by the realization that salvation from the world's terrors might be a dream that can never be realized.

ii

The sense of being dominated in the name of traditional values by some powerful and repressive minority is widespread in my culture, in contemporary Western civilization. The importances of the past are said to stultify, not liberate. Jacques Derrida captures this mood as well as anyone in his discussions of various French attempts to reject tradition in absolutely all of its manifestations.[7]

The notion of writing provides his controlling metaphor; tradition is to be understood as a vast Bible, a system of written and therefore objective assertions, a structure of truth serving as the guide and governor for all human activity. This one book of cultural articulation, to which all individual 'books' contribute, is precisely what I have meant by the totality of linked importances. It is an objective order of things, functioning to separate meaning from meaninglessness, rationality from madness, truth from error. Under the tutelage of this enduring value system, I learn how to think and act and feel in a civilized way, which is to say in a way that makes me confident that what I do is worthwhile and satisfying.

The key to a written work is repetition. Because it is embodied in a material medium it can be easily replicated, its content preserved by others imitating it, repeating its patterns within their lives, embedding them in cultural institutions and ideologies. The meaning of such objective structures of meaning is thus not exhausted in the moment of their emergence into experience. They overflow the present, and by their iterative power stretch out their significance into enduring strands of order.

But the problem with this, its abhorrence, is that such perpetuations force an unnatural conformity upon the world. The word, objectified in time and space, the word become flesh, defines in advance the boundary conditions for my life. In this sense, history, which is the process by which patterns of human order are concretely realized and sustained, is everywhere a matter of violence. It involves the subordination of the future to the past. The landscape of the historical is comprised by

totalitarian structures endowed with a unity of internal meaning, spiritual organisms in a sense, cultural worlds all of whose functions and manifestations are solidary and to which *Weltanschauungen* correspond correlatively.[8]

Thus tradition sacrifices spontaneity for the sake of survival, substitutes the dead hand of the past for the vitality of genuine life.

Derrida is intrigued by the poet Antonin Artaud, who attempted to devise a theatrical strategy for breaking out of this repressive structure. Artaud sees the theatrical tradition as an archetype of imposed order. The author of the play is God, himself absent from the scene but imposing a written document upon the space of the stage, a script that gives the marching orders by which the director then shapes the behaviors of actors so as to conform to predetermined ends. The author's script precedes the performance, controls throughout the meanings that will be communicated, and can endure despite the eventual perishing of the actors. In this sense the stage imitates historical reality: it is a structure of repression representing a structure of repression.

And so in the name of liberty and life, Artaud raises his standard of rebellion. There shall be no more written script in the theatre, nor even any speech forming sound by reference to inherited linguistic structures, no longer a syntax and grammar of cultural meanings. Spontaneous gesture and dance shall replace memorized stage movements; shouting and babble shall become the alternative to articulation. Artaud's whole project might seem to be utter madness, but that is exactly the reaction to be expected from those in power, Artaud argues, when they are confronted by an act of defiance that purposefully rejects the order of things that has defined sanity as conformity to its rules.

Another rebel identified by Derrida is Georges Bataille, who rejects all forms of Hegelian dialectic with its perpetual mediation of differences, its claim to be able endlessly to merge the apparently disparate into a single and truly real totality. Against this slavery to the whole, Bataille counters with a vision of the sovereign individual who prefers fragmentation, even ignorance, to the fascism of imposed importances. The instrument of this sovereignty is laughter, a refusal to take the webbings of cultural meaning seriously. I am to play the fool, to seek ecstatically the loss of sense, the embrace of unknowledge, and in so doing to escape the unrelenting clutches of an ever-conciliatory dialectic.[9]

Artaud calls this rebellion 'parricide,' for it asks that I murder my parents, deny utterly those who have given me life and have supported my growth into full personhood. The support is a lie, I am told; it breeds dependence by the demands of its love and chokes off creativity by the overweaning power of its importances. Life, individuality, distinctiveness requires liberation from the past. As someone perhaps influenced by Derrida has put it:

To live, the poet must *misinterpret* the father, by the crucial act of misprision, which is the rewriting of the father. But who, what is the poetic father? The voice of the other, of the *daimon*, is always speaking in one; the voice that cannot die because already it has survived death—*the dead poet lives in one.* . . . A poet . . . is not so much a man speaking to men as a man rebelling against being spoken to by a dead man (the precursor) outrageously more alive than himself.[10]

Rebellions are now a commonplace of my civilization. Initially my reaction to such acts of cultural defiance was simply to brand them as doomed to failure. Surely such gestures are parasites feeding on the very values they impugn. The more they rail against the times the more they simply exhibit the character of those times.

I was reminded of the ancient Hindu tale concerning a monkey who became upset with the scheme of things and with Krishna its source and exemplar. Perched in Krishna's hand so that he might the better see into the divine eye, this monkey shouts his defiance of the god and vows to venture forth into a life of true independence far removed from the familiar universe. And so the monkey boldly makes his journey to the end of the world and beyond, to the end of the stars and still beyond, to the edge of time and then further still. And at last, freed from the imposed importances, he stands alone and glorious, his own monkey at last. In a final gesture of disrespect and as a proof of his liberty, the monkey urinates upon the ground in front of him. And Krishna, smiling, wipes the pitiful drops from the index finger of his hand.

Yet Toynbee has been more perspicacious than I was in these initial reactions of mine. To be sure, the importances of my past are all-encompassing and define even the conditions of their opposition. But when these values cease being imitated by virtue of their persuasive power, they will need to be imposed by force as the only remedy against social chaos. And that is increasingly what has been happening in Western culture. But repression stirs up revolt as much as it quells it. I doubt that the monkey changed his mind after discovering that Krishna was omnipresent. The boundary of the monkey's prison was greater than he had thought, but it was still a prison.

The esoteric rebels come first, says Toynbee: the ranters, the hippies, the apocalyptic cultists, the Artauds and Batailles, those who withdraw their allegiance from the whole for the sake of some private fantasy. Of them, perhaps, I need only smile indulgently. But afterward comes the withdrawal into selfishness and cynicism of the general populace, and in consequence the collapse of the old order.

I need not be worried by Derrida's report on Artaud and the other rebels of our troubled age, therefore, but when Derrida moves from a discussion of such negative gesturings to the elaboration of his own positive argument, I should rightfully worry. His effort to deconstruct the edifice of Western meaning, his project of decentering all structures of social value, is threatening in the extreme. For it is one thing to claim that the importances of the past are not absolute, that some truths escape their envisagement. And it is fine occasionally for someone to rebel against that inadequacy in the name of the neglected truths. But Derrida has a different claim to make, a far more radical attack to launch against my citadels of meaning. He would claim that there are no ultimate meanings to be encompassed. No objective truth is omitted from my world because, since there are many worlds, not one, and hence many truths but no universal truth, there is nothing to be omitted.

A structure for Derrida is any set of internally coherent and interconnected relationships that has either an initial source or final end as its foundation, as that in virtue of which it comprises a totality, a single whole. An historical structure, a set of importances, endures by means of the varied ways by which its reality is repeatedly realized temporally. The rules governing those transformations, assuring the transition from one exemplification of a structure to its replica and to the replica of that replica, are already implicit in the origin or in the endpoint of the process. Such a controlling point of embarcation is an *arche*; its parallel, wherein the route of historical transmission is controlled by the destination, is a *telos*. The one, the other, or both thus provide the kind of overarching order, the structure linking together the subordinate structures, that permits meaningfulness to be sustained in time. In every meaningful structure the *alpha* and *omega* are united, and the in-between is their articulation.

This description of a 'centered structure' sounds very much like the definition of a monad in Leibniz, or the unfolding of the dialectic in Hegel, or a route of occasions in Whitehead, although choice plays a crucial role in the last of these structures, none at all in the first, and is somehow both free and determined in the Hegelian version. Insofar as Derrida's notion suggests such traditional philosophic concepts, I can be assured that he is not providing me with a two-legged stool, constructed in order to be toppled, but rather is offering a reasonably accurate generalization of the understanding in Western culture concerning the patterns that make for stability and objectivity.

But Derrida says that there are no such structures. The patterns of meaning that arise in history have no 'natural site' to which they are tethered, no natural destination toward which they are lured, nothing whatsoever outside themselves that might serve to ground them. The patterns of meaning regnant in one historical period or among the peoples of one culture will be different from those extant in other times or at other places. The differences are fundamental and irreducible, for there is no principle of sufficient reason to govern their transformation into one another, no dialectic to do the mediating, no lure for feeling to guide the creativity.

There remains only the play of differences, and the only ethic for how I should comport myself amid those differences is to retain a proper respect for the uniqueness of each.

I should contest all claims to the existence and efficacy of centered structures, says Derrida, for

The best liberation from violence is a certain putting into question, which makes the search for an *archia* [sic] tremble.[11]

The decentering of structures is true liberation. It is an approach to life that does not merely rant and rave, shaking its fist impotently at the massive order of repression that surrounds it everywhere. Instead it invites me to take up a playful stance toward reality, to set loose my imagination so that I might fashion my own worlds at will or frolic joyfully amid the creations of others, enjoying each for what it is, for its distinctive vision of how things might meaningfully be arranged. Each new structure I uncover or invent enriches my sense of what the possibilities for structure are. Human beings through the centuries have been so many artists constantly fashioning new works, new worlds of significance, out of the paint and wood and canvas of experience.

Nor is this artistic reference merely metaphorical exuberance. Nelson Goodman echoes Derrida's enthusiasm for the human capacity to make worlds,[12] and in careful detail explicates the characteristics of a meaning structure that make it very much like a work of art and not at all like a mirror reflecting some other, transcendental reality. Truth is not a matter of my mental image mimicking accurately some external reality that is its objective ground. I am cut loose from that oddly redundant expectation, able instead to find truth in the aesthetic requirements of internal coherence and clarity, and in the pragmatic criteria of relevance and utility.

This decentering of belief, this disappearance within my culture of the old confidence that human understanding can link itself securely to transcendent historical meaning, has itself a history. In addition to Derrida and Goodman, I will mention three other recent versions of the tale. Each lends its special perspective and thereby corroborates my growing realization that the twentieth century is heir to a trajectory in traditional belief that is approaching its nadir.

Michel Foucault approaches the question of cultural decentering by contrasting sixteenth-century European understandings with those that succeeded it.[13] Mimesis was central to a pre-Cartesian, pre-Newtonian perspective. The things of this world, including the human languages, were thought to be signs for interpreting the meaning of the natural order. This involved a threefold relationship: auspicious things or events, including the writings of the ancients; the world inhabited by humankind, the affinities and mutual resemblances of which being what those signs explicate; and the universe, the macrocosm of God's whole creation, for which the world known to human consciousness is a microcosm.

Here was a centered structure of the richest sort. The temporal, earthly order of things was thought to mirror the timeless, heavenly order, and both were imitated by a natural system of signs. The arts and sciences both had the same task: to read the symbols found everywhere throughout experience for clues regarding the way things relate, to sift the reports and commentaries on what these symbols meant, finding in them further and deeper relationships, unendingly engaged thereby in the pious effort to discern in the book of nature the purposes of its Author, the divine *arche* and *telos* of the cosmos.

But according to Foucault this mimetic sensibility is completely recast in the early seventeenth century. Words come to be taken as human inventions, not divine gifts. Speech is cut free from its tethering to a transcendent foundation. Words can still be true insofar as they refer univocally to a world analysable into units which are only interrelated accidentally, but the relationship is stipulated not discovered. A natural, objective relationship between human speech and the Word that created the world is replaced by the belief that human invention can create a word able to mirror truly a natural order that is independent of its musings. The atoms blindly run, while men and women fashion for themselves a mental replica of that process and call it truth.

By the nineteenth century, says Foucault, even this artificial mimicry in its turn gives way to a belief that the orders fabricated by human imagination are creatures of hedonistic desire, economic self-interest, and group survival. As the twentieth century draws toward its close, the last remnants of the older fabric have become so tattered that they are barely recognizable.

After listening to Foucault's arguments, I cannot avoid drawing the conclusion that objective truth has become no more than a nostalgia, a quaint belief tolerated in a world of stridently pragmatic purposing. Or worse, as Derrida argues, I must acknowledge that it has become a weapon of repression, a useful device for those bent upon snuffing out the bright candle of liberty. When my Western tradition abandoned its belief that language is a natural phenomenon able to disclose fundamental truth, a process of reconceptualization was set in motion that has eventuated in the conviction that every meaningful ordering of experience is subjective, and therefore lacks justification for excluding any other ordering's claims to truth or relevance. All systems of belief are equally viable, and any attempt to argue otherwise must be seen as an attempt at repression. Without objective norms, without defining importances, there are only differences to be noted and not values to be ranked.

According to Erich Auerbach,[14] the literary and artistic version of this devolution begins with the emergence in the Christian middle ages of a style of expression involving figural interpretation. In terms of this approach, for instance, Abraham's sacrifice of Isaac should be understood as a story with its own beginning and end, having a meaning that can be read directly from the account, a meaning that is about the demands of the divine and the loyalty of God's true servants. But the sacrifice of Isaac at the same time prefigures the sacrifice of Christ, the testing of the human race and the gracious salvation reserved for those who keep the faith. In any such figural reading of an event or person, a connection is exhibited between the immediately available subject matter and some other event or person unconnected with it temporally or spatially. The event being depicted in the story or art work signifies not only itself but something other as well, this other being taken as an extension or fulfillment of what has been directly given. The visible is a figure of the invisible.

Meanings that are hidden from sensory observation are in this way revealed. The supporting foundation that social importances provide is never directly available to me, for the origins of anything lie hidden behind the curtain of the past and the culmination of a process is always veiled by the future. But I may interpret what is present as having an origin and a destiny, an *arche* and a *telos*, by construing it figuratively. In doing so I will break it free from the surface sequence of causal linkages so as to disclose the bedrock upon which it rests. And since any foundation defines the essential character of whatever structures it supports, a figural interpretation discloses the transcendent meanings that lie behind observable reality, the truth behind the appearances, the steadfast behind the perishing immediate.

Thus, Auerbach argues, there emerged in medieval Christian culture a view of human life in which, overarching all earthly events, no matter how fraught with suffering and loss they might appear to be,

stood the towering and all-embracing dignity of a single event, the appearance of Christ, and everything tragic was but figure or reflection of a single complex of events, into which it necessarily flowed at last: the complex of the Fall, of Christ's birth and passion, and of the Last Judgment.[15]

This centered structure, replete with the mythic gods and heroes that give it vivacity and human relevance, is obviously one of the primary importances rescuing me from the terrors of temporal flux. If the iconography of the art that adorns my buildings and the meaning of the books that march across my shelf are always and repeatedly a figural expression of that enduring structure, then I will feel as well as understand its encompassing assurances. I will know with confidence that my world is truly a mirror of permanent realities.

Auerbach goes on to describe how the notion of figuration has been undermined over the centuries. The heroic epics of late medieval chivalry, including many of the articulations of my beloved Arthurian legend, separated their ideals from the practical and everyday, reserving for a few the realization of invisible truth while for the majority of humankind such mimesis was deemed irrelevant. In the resulting vacuum, a form of literary expression took root in which events no longer prefigured hidden realities. Boccaccio's accounts of mundane happenings, both comic and tragic in their immediacy, have no significance beyond themselves. They occur, they are gone; they tell a momentary tale which, it is hoped, a reader will find diverting.

By Shakespeare this untethering of the importances came to mean the absence of any single and all-encompassing significance. There is still "a basic fabric of the world," but it lacks permanence, has become "a world which is perpetually regenerating itself out of the most varied forces." Life's meaning and its value are perpetually woven and rewoven, these fashionings providing for the human actors on the stage of history some modicum of the guiding significance and ultimate meaning they crave. But the sense is not so much discovered as created, requiring as it does that each individual give his own distinctive final shape to the elements of flux and meaning that comprise the mystery of things. Hamlet or Lear make their own destinies by means of the character, the commitments and the ripeness, that they have themselves given to their lives.

The defiguring of centered structures of meaning culminates in contemporary fiction—Auerbach's examples are Proust, Joyce, and Woolf—where the subjectivity of a character predominates, overpowering and replacing even the last vestiges of the objective criteria of order and purpose that traditionally frame a narrative. The aim of a novel is to reflect the human condition just as it is in its daily, confusing immediacy:

We are constantly endeavoring to give meaning and order to our lives in the past, the present, and the future, to our surroundings, the world in which we live; with the result that our own lives appear in our own conception as total entities—which to be sure are always changing, more or less radically, more or less rapidly, depending on the extent to which we are obliged, inclined, and able to assimilate the onrush of new experience.[16]

I am on my own now. The 'onrush' of the fleeting moments is given a structure, a meaningful coherence, that is more or less adequate to my needs, depending on the degree of my motivation and ability to provide it. But there are no pre-existing patterns to draw from, no vaguely discerned prefigurings to clarify or sharpen. There is just the piling up of random experience and my own inventiveness. The teaching of twentieth century literature is that I am quite literally the solitary captain of my fate, the unassisted and unsupported maker of my own destiny.

Richard Rorty's account of this tale[17] confines itself to the epistemological controversies in modern and contemporary academic philosophy, but the message is the same. The traditional belief is that human beings are blessed with a "glassy essence"—the phrase is Shakespeare's—which is their ability to grasp universal truths by mirroring them in consciousness. I have a privileged access to my own mind and through it a privileged access to the fundamental truths, the necessary structures, of reality. But this notion turns out to be a quagmire of contradiction, and much of the history of modern philosophy has to do with various attempts to crystalize its viscoid ambiguities in order to provide it once and for all with the needed firm underpinnings. Each attempt in its turn has proven to be a failure: Spinoza gives way to Hume, Kant to Dilthey, Husserl to Davidson. But the critics are no better off than those they criticize, for

there is no way to make some empirical discipline do what transcendental philosophy could not do—that is, say something about the scheme of representations we are employing which will make clear its tie to the content we wish to represent.[18]

The only solution, says Rorty, is to abandon foundationalism altogether, this theory that epistemological mimesis is the condition for truth. In its place I am to find consolation in pragmatism, in "truth without mirrors," in an understanding of consciousness as the human capacity to make rather than find truth. The "incommensurability" of the rich embarrassment of attempted fabrications is to be celebrated not condemned, for it witnesses to the power of the human spirit, its glory, its priceless powers of accomplishment.

These four accounts of the collapse in centering beliefs—those offered by Derrida, Foucault, Auerbach, Rorty—are surely sufficient to make my point, but I should like to add one more nonetheless. The trajectory followed in the last century and a half by Hegelian interpretation is an instructive illustration of the decentering process at work.[19]

At first Hegel's dialectic is understood to trace an objective temporal process, the transformation of abstract Idea into concrete and universal self-consciousness. The process is believed to take place in time, *is* time articulating itself, and human history is its culmination. *Deus sive historia*: the perfection of divine understanding and the true order of historical change are one and the same. What is exhibited in the magisterial progression of Spirit through the ages is recapitulated again and again in the rise of each new nation onto the stage of world-historical significance, and repeated yet again in the coming to consciousness, to fully civilized consciousness, of each individual. Thus Hegel recaptures in his philosophy the mimetic layerings of reality, the figurational relatedness of things, that comprise the essence of Western understanding.

But soon the myth of God's incarnation as history had to be demythologized. Hegel, it was pointed out, had said that philosophy cannot predict the future but can only comprehend what has already happened. The owl of Minerva takes flight only after the day's work has been completed, at the dusk when at last reflection can begin to comprehend what has transpired, welding the momentary fragments of action into an intelligible, meaningful unity. For this new kind of Hegelian, philosophy is always an interpretation from a standpoint. The philosopher always stands at the end of history, discerning the order of things which that unique perspective provides. The vantage point is all-encompassing as regards the past, able to incorporate into some appropriate niche all of the prior perspectives devised by the human mind. But it must remain open toward the future which always transcends it. In this approach, thus, truth is seen as radically historical, in the double sense that it is both relative and developmental. The permanences and enduring significances disclosed by any one generation may be true for it but have no lasting truth, except insofar as they are taken up into each succeeding disclosure of significance. Hegel spoke the truth from the vantage of early nineteenth-century European understanding, but 150 years later another truth is needed, one that dialectically surpasses Hegel but in doing so retains all that remains living in his philosophy.

Only a simple step is required to move from this progressive kind of historicism to that of Oswald Spengler.[20] For him each culture has its own unique perspective, the structures and dynamic of which are fundamentally Hegelian. But the various cultures he describes are each closed in upon themselves, each a vantage point that knows not its predecessors, that succeeds them without surpassing them. Spengler's metaphor is of the flowers in a field. Each has its day, the Apollonian, the Magian, the Faustian, springing up into bud and blossom. And each perishes, to be followed willy-nilly by new buddings and further perishings. There is a structure to the birth and death of each example of human order, but there is no structure to the transition from one order to the next. Among the centers of order there is no order.

The conceit of some contemporary Hegelian scholarship is that this radical historicism can be avoided by introducing the notion of heuristic models. A philosophic system is henceforth to be taken as an *organon* for interpretation. It is a schema of the relationships among interpretive concepts, taken in abstraction from any specific content. In this sense akin to a mathematical system, it is to be judged pragmatically. Is it powerful enough to provide a way for analyzing, clarifying, and coordinating the complexities of any hypothesis proposed as a model for some aspect of experience? Is it adequate to the relevant details, internally coherent, and predictively fecund? The claim is then made that Hegel's system, including his notion of historical dialectic, is just such an *organon*. It makes no claims about the past, tells no tale of permanences and change over time, forecasts no future, implies no moral imperatives. But given any such claims, any attempts to describe, evaluate, or otherwise manipulate the elements of experience for some purpose, the Hegelian system will provide the most effective instrument for doing so. Its subtlety and sophistication are unmatched.

The final collapse into raw subjectivism comes when even this version of Hegel is said to be overly pretentious. Hegelianism, as any metaphysics, is then proposed as primarily a dream, a poem expressive of human hope. Its function is affective, rhetorical. I am to value it as I do all great literature: for what it tells me about myself and not for what it purports to say about the world. So there are as many metaphysical dreams as there are dreamers, and among them the Hegelian variety are especially attractive. Truth in even its most attenuated sense is no longer a relevant consideration, but rather beauty, harmony, and sublimity.

So what is the meaning of this twice-told tale, this account from so many perspectives of the demythologizing of truth? The moral is this: I am being offered trivialization as an alternative to blindness, and I find it no less unpalatable. The soaring, saving mythologies of my people were shown to be susceptible to dogmatic closure, prone to claim a universality and certainty they could not provide. But once I turned away from blind loyalty to a single truth and toward the possibility of multiple truths, I found that the controlling myths underwent a rapid devolution from expressions of profound truth to historically delimited partial truths. Then they became legends illuminative of an age or group, often used by that group as a repressive instrument for social control. And eventually my myths came to be seen as stories, merely the expressions of momentary rebellion and individual imagination, of public outrage and private deviance.

The power of a myth is its synecdoche, its capacity to embody the whole in a concrete particular. But the desacralization of myth has seemingly rendered it useless as a resource for living a meaningful life. Yet those who would decenter my confidence in the truth of traditional meaning have not wanted to leave me bereft of help. They each have had their own solutions to purvey.

Auerbach, for instance, celebrates "the wealth of reality and depth of life in every moment to which we surrender ourselves without prejudice." Having emptied the world of hidden meanings and orienting purposes, having reduced reality to the passing moment and my subjective perspective regarding it, Auerbach would make of this a virtue:

It is precisely the random moment which is comparatively independent of the controversial and unstable orders over which men fight and despair; it passes unaffected by them, as daily life. The more it is exploited, the more the elementary things which our lives have in common come to life.[21]

The moment, purified of the encumbrances of tradition, is proposed as a kind of nominalist substitution for universal structures. Although these moments are random and without depth, their very egalitarian directness gives them importance. Everyone experiences such randomness and such directness, after all, and somehow by sharing together these "elementary things," without an appeal to erudite interpretation and figural disclosures, humanity can find its common ground.

Derrida offers me the "play of the world" as his alternative to the work of tradition. I can linger should it be my wont in the graveyards of nostalgia, longing for lost foundations that in fact never did exist. But he invites me instead to take pleasure in being liberated from the tyranny of things past. I am to embrace

the Nietzschean *affirmation*, that is the joyous affirmation of the play of the world and of the innocence of becoming, the affirmation of a world of signs without fault, without truth, and without origin.[22]

The deconstruction of stultifying order is not chaos, says Derrida, but history, the middle way between reason and madness. To affirm the historicity of all things is to claim that becoming, the indeterminate, is not something to be transcended, to be fled from in terror. The becoming of worlds that I and others fashion is an innocent activity precisely because it does not mean anything other than itself. If the absence of determinate structure is not a failure, the result of some betrayal on the part of myself or my ancestors, our inability to perpetuate an archaic reality, then the present should be enjoyed for what in fact it is, the perpetual opportunity for new creation.

Derrida's celebration of play is reminiscent of the neo-Freudian rejection of those discontents that unavoidably result from the repressions required by civilized order.[23] And his adulation of becoming echoes the existentialist insistence that "ephemeral creation" is more true to human realities than an artistic expression that attempts to mirror a supposedly enduring Truth.[24] For Derrida, as for these others, the individual human being, defined in terms of his powers of creative self-expression and affirmation, is the one true, abiding locus for value. Such values are as multiple as the multiplicity of persons, as many as the myriad moments of their inventiveness. Social order distorts, attenuates, and destroys this plurality of meanings and so must itself be destroyed. Or rather it must be shown to be in fact merely the product of humans attempting to impose their own brief authority upon others. Playfulness substitutes the tolerance of difference for any attempt to mediate it into some wider, spurious unity.

Rorty's version of this kaleidoscope of momentary accomplishments is the image of a conversation. The worlds and worldviews of human inventiveness need to be rescued from their normal tendency toward closure, their typical penchant for silencing dissent. Let the philosopher pursue an abnormal discourse, therefore, constantly calling into question the claims to finality that are forever being raised, seeking to keep the conversation going by keeping it open. The role the philosopher should play

is that of the informed dilettante, the polypragmatic, Socratic intermediary between various discourses. In his salon, so to speak, hermetic thinkers are charmed out of their self-enclosed practices. Disagreements between disciplines and discourses are compromised or transcended in the course of the conversation.[25]

This is an educative role—Rorty's term is 'edification'—because it leads me out of my comfortable, tradition-bound self, helps me grow, aids me in becoming a new person. Closure is an intellectual proclivity, to be sure, but it is primarily and most threateningly a political expedient, the response of social authority to actual and perceived threats to a population's security and happiness. If only such repressive acts could be themselves repressed, the philosophic gadfly would surely suffice for assuring me that then each voice in the conversation will have an equal say:

The dangers to abnormal discourse do not come from science or naturalistic philosophy [in their quest for certainty and closure]. They come from the scarcity of food and from the secret police. Given leisure and libraries, the conversation which Plato began will not end in self-objectification [or any other denial of open-endedness]—not because aspects of the world, or of human beings, escape being objects of scientific inquiry, but simply because free and leisured conversation generates abnormal discourse as the sparks fly upward.[26]

So once again I am offered the natural rhythms of freedom and unconstrained self-expression as the antidote to a self-induced or societally imposed structure.

All these approaches deny centered structures and therefore may be persuasive in their deconstruction of the claims made on behalf of one or another *arche*. But none of them manages to shake off its belief in a *telos*. They remain at base eschatologies, for they have not abandoned hope in an ultimate order of things that might someday burst forth into history. Foucault speaks of instabilities in the soil of Western culture that have apparently been rendered immobile but which are now "once more stirring under our feet." Auerbach believes that he has been able to glimpse "the first forewarnings of the approaching unification and simplification" that shall rise from the ashes of political warfare and intellectual confusion. Rorty is confident that philosophers will have a newly important role to play in "the continuing conversation of the West" once their traditional concerns are fully swept aside. And Derrida envisions the near future as a birthing time, although for the present moment one can only catch the barest glimpse of "the as yet unnamable which is proclaiming itself," and which when it is born will surely appear to us, unfamiliar with its radical novelty, in "the terrifying form of monstrosity."[27]

These expectancies mean that in each case I am being offered centered structures after all. There may be no explicit point of origin functioning as the source and norm for what constitutes authentic selfhood and meaningful self-expression. Historical creations may be radically pluralistic in kind and number, and none reducible to another. But neither the egalitarianism nor the nominalism of these positions can remove the glaring fact that they each interpret the historical process as having a structure that is discovered, not invented.

The periodizing power of this structure is one of its salient features. According to each of the deconstructional analyses, there are times in human history when certain beliefs predominate, imposing some distinctive conceptual and political order upon the wider environment. There are also the transitions, usually abrupt and violent, to other times and other orderings of the world. And there is the apocalyptic expectation that the present moment is within or on the verge of a new transition, this one ushering in a better, brighter world.

The human adventure has a *telos* after all. A new age shall come, is now emerging. It will be one in which, at long last, societal privilege and privileged knowledge will be eliminated, in which the tyrannies of universal truth and centralized administration will be dethroned. The *telos* of becoming is the realization in history of the classless society, devoid of government or scarcity, permitting self-expression and free mutuality. It is the Kingdom of Heaven without a king, the Messianic Age with everyone his own messiah.

Wherever there is a foundational *telos* there is necessarily an *arche* as well, and upon closer inspection it can indeed be discerned in these various positions, despite the clever efforts to disguise it by iconoclastic rhetoric. This *arche* is the supremacy of presence over permanence, the moment over time, fulfillment over fidelity. This is the implicit credo of the deconstructionist rebellion, and it invokes one of the most noble of a culture's ideals, the insistence that human life, life lived within the vital present, is a value beyond price. But this conviction carries with it a terrible virus which all too soon infects both *arche* and *telos*. For to believe that the future promises, indeed is even now realizing, the values of presence, spontaneous expression, and individual fulfillment, is willingly to take arms against all that retards or denies that realization. And so rebellion all too often sacrifices the past for the sake of a future present, a future never in fact realized but always postponed, always just out of reach.

Thus a deconstruction of the deconstructionist project will reveal that it too presupposes certain enduring truths about the order of things. But this set of assumptions and hopes has no more standing than my mythologies. If my belief in the importances of the past is branded as a conservative ideology, then these others are merely the antithesis, dogmas regarding the importance of immediacy and revolutionary change. Or if my beliefs are dismissed as the trivial enchantments of an insecure mind, then these

others too are merely idle chatter, the fantasies of the disenchanted bourgeois intellectual. I am no better off with Derrida than I was with Arthur,
and far worse. For with the deconstructionists I have lost the permanence
of traditional value and in its place have been given only a fleeting cry in
the night, a night increasingly devoid of stars.

The Arthur legend, taken merely as Malory at play, offers an interesting insight into late medieval culture, provides some diverting entertain-
ments in lieu of television reruns, and proposes valuable insights regarding textual redaction and literary form. It may even teach lessons for the
reader's moral edification, prudential warnings about the consequences of
blind passion and deceit, political admonitions about delegating power to
untrustworthy subordinates, advice on love and law and leadership. And
all these aspects of the Arthurian materials are most certainly true to it.
The only problem is that, if Arthur's life and death do not show me what
is enduring in my culture and what is of passing significance, how will I
ever learn to distinguish the important from the trivial? If the Arthurian
vision does not explain to me how it can be that there are ideals worth
living for, worth dying for, even worth killing for, how shall I ever escape
the narrow prison of my selfish concerns? Without the greater values
provided by the enduring, objective meanings in the universe, without a
structure of significance surrounding me, the lesser values celebrated by
play and conversation and the delights of the commonplace are meaningless,
mere nihilistic gestures of defiance and pathetic acts of self-deception.
Arthur is king or I am nothing.

Derrida reports Husserl as claiming that historicism can avoid

neither relativism nor skepticism. For it reduces the norm to a historical
factuality, and it ends by confusing . . . the *truths of fact* and the *truths of
reason*.[28]

Certainly this is precisely what has happened to the assurances provided
by Western civilization as these have come increasingly under the barrage
of the attacks I have been summarizing. The sacred mythologies of my
tradition were accused of being dogma and then shown to be merely gossip,
which like dogma is language unconcerned with truth. Arthur was dethroned
and I with him. Whether my relationship to the importances of the past
be henceforth interpreted as one of blindness or of trivialization, whether
the proposed alternative be skepticism or relativism, the end result would
seem to be the same: the loss of the importances.

I cannot create the enduring structures of importance that give a culture a sense of its significance and so the capacity to be an effective steward of its inheritance. Yet it is only by such stewardship that the culture survives, for the power of the past was fashioned from acts of freedom constrained by loyalty to perpetuate a pattern of accomplishment, and unless I feel that power as equally demanding on my own loyalties it will not endure. Imperceptibly over the centuries of modernity and now in this century with increasing obviousness, the power of my tradition has been weakening, hardening into ineffective dogma and collapsing into self-indulgent relativism. So although it is through my cultural tradition that I have learned the importance of stabilizing structures of importance, I must also recognize that those realities are everywhere in disarray. The fabric of social meaning in Western civilization is coming unraveled, and it would seem that all I can do is bemoan the consequences.

iii

There is one other alternative yet to be explored, however. I can abandon my confidence in some single strand of order that gives meaning to the flux of things without having to settle for meaninglessness. Perhaps I can affirm the importance of novel creation and idiosyncracy without having to denigrate the old importances and the ancestral creativity that gave them birth. This would be possible were I able to combine my quest for order with a recognition of its inherent limits. Suppose that the search for order results in a plurality of orders but no single ordering of all things, and suppose also that this fact is itself the evidence of an orderless but underlying harmony which things have apart from all their various and partial forms of organization. Such a blend of anarchy and mysticism is Taoist in its flavoring, and it finds its most persuasive Western voice in the recent work of David Hall.[29]

According to Hall, my heritage is marred by its excessive attention to the ideal of what he calls "the single-ordered cosmos." His characterization of this belief accords with the one I have been explicating, but his analysis brings some of its key aspects into sharp focus. Hall claims that ethics and science are the hallmarks of the Western tradition. Both these forms of cultural activity seek to encompass all actions and understandings within a single normative structure. Right behavior is conduct that conforms to a pattern of intentions and actions which assure that, over the long run, individual lives will be rendered mutually compatible within a realm of social harmony and individual fulfillment. Science, in its search for a fully adequate grasp of the principles that describe natural phenomena, utilizes a similar insistence on compatibility, logical consistency, and ultimately completeness within a unified theory embracing all scientific knowledge.

This effort to tame chaos takes its cue, according to Hall, from the cosmogonic myths at the root of all forms of Western thinking. These myths proclaim that order has been wrested from chaotic waste by the act of a god. Nature is the result of this primordial act, its purpose to glorify its creator and to serve as the paradigm for all humanly created order. In imitation of Nature, therefore, a culture hero in collaboration with the gods creates the societal order in which I participate. Its purpose is also to glorify the divine creator and to realize in history its creators' purposes. I am a creature of both that nature and that culture, and my purpose is in turn to exemplify and further these wider purposes. Thus Western myths teach me that the *arche* for the layered mimetic structure of importances that comprise the cosmos is an act that imposes order on what resists it, a victory of purpose over purposelessness.

The implication of this, says Hall, is that both practical and theoretical activity become fundamentally instrumental. The aim of action and of thought is to fashion and preserve meaningful order in the face of the circumambient dangers posed by the incoherences of logical contradiction and cultural treason:

The cosmogonic myths and the cosmological theories that developed from them were stratagems for handling very practical problems associated with the experience of contingency and the sense of alienation from the natural world. The myths of cosmogenesis are myths of construal which provide models for the organization and control of our natural [and social] ambience.[30]

But such 'stratagems' of control, whether rational or political, cannot account for themselves. The order of creation does not explain why it was created nor why the possible alternatives to it were ignored or suppressed. Whatever is the means for an end is justified by reference to the end it serves, an end different from it, lying beyond its purview. Hence the rationality of science is grounded in an irrational belief in mathematically expressible truth, and the institutional matrix of the state is grounded in a belief regarding human fulfillment that is not itself an institution nor a law for defining and creating them. The sole justification is a utilitarian one. The beliefs work; the mathematical formulae provide trustworthy predictions and the governmental structures provide peace and plenty.

The corrective to this approach, Hall argues, is to turn to aesthetic and mystical appreciations of the rich variety of individual things and idiosyncratic accomplishments. The quest for logical order requires abstraction, exclusion, and compaction; the proper antidote is simply to let the multifarious plurality of the things of the world be themselves, to celebrate the details of experience without attempting to reduce them to any single totality, without seeking to comprehend them within any single vision. Aesthetic value does not require an imposed structure but rather its opposite, an appreciation of concrete individuality.

Theoria is the counterweight to theory. In the classical Greek sense of the term, theorial activity is contemplative. I open myself to the sheer givenness of reality without trying to impose practical concerns or other interpretive frameworks upon that reality. But whereas for Plato or Aristotle contemplation was purely intellectual, for Hall it is primarily imaginative and emotional. The reason for this is that uninterpreted experience, experience apart from any imposings and shapings, is felt not thought. Its truth, the factuality of it, its presence for me, is prior to any fashioning of that encounter into the objects and events, the obstacles and opportunities, of an ordered, meaningful, world.

Hall terms this contemplative appreciation of things "utopian", but the term is misleading. Utopias are actually utilitarian constructs, regulative principles guiding future action, whereas what Hall has in mind is an experience that is its own justification, that serves no end beyond its own immediate realization in experience here and now. *Theoria* is the experience of a realized utopia, the Kingdom of God that is already in our midst rather than some hoped for ideal we seek but have yet to find.

A world composed of things that are appreciated exclusively for what they are and not for how they function is necessarily anarchic. That is, it lacks an *arche*. There is no single foundation in terms of which the multiplicity of entities and events in the world are interrelated logically, causally, or valuationally. There is only the multiplicity, each item of which has its own principle of organization, its own purposes, its own unique characteristics, its own parochial *arche*. There are orderings but no overall order; many *cosmoi* but no cosmos.

For Hall, the practical implication of this refusal to move from multiplicity to unity is that I should cultivate an ironic stance toward life. By itself irony is merely another form of debilitating skepticism, but when combined with the contemplative appreciation of the whole congeries of things that are, it is a crucial component in a rhythm of experiencing. Theorial vision is mystical. It awakens in me a sense for the totality, the completeness, of things. My desire to realize this wholeness in practical or intellectual terms is the motivation behind scientific system-building and practical empire-building. Irony is a commentary on this double aspiration, asserting that, pragmatically speaking, no such ideal can be realized. Absolute truth, world government, and universal justice are at best unrealistic dreams, at worst rationalizations camouflaging failure or deceit.

In deference to the excellence of each thing, I must forgo efforts to organize all things into hierarchies. No purpose is less valuable than my own, nor more so; no truth more fundamental; no group of individuals more deserving or inherently more able. The voice of irony is iconoclastic. It reminds the political elitist that all humans are equal before the law, that they have equally valuable contributions to make to the social good, and that all of them have an intrinsic value beyond the control of society. Irony tweaks the nose of understanding, reminding it that there are perspectives equally as useful as the established one, and also just as likely to be fraught with paradox, omission, and inelegance.

Hall's recognition of the limitations inherent in any fashioning of a world is rescued from mere deconstructionist negativity by the emphasis on appreciation. Each specific one of the things that are, each person, each object, each event, requires my attention, deserves my respect. Consequently all of those things remain important for me even in the act of refusing to organize them. I retain a positive experience of the whole of things, a sense of the sheer fact that they all exist and together comprise the furnishings of reality, although I refuse the claim that this whole is an ordered whole. The deconstructionist rejects an ordering of the whole of things for the sake of certain specified parochial creations. Hall insists, in contrast, that I appreciate the whole by appreciating all of the specific things there are, every last one of them and all at once. He thus recommends that the proper term for the whole is 'chaos', that what I contemplate in my encompassing deference to all things is emptiness.

In my appreciation of the multiplicity of things, what I attend to is empty of any overarching logical order. But to be empty of that sort of order is not to be vacuous. Chaos is fecund, for it gives rise to an unending cascade of orders; it is rich in paradox, for it contains irreconcilable, incommensurable differences; it is mysterious because indeterminate, lacking the specificity needed for organization into an explicable structure. It is thus both the source and denial of order.

This aesthetic harmony devoid of any overarching logical unity is not unlike the universe as depicted in some contemporary physical theories. Hall is especially attracted to the metaphor of hologrammatic relationships, what David Bohm calls an implicate order.[31] In a hologram the whole is contained in any of its parts, but in such a manner that the order which defines a specific part is unique and cannot be defined alternatively in terms of the order characterizing some other part. Nor is there a way to order the sum of these parts. The whole, present in each, is always the whole from some particular perspective. It is never expressible apart from those several perspectives, in abstraction from them. As such it is chaos, that which although itself lacking order is the ground or source of all the orders there were, are, and will be.

This notion of chaos is akin to the Chinese notion of Tao. It would be foolish to attempt to delineate the kinship in a few quick brushstrokes, or even to attempt to do so in a long scroll painting or a technical treatise. But consider these lines from chapter 21 of the *Tao Te Ching*:

> That thing which is the Tao is chaotic.
> Chaotic! Yet within it are forms.
> Chaotic! Yet within it are things.
> Chaotic! Yet within it is the life force.
> This life force is truly real; it is the truth.[32]

The determinate structures of the world, the orderings that create inanimate nature, life, and human civilization, arise not merely by taming chaos but in virtue of its nurture. Disorder is not the enemy of order but its font, the resource out of which it arises. As another line from the *Tao Te Ching* puts it: "It can be regarded then as the mother of the world."

The Confucian tradition like so much of Western thought is at odds with Taoism precisely at this point. For Confucianism the beginning lies with the first creation of human order, the emergence of civilization out of the meaningless wilderness of the natural. The golden age is the time of the culture heroes, the time when wise kings ruled, whose wisdom the present generation is admonished to emulate. The Taoist, although not denigrating the value of such creative power and wisdom, hastens to point out that the orderings which thereby emerge are not enduring ones. Their limitations are their undoing and so eventually they falter and collapse, determinateness returning to the indeterminate.

For the Taoist, chaos and the *cosmoi* comprise a rhythmic interrelation, a process of eternal return, the *yin/yang* of temporal transition. I must understand myself and the social order to which I belong as part of a process that is more fundamental than the meanings in which I participate individually and collectively. Taoist fidelity to this truth therefore takes the form of a practice that seeks to recover at least the awareness if not the reality of the self prior to determinateness, the 'faceless' self of the primordial chaos.

In a story that concludes the 'inner chapters' of the *Chuang Tzu*, the Emperor Hun-tun of the Center, an eponymous representative of chaos, is killed by his well-meaning neighbors when they attempt to puncture his formless totality with the "seven openings" that make it possible to "see, hear, eat, and breathe," that give the formless a human form. This story teaches that I too will perish if I am reduced to a definitive order, my truth become the face I show to the surrounding world. Taoist piety typically involves meditative steps designed to 'close up' these openings spiritually, to reclaim the wholeness of self that is my true self, that is more fundamental than that of me that has a name and a face, that is part of a cultural tradition. Thus for me, as for each thing and all things, "at the end the beginning reappears and there is only order in relation to chaos."[33]

This third critique of the structure of importances is far more constructive than the others because it continues to affirm the need for some authoritative source of objective meaning. Hall provides an aesthetic criterion, however, in place of the logical one he criticizes. Or rather he subordinates logical to aesthetic kinds of order. In this way Hall attempts to retain the significance provided by a single enduring foundation to cultural experience while attacking the traditional manner in which that foundation has been construed. But ultimately this third way is no more a solution to my problem than were skepticism or relativism. Hall, and the Taoism that is his inspiration, make an assumption the authority for which seems to me as problematic as the authorities it proposes to replace.

Hall clearly has an *arche* which is the source, end, and foundation of his world. Its name is chaos. My life is meaningful, according to Hall, just insofar as I forsake the false god of some particular order, some logical structure of things, and give my allegiance instead to the true god, the God beyond the gods, that which is the source, support, and end of my existence. A particular order defines a norm for behavior, fashions a set of conditions the violation of which entails exclusion from the privileged realm of truth or goodness. But even though chaos as a foundational principle seems more tolerant, more indifferent to the orders of things, it is nonetheless normative. For example, creativity, spontaneity of self-expression, the splendor of exemplification, are all basic values within Hall's world-system. Their denial or distortion by the action of some individual center of order is not an excellence. My proper response is not deference but succor, an effort to liberate the creativity and to reform its enemy. Hall's aesthetic order, comprised by a harmony of individual excellences, is as foundational as any of the logical orderings he rejects. It is a principle for separating right action from wrong, truth from error. An *arche* need not be a logical principle to be nonetheless a normative one.

Hall's approach is normative in a second sense as well, for at the microcosmic level it clearly favors order over its denial. Creative expression is an act of ordering. For Hall, the problem with a single-order cosmos is that it excludes other creative achievements by proclaiming its own the only acceptable one. But the problem is not order; it is exclusivity. Hall's rejection of one kind of order should not prevent him from encouraging the continual appearance of order, applauding each individual center of order as it fashions its own distinctive meanings. The emptiness of chaos is its fecundity. My deference to individuality should mean my love for order, and this should impel me to encourage all forms of order and to condemn the absence of order-making centers of activity. An aesthetic appreciation of plurality includes respect for the achievements of logical order characterizing each item of that plurality. Let a thousand flowers bloom, and reject the demand that they grow in even ranks and rows, but abhor also the barren winter in which there are no flowers to bloom.

Hall's positive chaos thus tolerates the plurality of logical orders but it cannot afford to tolerate the negative chaos in which no orders arise, a chaos devoid of creativity. Hall insists upon the eternal return, the death of any finite achievement in time, but he cannot neglect the eternal outpouring of new order. Eros may need irony to correct its claims to absolutism, but were ironic criticism so to intimidate eros that the desire for order would wither, then irony would be the enemy and not the savior of creativity. Suppose the gadfly were to torment the horse until it died. Balance is crucial; it is the instrument by which creativity is exuberantly repeated, its drive toward order fostered but then constrained at the point where other creative ventures might be crowded out.

The *arche* of Hall's Tao, whether he will acknowledge it or not, is the same as that of nineteenth-century economic liberalism: that the only constraint to self-expression should be what is required to prevent one mode of expression from excluding others. Hall worries about the creation of any order that might predetermine or otherwise prefigure the authentic self-expression of each individual center of creativity. His sense of the totality of excellences is radically egalitarian. This self and this other self each deserve the opportunity to be spontaneous, to invent, to spawn their distinctive orderings of experience. If tradition were to impose strictures upon that enterprise, to define boundary conditions that are unnatural, to insist upon procedures and beliefs that impose values from the past upon the options available to the present, the result would be repressive. To defer to another's excellence means to treat that other as a creative individual liberated from the repressive orders of his inheritance. It would seem

that Hall ought to carry this point to its obvious conclusion and insist that
the results of each creative individual's activity not be passed on to successors,
whether by imposition or persuasion. For to do so would be to advantage
the inheritor unfairly or to constrain him within fetters not of his own
making. Insofar as tradition defines the conditions for individual action in
fabricated rather than natural ways, it is an imposed order and by the logic
of Hall's reasoning should be rejected.

Hall thus invites me into a reality populated by individual centers of
order that have no moral right to a heritage of achievement that can serve
as a funded resource from which they might draw strength and inspiration.
In his utopia creativity cannot legitimately fashion results that would permit a successor to see further and more deeply than otherwise. In the
fashioning of my own distinctive excellence, I am to begin the world anew
and to make sure it perishes with me. I should be a center of creativity
that like Newton's atom is self-contained, autonomous, lacking any internal relationships with the rest of the creation because obliged to rely only
upon myself for the value born of my travail. But this is precisely the
point of maximal entropy in which all basic units of the real are identical
except for their spatio-temporal location.

This would seem to reduce Hall's position to absurdity, but I do not see
how that can be avoided except by being more deferential than he wishes
to cultural traditions and world-defining orderings. Thus order really needs
to be a foundational notion for Hall: the orders exhibited in each individual achievement and the wider orders that promise qualitative enhancement
to those individual efforts. That the one level of order should not exist at
the expense of the other does not imply that either can exist without the
other.

The creation of an environment favoring extraordinary kinds of creative accomplishment: this is what the search for enduring importances
has been all about. The *arche* of this ideal is the intensification that emerges
when mythologizing processes make accumulated achievements of the past
available as a resource for present accomplishment. The excellence of my
sculpture must be grounded in Praxiteles, Michelangelo, and Brancusi to
whom I am apprenticed and who make my unique artistry possible, and
thus make possible their own transcendence. The excellence of my practices as a citizen must be rooted in the confidence that flows from my
sense of belonging to the Arthurian tradition, commanded by its commitment to a form of justice and human dignity that will be administered by
morally frail people like myself, people whose intentions and energies cannot be trusted although they can indeed be harnessed.

In the absence of such an environment of mentoring, the result cannot but be some drab uniformity of things where even the ordinary is an excellence and all students deserve an 'A' for effort. Life is indistinguishable from death when each moment of it must begin anew. Genuine life is the emergence of something at odds with the reigning excellence, but its necessary condition is the community of support that this very repudiated excellence provides. Improvement in the value of creative activity and its results requires an environment conducive to progress, which is to say it requires a history, an accumulation of value-making for values beyond the ordinary.

The foundation of Hall's aesthetic is reflexively self-destructive because in the name of value it eradicates one of the two conditions for value. Certainly creativity is necessary to the emergence of excellences that can be appreciated for their own sake, but so is a milieu of opportunity, a heritage of other excellences, complete with their constricting impositions and demanding obligations. Whenever I do anything important, anything truly valuable, I stand on the shoulders of giants who agree to hold me aloft only if I will do their bidding. The distinctive way by which I carry out that bidding, my misinterpretation of their command, gives novelty and refreshment to the world. But in the absence of these blackmailing giants, my novelty although unbounded will inevitably be unrefreshingly trivial.

So Hall's emphasis upon the present with its indeterminate openness, its reservoir of creative energy, comes to the same old impasse. I have been taught that too strong a loyalty to the past results in dogmatism. Old achievements slavishly followed can be stultifying and lead to their own demise. I have also learned that to rebel against this fetishism toward the past is simply to substitute a future possible order for the actual one called into question. But the future is too often never realized, and the work of deconstruction ends in the illusion that criticism can be a substitute for creativity. So I was offered creativity instead, but the present as a receptacle for everything resulted in a kind of entropic leveling where spontaneous expression, unconstrained by either memory or hope, deprived me of criteria for distinguishing excellence from its substitutes.

Dogmatism, skepticism, and spontaneity are each alternatives to a living tradition, and each is growing ever stronger, ever more virulent, in the contemporary world. But each collapses temporal duration into just one of its three modalities: dogma focuses exclusively upon the past, skepticism on the future, and spontaneity on the present. Reality, however, is fully temporal and human reality is fully historical. Therefore by pursuing any one of these three alternatives in lieu of an embrace of its richly dimensioned tradition of importances, my civilization and I with it are soon left with nothing.

iv

Beginning with immediacy, I have been led back to it. Nor have the confident assurances about on-going conversations, the play of the world, and the fecundity of chaos assuaged the fear that first set me on my journey. Worse still, the problem is not mine alone but characterizes my civilization as well. Not only I but all my people, my ancestors, my compatriots, my dearest friends, we all once believed that there were enduring structures of importance and that we could find a way to them across the confusions of historical change and personal ignorance. We saw ourselves as linked to those importances in ways that laid a claim upon our purposes, that gave us a task to do, that gave our lives joy and profound fulfillment.

But these centering beliefs having been attained, I found that the very instruments for their construction could be used equally well for their demolition. I discovered to my horror how across the generations belief could fade into superstition, reappear as subjective taste, and finally dissolve into irrelevance, the victim of a criticism that in destroying the old was unable to offer anything of value in its place. Nor is there any turning back. Belief that sees itself merely as belief can no longer be belief at all. Truth understood as merely a function of imagination is truth devaluated and fragmented beyond recovery.

The mix of dogmatism, skepticism, and immediacy that plagues this present age is undermining its traditional foundations without being able to offer any meaningful alternative. The importances of the past can save me and all of us from aimlessness, from ignorance and insecurity, only if we believe in their power. But this means to fill our action with their authority, our understanding with their truth, to take tradition as an *arche* and *telos* to the excellence of which alone I must defer by serving it creatively, loyally, joyfully.

I wonder if this is any longer possible, or whether I, and you, and all of us, might be losing not only the old assurances of tradition but also the very capacity for fashioning new assurances in their place. Am I part of a cultural collapse that is destroying even the very conditions for subsequent renewal? The fabric of tradition, once unraveled, cannot be woven anew should the weaver's art itself turn out to be among the threads that have been lost.

Nine

THE END OF TRADITION[1]

Philosophy is akin to poetry, and both of them seek to express the ultimate good sense which we term civilization. In each case there is reference to form beyond the direct meanings of words.
                              Alfred North Whitehead, *Modes of Thought*

i

The poet kindles a watchfire of imagination, and I huddle beside its
warmth in order to survive the chill of an impending winter. Bear with
me, then, as I muse upon the meanings of some verse.

I recently came across some lines from a poem written by a woman
raised among the Cheyenne of Oklahoma.[2] She has returned to the places
of her own childhood and approaches a creek that cuts through those
rolling prairie hills. I stand with her, am become her, as I, we, look around.

The log I used to cross
is no longer here,
but I still see it,
feel it in the footbridge of cut timber
I stand on now.
The foliage is less dense,
leaving more space for sunlight
to dapple the red creek and its banks.

227

In looking at a wooden footbridge I see the fallen log that once was ample enough a bridge for my purposes, and I note that the shade from the trees growing along the creek bank is far less thick than it once had been. My experience involves a comparison between an immediate present and another present long since perished. But this is not a contrast involving both memory and perception, for the log no longer here can still be seen. Both the old and the new are aspects of what I am currently seeing. Today's dappled shade falls on yesterday's shallow-watered stream. Is it really possible thus to see the past?

- - - - -

> How I used to crave the shade
> of these cottonwood trees!
> Walking barefoot down the sheep path,
> skirting lances of soapweed,
> avoiding sandburs in sun hot enough
> to hush the sound of insects,
> I could hardly wait for shade,
> the cool clay bank,
> water filtered through brush
> running clear over pebbles
> deposited who knows when.
> Oh, the coolness of it!

The seeing does not come at first. For in the beginning emotion is what predominates. As I look toward the creek I am engulfed in a tide of familiar, often repeated, emotions, feelings that were the content of a myriad of specific happenings and that gave them their importance. There is the feeling of overheated skin and the tickle of soothing water; there is another feeling of purposes pursued successfully; and yet another vague feeling wells up, of an environment predating both those purposes and the agencies of their satisfaction. These emotions then become for me the sensation of hot bare feet, protectively maneuvering themselves toward the cooling clay. I place my foot upon a plank of the footbridge, and immediately my sensation is not simply of that carefully milled lumber but also of a cottonwood log long since decayed, and of it as the objective of a thousand journeys leading from desire to desire's satisfaction, and of water running over stone a thousand thousand times before the first of those many journeys was begun. The new sensation recreates the older ones, not just remembers them.

- - - - -

It was my creek and yours.
To the north we could see
the smoke from the Rock Island;
south and east, smoke from tipis and tents.

I turn to my companion: it was our creek, my creek and yours. But this companion is a part of that former time and not someone who is physically with me now. My feelings have been transformed into visual images, emotion objectified as places, persons, and performances. And the private images of wading in the creek have given way to the more public ones that comprise the nearby landscape. Now as the Cheyenne settlements appear, and the railroad that linked them to the world of the white oppressor, so also does my friend appear beside me. Nor is she merely one person, this companion, but a people. She is the Cheyenne, and I and she are one together as we stand. As real as life our unity, for life is a matter of what one feels and hears and sees.

- - - -

I walk south.
There is no present. Even the rays
against which I shield my eyes
left their star minutes ago.
Everything is history. Scene upon scene
shimmers in this air.

I look through time-tinctured air. Just as the distant, ancient star is present to me in its current twinkling light, so that I close a gap of minutes—no, of years and of millenia—in my contemporary grasp of it, so likewise the human past. A parcel of geography, this sunbaked expanse of Oklahoma redclay, is not just the two dimensions of its cartographic surface, nor merely the third dimension of ground and air that cubes its shape. The land is dimensioned also in time, layer after layer piling up as from the flux of things the determinate ordering of the successive moments precipitate themselves into existence. This four-dimensioned thing, opaque to those without a sense of the enduring importances that structure it, is made transparent to emotion's eye. How rich, indeed, the sight!

I am walking on Red Wheat's land—
hers according to men who insist
parts of earth can be owned and given away.
Where one time or place leaves off
and another begins has never been clear.
When Soar Woman walked over our hill,
head wrapped in a kerchief
that half covered blind eyes,
dark shawl held close,
her daughter Sarah beside her,
what land was she treading?
What landscapes did she see?
Not always tipis on hot red clay,
sandy draws with cottonwoods.

I have felt the reality of this land through my own emotioned experiences and it has shown me contours involving cool creekbeds with trains and tipis on the hilled horizon. For Red Wheat, the land had been assigned to her by white conquerors in Washington who had displaced her people from better land in order to fulfill their own unseemly purposes. She and her daughter have had other emotions than mine, emotions that allowed them to see more deeply than I into the past. For Soar Woman's present blindness could not blind her to the goodly heritage her eyes once knew directly and with the confidence of youth. She sees her people in the land, and the meanings she glimpsed, and glimpses still, make it possible for her to persevere amid an exile from which she knows there can be no return. As my world unfolds, enfolding hers, my eyes see further too.

- - - - -

She remembered her people
in cool marshes with tall reeds,
lakes, rivers, prairies with birds,
fat skunks, deer in snowdrifts
not far from winter wigwams,
cornfields near the Missouri,
and especially buffalo plains,
plains without buffalo where Mother Red Wheat
packed her bundles for river after river
of waiting—
and, finally, Turtle Creek.

Before the white settlers came, before land was something bought and sold as though it were private property, the ancestors of Mother Red Wheat had enjoyed a satisfying life lived off a land bountifully suited to their needs. And if the years of absence from that land had served to temper its realities and idealize its possibilities, such is the soil in which traditions thrive. All of this Soar Woman could see as she walked with her daughter under the noonday sun because she had felt it in the campfire talk, sensed it in the customary shapings of clothing and design, touched it in hugging her children to her and in preparing the bodies of her parents for burial. There was more to Soar Woman than Turtle Creek, and seeing this she could walk on. And there is more to me than this footbridge upon which I hesitate, and so I can make sense of my dimmed heritage and the disintegration of so many treasured things.

- - - - -

> From the hill, I see the creek winding
> past Dog Patch, past our house,
> bending toward the town.
> The Rock Island whistles
> at a crossing.

So I am here now in this present, with its concerns. And here with me are those other presents, with their concerns. Each gives a new dimensionality to my world. Each removes another veil of ignorance to disclose some truth about who I am, what it means to be an American, to be an instance of the human race, to be only a moment of actuality birthed and perishing amid the flux of time. The tinctured space of my experience, the hues of temporality like dust particles suspended in the air surrounding me, have become a rainbow of significance. Can I, as did Soar Woman before me and Sarah after her, endure the wilderness if indeed this rainbow fills the sky?

ii

Another voice, a different mood. The poet leads me once more, and further still, into this dimensioned reality of mine.[3] The poem begins—

- - - - -

> Once I am sure there's nothing going on
> I step inside, letting the door thud shut.
> Another church: matting, seats, and stone,
> And little books; sprawlings of flowers, cut
> For Sunday, brownish now; some brass and stuff
> Up at the holy end; the small neat organ;

And a tense, musty, unignorable silence,
Brewed God knows how long.

Once more I have journeyed into the nearby mountains, returning to the churchyard where this odyssey began. I realize, in a way I had not before, how I am in danger of becoming little more than a tourist now in the world of importances my ancestors made. That magnificent edifice of theirs is very like a church, and something about it pricks my curiosity, draws me to inspect it from up close. Constructions of this sort are scattered across the landscape of human history, and this is yet another one, although it is more familiar than the rest because my father and mother once worshiped here and I may even have attended as a child myself. I enter, and the sanctuary encloses me, defining for a moment the perimeter of my concerns.

There is nothing going on here anymore, even though once, and that not so very long ago, there was. The signs of recent activity still abound. But all is silence now, and yet a special, pervasive kind of silence. The atmosphere is redolent with the history compacted into it. The memories, the hopes, the obligations and expectations of the people who once flourished here comprise a mute chorale of values that still clamor for attention. But there is no one to heed the call. Those ancient voices have had their tongues immobilized. Yet nonetheless they are not to be ignored. The silence is not wholly silent. What has died away still lingers as an echo in the air. I may brush it all aside impatiently, or shed a nostalgic tear in recognition of what might have been, or I may even study it with care as the expression of some once distinctive way of life. But it will not go unnoticed, up there at the holy end, that silence that is not nothing.

Whatever lingers in this ancient church was brewed so long ago that neither I nor anyone among my friends has any idea when it all began. God knows how long it's been, which is to say that no one knows—or even cares. Whatever it was, that musty tension in the air, was brewed not found. It was no gift of nature to nature's children, plucked raw to fill some human moment with delight. It was cooked up by folks who must have taken time to do their work, perhaps enjoying the process as well as the result. A tenacious concoction, for its odor lingers. Nor is the smell a putrid stink, the evidence of dead and dying things. Musty, yes, but yet, somehow, still fragrant. A silence in the air that catches at my consciousness.

- - - - -

Hatless, I take off
My cycle-clips in awkward reverence,

Move forward, run my hand around the font.
From where I stand, the roof looks almost new—
Cleaned, or restored? Someone would know: I don't.
Mounting the lectern, I peruse a few
Hectoring large-scale verses, and pronounce
'Here endeth' much more loudly than I'd meant.
The echoes snigger briefly. Back at the door
I sign the book, donate an Irish sixpence,
Reflect the place was not worth stopping for.

Good tourist that I am, I hastily make a canvas of the place as though it were an object I might decide to buy. I run my hands along the merchandise, check out the record of repairs, see how it functions with me at the controls. I conclude that it is not worth the price. So I sign up for the doorprize, contribute to the local charity, and depart.

First looks, the tourist's sole relation to a world, are always in terms of surfaces. Wednesday I will do the Prado and then be assured that on Thursday Toledo will have my undivided attention. In such high speed encounters, my eye has no choice but to glance off the depths, to slide over the details and fix itself intently upon the obvious. My purpose in this is often a pressing one and practical, a decision needing urgent attention and dependent on my glance for crucial information. And so the rough and ready surfaces will do. But surely practicality does not always entail urgency. The skill of patient observation is also well worth acquiring.

By the hundredth examination of an object I may have learned the spatial detailings that at first slid by my gaze, and I may have discovered how they bear up the surface which is their approximation and fulfillment. The details of an object's past are even more difficult to perceive, requiring more discipline than is needed for discerning the contours of its present. Yet derivational trails lead out from the momentary surfaces, and by following each pathway with diligence I am able to explore the thickness of the past, and to know the object of my investigation in all its full-bodied four-dimensionality.

This skill of perspicacity is learned, but it does not require specialized knowledge or technical preparation. I learn to see more clearly by trying to see more deeply. The more I know the better I can see; the more I see the sturdier my knowledge grows. Coming to see the complex geometry of an oak leaf stem, catching a glimpse of the god who promises a fuller life to those who would honor him through honoring the oak that is his symbol, seeing Arthur in an odd shaped stone and England in the gesture of a queen, these are the fruits of an eye apprenticed to the past.

But it is easier for me to be only a tourist in the world, impatient to get somewhere, to reach some end I have in mind. And so I skip over the space that intervenes between where I am and where I want to be. I abolish the distance, traverse its expanse along the superhighways of earth or sky, seek out the limited access routes that carry me smoothly through experience and understanding to my destination. And likewise I neglect the thicknesses of things. I attempt to smooth over the ragged edges of their historicity, to avoid carrying the excess baggage of the imponderables they insist upon, to collapse the time that puffs them out and makes them so unwieldy. As a tourist, the moment of my fulfillment is where the value is, and so I can neglect the getting there. The end and not the journey is what counts.

- - - - -

> Yet stop I did: in fact I often do,
> And always end much at a loss like this,
> Wondering what to look for; wondering, too,
> When churches fall completely out of use
> What we shall turn them into, if we shall keep
> A few cathedrals chronically on show,
> Their parchment, plate and pyx in locked cases,
> And let the rest rent-free to rain and sheep.
> Shall we avoid them as unlucky places?
> Or, after dark, will dubious women come
> To make their children touch a particular stone;
> Pick simples for a cancer; or on some
> Advised night see walking a dead one?

Some places, despite my tourist's mentality, manage to stay me in my course, to make me pause despite myself. This church is such a place. Its power may be weak and fading, but it has not vanished completely into nothing. The silence is eloquent with a sense of importances that once shouted their meaning from the rooftops of the sanctuary. This meaning brewed beyond my ken is a creaking in the rafters that I can disparage but which I cannot ignore.

I played my little game of preacher in the pulpit, and spoke the ritual words that declare the link between divinity and the sacred documents of that tradition. "Here endeth" that tradition was what I meant, for I only mouthed the words, not intending the beliefs they were formulated to evoke. Yet my mimetic mockery sounded more loudly than I thought it would. The vaulted chamber resonated to the sound. The silence had been awaiting my speech, still latent with the power to amplify impressively the single voice of piety. The echoes sniggered. Were they making fun of a hapless tradition that is no longer voiced, or was it at me they laughed whose voice is silent in the world except when amplified by such a place as this?

This ambiguity, this confusion, translates itself into the problem of deciding how best to make use of a once important past. I might reduce it all to art, to something worth appreciating but only from a safe distance, objectively. Cathedrals and other sacred places can be admired for their architecture, and the music of their rituals performed in concert halls. The speech and writing that celebrate the sacred deeds of the past can be enjoyed as literature, as folk-stories of anthropological value and sometimes even as viable exemplars of style, of meter, metaphor, and metonymy. The ancestors themselves, the saints and heroes, can be transmogrified into embellishments of the buildings and the literature, their bones mortared into the walls, their names inscribed above the doors, their character made over into the characters inhabiting a story or a poem.

The tradition become a museum for aesthetic appreciation is thus still revered, still retains the glimmerings of its ancient power, but it has been all reduced to surfaces. No matter how long the tourist stands before the icon hanging on the wall, no matter how informed the museum patron might be about the history of an architectural style, the look remains a glance. For the artifacts of my heritage, set off from the practical world by their new-found status as national treasures and artistic masterpieces, are but shadows of themselves.

The superstitious folk still wonder if the shadow might reflect some more substantial reality. And so they touch the stone-carved image of a buried saint or chip souvenirs of Arthur from the abbey walls at Glastonbury. Perhaps they kneel briefly in the graveyard beside the headstone of that pioneer wife, in the vague hope that such intimacy might leech out the hidden powers therein contained. These dead things still have power, to heal a dread disease, to raise spirits from the deep, to wreak bad luck on those who scoff. This art is not merely art, they say, but somehow something more.

- - - - -

Power of some sort or other will go on
In games, in riddles, seemingly at random;
But superstition, like belief, must die,
And what remains when disbelief has gone?

Grass, weedy pavement, brambles, buttress, sky,
A shape less recognisable each week,
A purpose more obscure. I wonder who
Will be the last, the very last, to seek
This place for what it was; one of the crew
That tap and jot and know what rood-lofts were?
Some ruin-bibber, randy for antique,
Or Christmas-addict, counting on a whiff
Of gowns-and-bands and organ-pipes and myrrh?

Yes, superstition like belief must die. And when it does, when all that
remains is the tourist's glance at objects in a world made only of surfaces,
then what? The buildings, it would seem, can be handed over to the rain
and sheep, the rituals allowed to grow up along the roadside like exotic
weeds which when chewed or smoked might bend the mind a bit. The
names will simply perish, lost by forgetfulness. In such a vacuum even
disbelief will be no longer possible, for skepticism like superstition feeds
solely on belief and in its absence must starve. Such is the devolution of
my heritage that soon it may no longer even be the target of a disbelief.
What then? What then, indeed.

Recently the American Museum of Natural History in New York City
exhibited an extraordinary collection of ancient bones.[4] The skulls of my
ancestors were put on display, the actual bones themselves and not some
reconstructed plastercast replicas. The actual skulls: my Cro-Magnon mother
reaching out to me across the 25,000 years that separate us, my father the
Neanderthal whose 50,000 years do not obscure his stern authority, and
all the far older relatives and friends back to my child, the five year old
Australopithecine girl, who 2,000,000 long years ago was ripped untimely
from my arms. I wept; this tourist cried; and cried out in anguish, not in
scorn nor in romantic foolishness. For is this not appropriate, that I should
shed my tears at the perishing of those so dear to me?

Or did I cry because they are not dead? These bones were the originals,
the real bones. They were not imitations of the past but the past surviving
into the present moment of my seeing them. In virtue of their physical
density and the fortuity of their resting place, these bones endured the
millenia. Two million years is a minor achievement for a slab of rock, but
even though I am awed by the four billion years of Earth's oldest stone my
emotions before these human skulls is infinitely more intense. Because I
am they, their bones and mine linked by a transmission from flesh to
flesh, perhaps 100,000 times repeated as the fruit of one womb became

the vessel for the next, replicating itself endlessly until myself. They live in me, even if I may have forgotten them.

As of course I had, for insofar as I am only a tourist now, a creature of surfaces, I have no ancestors, at least for all my actions and beliefs would tell of it. But nonetheless I came that day into the museum to see those bones. I reached out and contacted their surfaces with my eyes, and then those surfaces reached out in turn and pulled me in, taught me the 100,000 replications my glance had glided over, displayed the origin and end of the trajectory we share, gave me a heritage once more. The full dimensionality of my humanity was awakened in that experience, despite my disbelief, despite the outright ignorance that was its imminent destiny.

Nor was my experience unique. Said one of the anthropologists involved in unpacking the bones for the exhibit,

I sat down on the carpet and pulled open the tray. When I touched its jaw it happened. I consider myself agnostic. I don't buy religious mumbo-jumbo, never did, not even as a kid. But something shot through me, a thrill, a sort of tingle. I felt it in my feet, I felt it in my hands. It lasted for a few seconds, and then it was gone.

Or as someone else remarked, commenting on the attitude of patrons and anthropologists alike toward the skulls, "This is a little like discussing theology in a cathedral." Indifference, it would seem, had been unnerved, the ruin-bibbers and Christmas-addicts, the dubious women and ghost hunters, joined in their foolishness by sober scientists and sophisticated museologists.

A living tradition transmits the past by sustaining the original presence of former accomplishments despite the perishing of the details that embody it. The current embodiment does not preserve the past; it recreates it. So over time the power of the beginning grows instead of dwindling. I am not confronted with fainter and fainter copies of some original but rather with its ever more complexly articulated reality. The mature oak is not a faint shadow of the acorn but instead its full embodiment.

When the tradition dies, that is when the original begins to fade. After the tradition dies, the present only mirrors the past but does not resurrect it any more, does not reconceive and nurture it so that it is continually born anew. And so soon the mirror mocks the image, the voice falls silent. Forever silent, unless by chance or by some other means the present learns to see beneath the surface of its world, to peer into the hollow hill of time, and to rediscover what never dies but only sleeps.

I wonder who
Will be the last, the very last, to seek
This place for what it was; . . .
. . . .
Or will he be my representative,
Bored, uninformed, knowing the ghostly silt
Dispersed, yet tending to this cross of ground
Through suburb scrub because it held unspilt
So long and equably what since is found
Only in separation—marriage, and birth,
And death, and thoughts of these—for which was built
This special shell?

Things fall apart unless there is a center holding them. Surfaces are just so many different facets of a center that makes them possible and gives their variety a sense. The center is no more the reality than are the surfaces, of course, but the one is the structure of the others and thus what gives them meaning. A surface is the face a center turns toward some wish, some need, some special interest that probes it for its relevance. Were I to live only on the surface of life, my thoughts and actions would be always at the mercy of whatever playful purpose might have just welled up to give a momentary shape to things.

Tradition gives these surfaces their center. It does not thereby render them illusion or judge them unimportant, for only when my wishes, needs, and interests are able to glance off of surfaces can they attain the ends they seek. And since a surface is the details of a complexity melded by a glance into a simple fact, then were surfaces unreal so would be the details comprising them. No, what tradition offers is not another reality but the same one now rendered meaningful. Tradition is a way not only to focus a concern, to serve its immediate demands, but also a way to take it seriously, to keep it a concern beyond the fading of demand.

My life is packed up full with transitions in mood and purpose. The world around me is in flux, and my responses shift to cope with its shifting forms. But I change even when things around me are relatively calm. My restless urge for food and shelter, warmth and happiness, my curiosity and my dread, are a whip that will not let me stop. And then there are those transformations in my life that my life cannot contain: my birth, my giving birth, my death. If I must deal with all these things by glancing off their presence to me, by using them as aids or finding them as obstacles for my ends, then I need some sense of what I might expect, some confidence I have the needed skill, some integrating eye to see the whole amid the sequence of the parts.

It need not be logical nor even consistent, this center that gives my interactions with the world a sense. But it needs to define the central tendency of things, to set an outer boundary of significance, and to distinguish the crucial arteries of dependency. This structure which tradition is thus provides an environment for my aims, a sense of the possible, a criterion for assessing importance. A tourist travelling in a strange land must of necessity impose some structure on his itinerary. Most likely it will be a plan composed of abstract, schematic purposes, drawn perhaps from other journeys to quite different places, its insensitivity to the particularities of the current trip softened by opportunities for whim or the unexpected to play a role in shaping the intentions of the day.

Such a double arbitrariness, imposing an abstract plan and then embellishing it with bits of fancy, is what tradition is so often accused of doing. But when the land and its distinctiveness are known more fully than a first glance could hope to know, when the fundamental tendency of things is sensed, the contours felt that canalize its drift, the horizon scanned that delimits its relevance, then the journey will be well begun and the new world truly experienced in all its complexity. The path I take will be my own, but it will be pursued in that special way because I am sensitive to where I am and what might lie ahead or lurk on either side.

I can remember still, have not forgot, that this was why that church was built. Its noisy rituals have given way to empty silence, its walls have fallen into ruin, and before another year is passed the bulldozers down the road a bit will be here too, turning the rubble under for a housing tract. But I have not lost the sense of unity for which that church was built and which for many years it served. However loudly I may boast my disbelief, and however complete the distruction of the tangible symbols of belief might be, the sense remains.

As a child of my times, I might proclaim the value of unfettered purpose, of self-expression, of the liberation of the human spirit from all forms of tyranny. But I must not forget that it is by means of this culture-wide unfettering that my life has become scattered across a thousand unconnected purposes. This indulgence of spontaneity has fragmented my values into endless shards no longer fit to hold my sense of worth. This liberty has turned me over to the tyranny of moments following one another without rhyme nor reason, a rhymeless flux, an unreasonable cacophony.

And thus I know there is a better way even if I do not recall its name.

- - - - -

> For, though I've no idea
> What this accoutred frowsty barn is worth,
> It pleases me to stand in silence here;
> A serious house on serious earth it is,
> In whose blent air all our compulsions meet,
> Are recognised, and robed as destinies.
> And that much never can be obsolete,
> Since someone will forever be surprising
> A hunger in himself to be more serious,
> And gravitating with it to this ground,
> Which, he once heard, was proper to grow wise in,
> If only that so many dead lie round.

Tradition is a serious house, built by human workmen on this serious earth. It was constructed out of the recognition that time is all there is, that the flux of things is the sole repository of whatever is of value in the universe. This house was raised up in response to the tragic fact that what is lost is irretrievable and therefore that what is won is of inestimable worth. The achievement of some determinate actuality, the shaping of a 'this' from the vague possibilities of the flux, is precious for itself and is the sole base of all significance. Tradition is the serious attempt to rescue some of what is precious from the ravages of a process that constantly destroys what it permits, that offers death as life's reward.

The continual recreation of the past is the way humanity has chosen, perhaps mimicking all life in this endeavor, for overcoming the death of its accomplishments. But a cultural heritage is an especially difficult structure of inheritance because it is completely dependent upon freedom. Lacking the relative assurances of biological transmission, tradition seeks its end by the discipline of freedom, by turning spontaneity into a servant of the orderly. Tradition is imagination at work, its mere playful fantasies harnessed to a daring purpose. Freedom if pinned down by habit, sloth, and custom only then truly makes me free. Liberty if shackled by resolve, loyalty, and commitment can only then fully liberate. Tradition is the well-spring of human fulfillment and not its enemy, for under the tutelage of the past values are created that are richer, deeper, more intense than could ever be otherwise attained.

The natural drift of things, the standard journey of the world, is toward fragmentation, toward increased entropy. The effort at making something, the struggle even to repeat the past much less to improve upon its craftsmanship, is an energy that cuts against this drift. Creativity requires, therefore, far more than its own excitement, its own originalities. The creation of anything of value requires a supporting environment. For me, a single human being bounded by a birth and death, tradition is the only way I know to overcome the insistent entropy. I need to find a broadly gauged unity, a general structure of accomplishment, that can be the foundation for lesser accomplishments, and for my own. My mind, my consciousness, in order to survive requires a complexly organized environment, a human body functioning within a natural order conducive to its metabolic demands. So also the higher reaches of my consciousness, my capacities for cultural expression, for performing the duties of the citizen and for fashioning poems or cabinetry, require tradition. The enduring importances are the body of my higher self.

And so, despite and even because of my delight with life, the moment's joys and individual liberties, my hunger to be more serious runs deep. I know how high the stakes are in human history and that what takes centuries to build can be pulled down in years. As I criticize my tradition for its weaknesses, and even as I abandon it for disbelief, it reminds me of a truth too easily forgot. The very capacity I have to criticize some social practice as dogmatic and to keep a distance skeptically from all forms of intellectual and cultural closure is a capacity I was taught. I could grow wise if only I would find myself once more within the nurture of that tradition.

Perhaps I am still within it but do not know I am, blinded by my arrogance and ignorance, blinded by the very vices against which I have been rebelling. In the company of so many dead ones, ancestors I know if not by name, the dead who gave me a life transcending my natural powers and who asked only that I pass it on to those who will follow me, perhaps I am not alone and traditionless after all.

Here on these ruins all my compulsions meet and find the form they need to make me who I am. I only stand silent now, bemused by all I've thought and said, convinced that once I and this people have gone beyond belief there is no turning back, convinced that the way forward does not lead on to light.

And yet. And yet if only I could speak again. If only I could speak those sacred words once more: "Here endeth." If only I could say here is the end of my tradition, which finds its end in calling me forth to speak its truth once more and to hear the chapel and the world resonate in response. Ah, yes, if only I could speak and raise up Arthur out of Avalon. If only I could speak again.

iii

A fisher king sits by the shore, maimed ruler of a wasteland devoid of the fulfillment promised in ancient oaths and divinations. He fishes and his back is to an arid plain across which he has journeyed long and painfully. Some fragments of the world that he had left behind, some shards rescued from the desolation of his lands, he hugs to himself as the sole source of his comfort.—"These fragments I have shored against my ruins."[5]

One fragment, beloved Tiresias, I would add to the four you clutch at your wounded side. There is a dream that haunts the house of our tradition, a dream with many names and countless forms. Cosmopolis; the Kingdom of God; the Classless Society; Galactic Federation; Omega Point. It hears individual freedoms as a harmony, sees the enrichment of the whole in the diversity of its parts, touches no exclusionary boundaries in its open embrace, tastes the sweet essence of humanity in every life, and knows the scent of otherness as an intimate perfume.

The English-speaking peoples were beginning an ascent to the apogee of their cultural domination in voyages of discovery and settlement during the sixteenth and seventeenth centuries. Their contribution to your neglected dream was the patient and repeated reading of the three books carried on all ships flying the British flag at the time: *The Bible*, Hakluyt's *Principal Navigations*, and Foxe's *Book of Martyrs*.[6]

One told tales of a nomadic minority struggling for survival in a narrow corridor between big power frontiers. One recounted stories of adventure and plunder by selfish and narrow-spirited men. And one detailed the sufferings of a minor religious sect noted for its intolerance and narrow-mindedness. Yet amid all this rushing torrent of narrowness, a different current flowed its course as well, a dream of mountains brought low and valleys lifted up; of Jew and Gentile, male and female, made one; of the linking of peoples through commerce and travel into a single commonwealth; of a promise that even petty origins and sordid disloyalties can serve a reconciling destiny. Universality arising from particularity as its child and redeemer.

A strange idea, although an ever-present seam running through the fabric of those enduring importances that characterize the Western peoples, its light fading now in these times of cultural forgetfulness and breakdown. Certainly neither constitutive of my current beliefs and practices nor regulative of them. Yet worth the remembrance; a fragment to be preserved. A fantastic notion, an idea no longer fit for the sober realities of the contemporary world I inhabit and the human nature that circumscribes my possibilities. But even what seems fantastic need not be nothing, and so I offer it as a fragment for the dying king.

In other worlds, where human nature is a possibility beyond my ken, it may be that such dreams are truth and the ruins of this vast and splendid heritage can serve as the foundation for a new heaven and a new earth. Meantime my tasks call me in freedom away from the shores of fantasy and toward the terror and uncertainty of history and its duties. I shall leave the fishing to Tiresias.

NOTES

Preface

1. This is one of a set of similar myths discussed in terms of this and other cultural significances by J.-P. Vernant, "The Union with Metis and the Sovereignty of Heaven," in R. L. Gordon, ed., *Myth, Religion and Society* (Cambridge: Cambridge University Press, 1981), pp. 1-15.

2. *Republic* VI: 509e-511e

Chapter One

1. This tale is told with impelling clarity by Loren Eiseley in *The Firmament of Time* (New York: Atheneum Publishers, 1960).

Chapter Two

1. These texts, with the Latin version in its more accurate 1642 form, are contained in Descartes, *Oeuvres philosophiques* (Paris: Garnier Frères, 1967), Tome II, ed. Ferdinand Alquié. I will be utilizing the English translation by Elizabeth Anscombe and Peter Geach which is contained in Descartes, *Philosophical Writings* (Indianapolis: Bobbs-Merrill, 1971); page references in square brackets are to this volume.

2. George Santayana, *Scepticism and Animal Faith* (New York: Dover Publications, 1955 [1923]), pp. 9-10.

3. Bertrand Russell, *The Problems of Philosophy* (New York: Galaxy Books, 1959 [1912]), p. 16.

4. How misleading, therefore, the French use of a dependent clause; the radical notion of the self as *res cogitans*, a reality the essence of which is activity, becomes *une chose qui pense*, a substance with activity as its attribute.

5. "I call a perception *clear* [*clare*] when, if the mind attends to it, it is present and manifest. . . . I call a perception *distinct* [*distincte*] if it is not only clear but also precisely distinguished from all others. . . ." *Principles of Philosophy*, 1644; section XLV. In Anscombe and Geach, p. 190.

6. The French version turns this spontaneity into a disposition, *une certaine inclination*. But in either case the point is that a person usually trusts experience, and does so without stopping to reflect critically or analytically upon the grounds for that trust.

7. "It is only will, or freedom of choice, that I experience in myself in such a degree that I do not grasp the idea of any greater; so that it is in this regard above all, I take it, that I bear the image and likeness of God. For although God's will is incomparably greater than mine . . . yet it does not seem to be greater when considered precisely as will." [95-96]

8. Locke's parallel list is more ambiguous: "whiteness, hardness, sweetness, thinking, motion, man, elephant, army, drunkenness." But he intends them to illustrate the same unequivocal assertion: "It is past doubt that men have in their minds several ideas . . . [and that they all derive] from EXPERIENCE. In that all our knowledge is founded; and from that it ultimately derives itself." Locke, *An Essay Concerning Human Understanding*, Book Two, Chapter I, sections 1,2 (New York: Dover Publications, 1959).

9. I shall return to these 20th-century constructionist views in Chapter Eight.

10. For the details of this quest in modern Western philosophy, see Richard Rorty, *Philosophy and the Mirror of Nature* (Princeton: Princeton University Press, 1979). I will return to Rorty in Chapter Eight.

11. Bertrand Russell has many faces. I have in mind this time the arguments in probably his most systematic work: *Human Knowledge: Its Scope and Limits* (New York: Simon and Schuster, 1948).

12. Alfred North Whitehead, *Process and Reality* (New York: Free Press, 1978, Corrected Edition).

13. My reading of Whitehead on this and related matters is controversial and probably revisionist. It obviously needs to be defended in more lengthy and detailed fashion. But not here.

Chapter Three

1. Charles Sanders Peirce, *Collected Papers*, edited by Charles Hartshorne and Paul Weiss, six volumes (Cambridge: Belknap Press, 1960 [1934]). Citation is from volume 5 paragraph 45.

2. Peirce, vol. 5 para. 58.

3. Whitehead, *Process and Reality*, p. 176.

4. Herbert Butterfield, *The Whig Interpretation of History* (London: G. Bell & Sons, 1963 [1931]). The Whig interpretation of history is "the tendency in many historians to write on the side of Protestants and Whigs, to praise revolutions provided they have been successful, to emphasise certain principles of progress in the past and to produce a story which is the ratification if not the glorification of the present."[v]

5. Alfred North Whitehead, *Modes of Thought* (New York: Free Press, 1968), p. 11.

6. I shall return to these thinkers in Chapter Eight when the position they criticize has been fully deployed, when the confidence in importances they importune has first been adequately elaborated.

7. William James, "The Dilemma of Determinism," in *Essays in Pragmatism* (New York: Hafner Publishing Co., 1948). "Indeterminism . . . admits that possibilities may be in excess of actualities, and that things not yet revealed to our knowledge may really in themselves be ambiguous. . . . Possibilities that fail to get realized are, for determinism, pure illusions: they never were possibilities at all." [p. 41]

Chapter Four

1. I have been drawing in these paragraphs from Roy Andrew Miller, *The Japanese Language* (Chicago: University of Chicago Press, 1967), chapter 7.

2. My information on Dodona comes from two sources: (1) H. W. Parke, *The Oracles of Zeus* (Cambridge: Harvard University Press, 1967); (2) Nicholas G. L. Hammond, *Epirus* (Oxford: Oxford University Press, 1967). I have personally never been there, but after reading these books it is as though I had.

3.   "He said it was ordained by the gods: the end
      of the labors of Herakles. It's what the sacred oak
      told him through the twin dove-priestesses
      at Dodona. . . ."

Sophocles, *Women of Trachis*, tr. C. K. Williams and Gregory Dickerson (New York: Oxford University Press, 1978), lines 168-171.

4. "It was when they were mad that the prophetess at Delphi and the priestesses at Dodona achieved so much for which both states and individuals in Greece are thankful." *Phaedrus* 244b. Tr. R. Hackforth in *The Collected Dialogues of Plato*, eds. Edith Hamilton and Huntington Cairns (New York: Random House, 1961).

5. Herodotus, *Historion* 2.52. Tr. A. D. Godley in *Herodotus* (New York: G. P. Putnam's Sons, 1921). References are to book and paragraph.

6. *The Iliad of Homer*, tr. Robert Fitzgerald (Garden City: Anchor Press/Doubleday, 1975), book 16, lines 233-235.

7. Thorkild Ramskou describes his trip to the sacred oak in an article published in *Skalk* 2 (1960). The story of the child appeared in a 1966 Copenhagen newspaper interview with a 90 year old woman. Both events are discussed in "Editorial", *Antiquity* 42: 167-168 (1968).

8. Clifford Geertz, *The Interpretation of Cultures* (New York: Basic Books, 1973).

9. Geertz, p. 75.

10. Geertz, p. 81.

11. Geertz, p. 99.

12. Arnold Toynbee, *A Study of History*, twelve volumes (London: Oxford University Press, 1934-1961), vol. I, p. 191.

13. Toynbee, vol. III, p. 234f.

14. Toynbee, vol. VI, pp. 175-176.

15. Toynbee, vol. I, p. 205.

16. In the following paragraphs I have been helped with my facts by Franklin Littell, *The Origins of Sectarian Protestantism* (New York: Macmillan Company, 1964 [1952]).

17. Littell, pp. 70, 186. I cannot help but note this passing reference in the Anabaptist sources to the role of the oak as a gathering place where sacred deeds are performed.

18. John Winthrop, *A Modell of Christian Charity*, from *Winthrop Papers* volume III (The Massachusetts Historical Society, 1931), pp. 292f. Reprinted in countless places, including Conrad Cherry, *God's New Israel* (Englewood Cliffs: Prentice-Hall, 1971).

19. Here I rely for my facts on Harold T. Parker, *The Cult of Antiquity and the French Revolutionaries* (New York: Octagon Books, 1965).

20. David Dowd, *Pageant-Master of the Republic: Jacques-Louis David and The French Revolution.* (Freeport: Libraries Press, 1948).

21. Jaroslav Pelikan, *Obedient Rebels* (London: SCM Press, 1964), devel-

ops this point at great length. His book is built around an exploration of the phrase with which Paul Tillich (*Systematic Theology*, v. III) describes the middle way of the Reformers: seeking simultaneously to embrace "Catholic substance and Protestant principle."

22. Pelikan, p. 29.

23. Richard Hooker, "The Laws of Ecclesiastical Polity," in Harry Emerson Fosdick, *Great Voices of the Reformation* (New York: Random House, 1952), p. 354.

Chapter Five

1. Søren Kierkegaard, *Either/Or*, vol. I (Princeton: Princeton University Press, 1971 [1843]). This volume purports to be comprised of a number of hedonistic documents, including a diary detailing the seduction of Cordelia Wahl by a local 'gentleman' known to us only as Johannes.

2. One speaks the unspeakable truths of Zen only with trepidation and an ample sense of irony. I am emboldened, at least, by the existence of a voluminous literature on the subject.

3. The concepts of Truth and Beauty as they are developed in what follows derive from the arguments in Whitehead's *Adventures of Ideas* (New York: Free Press, 1967 [1933]), chapter 17.

4. I am thinking of Peirce's difference between Firstness, which is monadic characterization and so includes all qualities, and Secondness which is a matter of sheer dyadic encounter. The latter is the experience of undeniable otherness; the former is the source of aesthetic contrast, of higher but also more subtle experiences.

5. William Shakespeare, *Henry V*, Act IV, Prologue.

6. *Henry V*, Act IV, Scene III.

7. See Marx's familiar example of the cherry tree in *The German Ideology* (New York: International Publishers; 1947 [1846]), p. 35, or Sartre's less well known example of the denuding of Chinese hillsides in *Critique de la raison dialectique* (Paris: Gallimard; 1960), pp. 232-235.

8. The Indians who inhabited the upper reaches of Lake Michigan in the 17th and 18th centuries had their own distinctive names for that lake and the surrounding hills, and saw the past importances there enshrined without requiring metal markers to open their eyes. Their great hero was Manabozho, who fought valiantly to save these transcendent meanings from the unsettling encroachments of the white adventurers. Hiawatha is an invention of Longfellow, and as such just one more evidence of the European tyranny that so quickly replaced the Indian's world with its own

alternative mythologies. I am a creature of those latterday mythologies, and so have chosen to weave them into my story rather than to use references that although historically more accurate are for me, due to my ignorance, affectively pallid.

Chapter Six

1. Geertz, p. 100, supplies my labels for these threats. The whole of his chapter 4 is relevant to what follows, as well as three works by Ernst Cassirer: *Language and Myth* (New York: Harper Brothers, 1946); *Philosophy of Symbolic Form*, vol. II (New Haven: Yale University Press, 1955); and Cassirer's briefer restatement of the whole three volumes of PSF, *Essay on Man* (New Haven: Yale University Press, 1944).

2. Geertz, p. 126.

3. Cassirer, *An Essay on Man*, pp. 224-225.

4. Recall my earlier examples of naming and renaming during the French Revolution (Chapter Four), and my passing reference to Blacks and Québécois (Chapter Five).

5. To remind the Hebrew rabbi of this, the scriptural texts used in the synagogues would replace the appropriate vowel pointing for 'Yahweh' with the pointing appropriate to the synonym 'Adonai.' 'YHWH' plus the vowels for 'Adonai' yields 'Jehovah', the term used in an early modern translation of the Hebrew scriptures into English and then picked up by at least one Christian sect as being the true name of God. This demonstrates the way in which even a blatant misreading of ritualistic requirements can nonetheless have a significant impact on historical developments.

6. Roland Barthes, "Myth Today," the last part of *Mythologies* (New York: Hill and Wang, 1972), tr. Annette Lavers [*Mythologies*, Paris: Editions du Seuil, 1957]. Because in what follows I am not subscribing to all of Barthes' claims regarding semiological systems, I have used his technical vocabulary only minimally.

7. Barthes calls this the process of "ex-nomination": the source of the ideology becomes anonymous. When history (*anti-physis*) becomes what seems to be nature (*pseudo-physis*), it can no longer be questioned because there is no one, no group, to whom the question can be directed. There is no longer any reason for why 'this is what one must do': it is just the case that it is, that's all. "Myth has the task of giving an historical intention a natural justification, and making contingency appear eternal." [Barthes, p. 142]

8. Barthes, p. 155.

9. This phrase is taken from Brian Wicker, *The Story-Shaped World* (Notre Dame: University of Notre Dame Press, 1975). The distinction between narration and authorship in what follows draws in important ways from Wicker's book.

10. I find it delightfully ironic that this line of argument should coincide with that of the deconstructionists whose attack on tradition I will be discussing in Chapter Eight. Traditional literary criticism is based on the assumption that the narration of a story or a concept by an author implies a 'privileged interpretation' of the resulting text, namely the one intended by the author. Contemporary deconstructionism undermines this notion of an objective or primary reading for any text by denying that it actually has a specific author. Each reader is its author, the creation of the manuscript being merely the first such reading, and all these authorings are equally valid. The argument I am making here, with Wicker's help, is that it does not follow from the fact that a text has no single human author that it has no privileged interpretation. The authorship might be anonymous because, as the deconstructionists claim, everyone who encounters it transforms it, and so no one can claim it as his or her own private property. But this ownerlessness might be because the text is a work of the culture itself, including the heroes and the gods that ground its truth. Anonymous authorship can be the basis for objectivity rather than its denial. What transcends an individual can also transcend all individuals.

11. Key ideas in what follows are drawn from Louis Gernet, *The Anthropology of Ancient Greece* (Baltimore: The Johns Hopkins Press, tr. 1981 [1968]), chapter 4: "The Mythical Idea of Value in Greece."

12. I have no intention of attempting to do justice to the mythic materials regarding the house of Atreus, Jason, or the golden fleece. This simple version of the story, like any story, has a purpose—to highlight the relation of the fleece to kingly authority. For more on the complexities of the myth, see Robert Graves, *The Greek Myths* (New York: George Braziller, 1955), vol. 2: no. 111, 148, 152.

13. In what follows I draw from Parke, *op. cit.*, and (with care) from James Frazer, *The Golden Bough*, one volume abridgement (New York: The Macmillan Company, 1951 [1922]).

14. Frazer, pp. 686-687. Frazer's interest in agricultural myths leads him to neglect to mention the political and cultural continuities that are also, and just as importantly, assured by this eternal succession.

15. I am still relying on Frazer, but here also, and with appropriate qualms and qualifications, I draw a couple of notions from Robert Graves, *The White Goddess* (New York: Farrar, Straus and Giroux, 1966).

16. This information was provided by a friend of mine, Susan Nichols, who is one of Bardi's grandnieces. The original manuscript of his genealogical investigations is in the Library of the New England Historical Genealogical Society.

17. John Foxe, *Actes and Monuments of these latter and perillous dayes* . . . (London: John Day, 1563 et seq). I have used an 1843 edition: *The Acts and Monuments of John Foxe* (London: Seeley, Burnside, and Seeley, 1843), vol. I. Relevant information comes primarily from Book II, pp. 306-328. Foxe depends heavily on the *Anglica Historia* of Polydore Vergil who half a century earlier had consolidated the various chronicles and legends of Britain into a single account. The best secondary source on this aspect of Foxe's book is William Haller, *Foxe's Book of Martyrs and the Elect Nation* (London: Jonathan Cape, 1963).

18. Geoffrey of Monmouth, *Historia Regum Britanniae*, tr. Lewis Thorpe, *The History of the Kings of Britain* (London: Penguin Books, 1966).

19. Geoffrey, p. 74.

20. Geoffrey, p. 65.

21. The contemporary dispute regarding historical explanation is usefully summarized in Dale Porter, *The Emergence of the Past* (Chicago: University of Chicago Press, 1981), ch. 1-3.

22. The politics of this conviction are usefully recounted in Frederick Merk, *Manifest Destiny and Mission in American History* (New York: Random House, 1963).

23. This phrase is the basis for the title essay in Perry Miller, *Errand into the Wilderness* (New York: Harper & Row, 1956). This is the classic interpretation of Puritan self-understanding in 17th-century America.

24. How Winthrop's apocalyptic justifications are turned into the more secular ones required of manifest destiny is explored in Albert Weinberg, *Manifest Destiny: A Study of Nationalist Expansionism in American History* (Baltimore: Johns Hopkins University Press, 1935). See also Ernest Tuveson, *Redeemer Nation* (Chicago: University of Chicago Press, 1968, pp. 91-136).

25. See the study of Whitman's poetry in Henry Nash Smith, *Virgin Land: The American West as Symbol and Myth* (Cambridge: Harvard University Press, 1950), ch. 4. Chapter 3 deals with notions of manifest destiny expressed through theories regarding the inevitable westward course of Empire.

26. Walt Whitman, *Leaves of Grass* (New York: Random House, 1950). I have selected out these particular and often non-consecutive lines to convey by condensation the point of the whole poem.

27. Baruch Spinoza, *Ethics* [1673]. E.g., in John Wild, ed., *Spinoza Selections* (New York: Charles Scribner's Sons, 1930).

28. Jean-Paul Sartre, *Being and Nothingness* (New York: Philosophical Library, 1956) [*L'être et le néant* (Paris: Librairie Gallimard, 1943)], especially Part Four, Chapter Two, and Conclusion, pp. 557-628 [643-722].

29. "It is as consciousness that it [the human self] wishes to have the impermeability and infinite density of the in-itself. It is as the nihilation of the in-itself and a perpetual evasion of contingency and of facticity that it wishes to be its own foundation. . . . It is this ideal which can be called God." [Sartre, p. 566]

Chapter Seven

1. This puts me at odds with Otto Rank who in *The Myth of the Birth of the Hero* (New York: Random House, 1959 [1914]), argues that all myths are "retrograde childhood fantasies" expressing universal parent-child tensions. Joseph Campbell, in *The Hero With a Thousand Faces* (New York: Pantheon Books, 1949), and then more fully in the multi-volumed *Masks of God* (New York: Viking Press, 1959-68), takes a similarly universalist approach: there is one story, a thousand particular expressions of it.

2. My principle sources for historical information are Leslie Alcock, *Arthur's Britain: History and Archeology AD 367-634* (Middlesex: Penguin Books, 1971); Kenneth Jackson, "The Arthur of History," in Roger Loomis, ed., *Arthurian Literature in the Middle Ages* (Oxford: Oxford University Press, 1959); F. J. Haverfield in *The Cambridge Medieval History* (New York: Macmillan Co., 1911), vol. 1.

3. Gildas, *De Excidio et Conquesto Britanniae*. Relevant passages from all the pre-Monmouth chroniclers are available in Latin in E. K. Chambers, *Arthur of Britain* (London: Sidwick & Jackson, 1927), pp. 233-281.

4. Nennius' history is part of a conglomerate manuscript, the prefered copy of which dates from the 12th century (British Museum Harleian MS. 3859) and is likely a direct copy of a 10th century predecessor. The Arthur material, appearing in folio 187A-B, section 56, is probably a summary by Nennius of a Welsh poem already well known in his day. Because there is no mention of Arthur's death, Alcock speculates that the poem was composed in the early 6th century while Arthur was still alive [Alcock, p. 59]. By such tenuous and indirect means is the historical record of Arthur constructed.

5. So Alcock, p. 320. Kenneth Jackson, p. 9, insists, however, that a

'leader of battles' is a descriptive term and not a title. Arthur is being described as the man who was the leader for the Britons in the twelve battles of which Badon was the last. He is not being assigned the title of *dux* to indicate he is of lesser status than the *regi*. In following Alcock's interpretation, I nonetheless agree with Jackson that Nennius' point is not to label Arthur as inferior to the kings but rather to indicate his key military role in this particular set of encounters with the Saxons.

6. However, John Rhys, *Studies in the Arthurian Legend* (New York: Russell & Russell, 1966), p. 8ff, argues that 'Arthur' derives from 'Airem', the name of one of the early High Kings of Ireland, which is in its turn derived from the name of his sky god progenitor. Mordred's name derives from Mider, the god of darkness, and Guenivere takes her name from Etain, the shining one, goddess of the dawn. The tale of Arthur is thus a solar myth, a struggle between the gods of light and darkness for possession of the dawn. E. K. Chambers, pp. 206-210, rejects this as an over-interpretation, and most other commentators agree. Attempts to trace the origin of 'Arthur' through the root 'Ar'—possibly meaning 'to plow or to fit together', and just as possibly meaning a bear—are similarly unfruitful. The historical origin of the name resists dissolution into universal symbolic meanings.

7. Geoffrey of Monmouth, *Historia Regum Britanniae*, Cambridge University Library MS. 1706. Published in a critical edition by Acton Griscom, *The Historia Regum Britanniae of Geoffrey of Monmouth* (London: Longmans, Green and Co., 1929). The best available translation, as I indicated in Chapter Six, is by Lewis Thorpe, *The History of the Kings of Britain* (New York: Penguin Books, 1966).

8. Charles Williams and C.S. Lewis, *Arthurian Torso* [along with Williams' *Taliessin Through Logres* and *The Region of the Summer Stars*] (Grand Rapids: Eerdmans Publishing Co., 1974), p. 211.

9. See John J. Perry and Robert A. Caldwell, "Geoffrey of Monmouth" in Loomis, ed., p. 72.

10. Chambers, p. 20.

11. E.g., James Douglas Bruce, *The Evolution of Arthurian Romance* (Gottingen: Vandenhoeck & Ruprecht, 1928), vol. 1, p. 23.

12. Roger Loomis, *Wales and the Arthur Legend* (Cardiff: University of Wales Press, 1956), pp. 180-182. This book, especially Chapter X, provides the classic argument for Geoffrey's dependence on Welsh sources. Folk traditions, not the inventions of a cultured elite, are the reason why the Arthurian materials exist.

13. Loomis, *Wales and the Arthur Legend*, p. 214.

14. Such would seem to be at least one implied meaning of this obscure line from the 6th century poem *Y Gododdin*: "He gutted black ravens on the wall of the fort, though he was not Arthur."

15. This epic tale is one of eleven from the *Mabinogion* (London: J.M. Dent, Everyman's Library, 1949), tr. Gwyn Jones and Thomas Jones. It is reprinted in Richard L. Brengle, *Arthur King of Britain* (Englewood Cliffs: Prentice-Hall, 1964).

16. Roger Loomis, *Celtic Myth and Arthurian Romance* (New York: Columbia University Press, 1927), p. 354. Elizabeth Jenkins, *The Mystery of Arthur* (New York: Coward, McCann & Geoghegan, 1975), takes this line of reasoning in a more psychological dimension, arguing that culture heroes such as Arthur and Beowolf provide individual consolation [p. 35]. Threatened by freezing weather, dark nights, hungry wolves, and prowling enemies, people identify with the heroes, finding in their immortal deeds the possibility of similar accomplishment themselves. Clanish and even cultural differences are not as significant as the individual psychic value offered in this identification of oneself with a significant other.

17. Bruce, pp. 58-59, 70; Loomis, "The Oral Difusion of the Arthurian Legend," in Loomis, ed., p. 60.

18. The first number within the square brackets refers to the chapter in Monmouth's *Historia*, the second number to the appropriate page or pages of the Thorpe translation.

19. Perry and Caldwell, p. 83.

20. I realize that this claim to thirdness does not square with the earlier statement [7,233] that three conquests prior to Arthur's justified a fourth one. Maximianus is forgotten in the recount. Monmouth is not noted for his consistencies.

21. Another one of the eleven tales comprising the *Mabinogion*.

22. Bruce, *op. cit.*, provides an excellent summary of the prose and poetry comprising this complex flowering of Arthurian literature.

23. Eugène Vinaver, ed., *The Works of Sir Thomas Malory* (London: Oxford University Press, 1967), 2nd edition, three volumes. This critical edition with commentary and notes is based on the 1475 Wincester manuscript, which Vinaver thinks more accurate than the 1485 Caxton manuscript typically utilized. Subsequent quotes from Malory are referenced in square brackets referring to the appropriate page in the Vinaver edition.

24. Charles Moorman, *The Book of Kyng Arthur* (Lexington: University of Kentucky Press, 1965), p. 87.

25. Thomas L. Wright, "The Tale of King Arthur: Beginnings and Foreshadowings," in R. M. Lumiansky, ed., *Malory's Originality* (Baltimore:

Johns Hopkins Press, 1964), pp. 61-66.

26. Wilfred L. Guerin, "The Tale of the Death of Arthur," in Luminasky, ed., p. 233.

27. Vinaver, vol. I, p. xcvi.; and see also vol. III, pp. 1625-26. Other commentators insist that the dilemma has three horns rather than two, the additional one being the Christian ideal of service to God. This is part of Guerin's argument, echoing Vida Scudder, *Le Morte Darthur of Sir Thomas Malory* (London: J.M. Dent, 1921), p. 77f.

28. Guerin, p. 273.

29. Alcock, p. 35.

30. Quoted in Williams and Lewis, pp. 227-228.

Chapter Eight

1. Santayana, p. 7. My present line of reasoning is tutored by Santayana's arguments in Chapter II, pp. 6-10, and it is from there the rainbow example comes.

2. Toynbee, vol. 3, p. 374.

3. Toynbee, vol. 4, p. 129.

4. All of the information and some of the argument for what follows is taken from Peter M. Briggs, "Tall Tales, Unfinished Meanings, Restless Imaginings: The Discovery of America," *Bryn Mawr Now*, 12.2: 1, 10-12 (Spring 1984).

5. Briggs, p. 12.

6. Not everyone, of course. Montaigne's delightful and ironic essay "On Cannibals," for instance, shows a mind at work that could draw up the blinds on cultural parochialism, flooding the issue with genuine enlightenment.

7. Jacques Derrida, *Writing and Difference*, tr. Alan Bass (Chicago: University of Chicago Press, 1978 [*L'écriture et la différence*, Editions du Seuil, 1967]).

8. Derrida, p. 160. He is here providing a description of what Dilthey 'taught' Husserl, but Derrida finds the lesson apt.

9. The key chapters in Derrida on Artaud are ch. 6 and ch. 8; on Bataille, ch. 9.

10. Harold Bloom, *A Map of Misreading* (New York: Oxford University Press, 1975), p. 19.

11. Derrida, p. 141.

12. Nelson Goodman, *Ways of Worldmaking* (Indianapolis: Hacket Publishing Co., 1978).

13. Michel Foucault, *The Order of Things* (New York: Pantheon, 1970 [*Les Mots et les choses*, Paris: Gallimard, 1966]).

14. Erich Auerbach, *Mimesis: The Representation of Reality in Western Literature*, tr. Willard Trask (Princeton: Princeton University Press, 1953 [Berne: A Francke Ltd, 1946]).

15. Auerbach, p. 317.

16. Auerbach, p. 549.

17. Richard Rorty, *Philosophy and the Mirror of Nature* (Princeton: Princeton University Press, 1979).

18. Rorty, p. 295.

19. I am benefited in this thumbnail sketch by an interesting set of papers given at a Symposium on Hegel and Whitehead, Fordham University, June 1984. These will be published by the State University of New York Press in 1985 in a volume edited by George R. Lucas.

20. Oswald Spengler, *The Decline of the West*, tr. Helmut Werner (New York: Alfred A. Knopf, 1962 [*Der Untergang des Abendlandes*, Munich: C.H. Beck'sche Verlagsbuchhandlung, 1959]); abridged edition.

21. Auerbach, p. 552.

22. Derrida, p. 292.

23. Remember the torch raised high on behalf of 'polymorphous perversity'? —Norman O. Brown, *Life Against Death* (Middletown: Wesleyan University Press, 1959).

24. I have in mind, of course, Albert Camus, *The Myth of Sisyphus*, tr. Justin O'Brien (New York: Vintage Books, 1959 [*Le Mythe de Sisyphe*, Paris: Editions Gallimard, 1942]).

25. Rorty, p. 317.

26. Rorty, p. 389.

27. Foucault, p. xxiv; Auerbach, p. 553; Rorty, p. 394; Derrida, p. 293.

28. Derrida, p. 160.

29. David L. Hall, *Eros and Irony* (Albany: State University of New York Press, 1982).

30. Hall, p. 45.

31. Hall's discussion, pp. 138ff, draws from David Bohm, *Wholeness and the Implicate Order* (London: Routledge & Kegan Paul, 1980).

32. These comments on Taoism draw in part from what Hall has to say, but primarily from N.J. Girardot, *Myth and Meaning in Early Taoism: The Theme of Chaos* (Berkeley: University of California Press, 1983). The above quote appears on p. 65.

33. Girardot, p. 304.

Chapter Nine

1. The meaning of this phrase is purposefully ambiguous, as will become clear in the unfolding of the chapter. The play on contrary meanings of 'end' first arose for me in a delightful conversation some years ago with my colleague Sam Banks, who was then working on a book entitled *The End of Education*, a book dealing with not only the current decline in but also the hopeful prospects for American higher education.

2. Anne-Ruth Ediger Baehr, "The Bridge," from *A Glimpse of Dragonflies*; a collection of poems still in process of composition.

3. Philip Larkin, "Church Going", in *The Less Deceived* (London: Marvell Press, 1955). This poem caught my attention because of a brief essay on it by Noel Perrin in the "Bookworld" section of the *Washington Post*. I have used some of Perrin's insights in what follows.

4. "Ancestors: Four Million Years of Humanity" was on display at the Museum from April through August 1984. I am drawing from my own experience and from an article about the exhibit that appeared in the *Washington Post* on April 28, 1984: Paul Richard, "Tracing Mankind's Family Tree," pp. C1,C7.

5. The allusions here and in some of what follows are, of course, to the closing section of T.S. Eliot, "The Waste Land."

6. *The Geneva Bible*, 1560. Richard Hakluyt, *The Principle Navigations Voyages Traffiques and Discoveries of the English Nation*, 12 volumes, 1589. John Foxe, *Actes and Monuments of these latter and perillous dayes*, 1563 expanded 1570.

INDEX

Abstraction: *see* Simplification
Anabaptists, 86-87, 90
Anarche, 216-225
Apocalyptic, 105, 155, 167-168, 170-171, 202, 213-214
Arche, 203, 205, 206, 213, 214, 217, 218, 221, 222, 223, 225
Aristotle, 13, 36, 59, 156, 218
Artaud, Antonin, 200-201
Arthur, historical sources 156-159; literary sources, 161-162, 172-173, 186-187; Malory's version, 173-185, 187-189; Monmouth's version, 159-172, 185; at Avalon 185-189; meaning of, 185-186, 198, 207, 215, 223, 233, 235, 241; why selected, 155-156
Auerbach, Erich, 206-208, 211, 213
Augustine, 147, 184
Beahr, Anne-Ruth Ediger, 227-231
Barthes, Roland, 132-135
Bataille, Georges, 201
Berger, Peter, 31
Bloom, Harold, 201
Bohm, David, 219-220
Briggs, Peter, 196-197
Brumbaugh, Robert, viii
Butterfield, herbert, 49, 81
Cassirer, Ernst, 31, 130
Confucianism, 220
Constructionism, 30-32, 42
Cumulation, 106-108
David, Jacques-Louis, 89
Deconstructionism, 31, 199-216, 224
Derivational feeling, 43-51, 53, 56, 59-60, 65, 71, 79, 92, 191, 233; directionality, 47-49; importance, 50-51
Derrida, Jacques, 200-204, 205, 211-212, 213, 215
Descartes, René, 13-28, 29, 32-33, 36, 38, 40, 44, 46, 53, 54, 55-56, 62, 117, 123, 130, 150, 153; *Meditations*, 15-27, 41; modes of thinking, 23-24, 37; certainty/importance, 18-21, 27, 28, 41, 56; doubt, 15, 16-20, 36, 43, 49; dread, 16, 17, 20, 28, 29, 41, 43, 85, 93, 108
Dewey, John, 30
Dogmatism, 193-199, 224
Dylan, Bob, 113
Einstein, Albert, 36
Elimination, 99-102
Eliot, T.S., 242-243

Foucault, Michel, 204-205, 213
Foxe, John, 143, 242
Frazer, James, 139
Freedom, 10, 24, 51, 52, 62, 63, 64-65, 90, 92-93, 112, 118, 133, 134-135, 145, 151, 173, 180, 182-183, 216, 240
Galileo, 36
Geertz, Clifford, 81-84, 129
Genealogy, 96-98, 142-144; Luke, 102, 104, 142; Matthew, 103-104, 105-106; Plantagenet, 100-102, 104, 106, 107-108, 113-117, 119, 185-186
Girardot, N.J., 220-221
Gods: Diana, 139, 141, 144; God, 26-27, 56, 77, 87-88, 102-104, 134, 136-137, 142, 145, 147-148, 150-151, 200, 205, 209; High Gods, 96, 140; Jupiter, 139, 141; Krishna, 202; Odin, 143; Yahweh, 107, 137; Zeus, 74-76, 131, 137, 141
Goodman, Nelson, 204
Hakluyt, Richard, 242
Hall, David, 216-219, 221-224
Hegel, G.W.F., 31, 203, 209-210
Heisenberg, Werner, 36
Herodotus, 75
Heroes, 110-111, 117, 120-121, 122, 128, 131, 142-143, 162, 171-172, 235; Archiles, 75-76, 131; Arthur, 155-189; Atreus/Jason, 138; Brutus, 121, 144-145; Captain Marvel, 131; Elizabeth II, 119, 132-134; Henry V, 106, 107, 108, 114-117, 119; Hiawatha, 120-121; René Robert LaSalle, 120-121; Marduk, 137; Martin Luther King, 119; Zebulon Pike, 120-121; René Lévesque, 119; Romulus, 139; Tiresias, 242-243
Homer, 75
Hooker, Richard, 91
Hume, David, 30, 37
Husserl, Edmund, 215
Imagination viii, 7, 112-116, 118, 133, 136, 225
Importances, ix, 50-51, 52-54, 55, 56, 60-61, 62-63, 68, 77, 79, 80, 85, 90, 92-93, 95, 106, 108, 117-118, 121-122, 129, 142, 145, 151-152, 153-154, 176, 178, 184-185, 189, 192-193, 197-199, 202, 206-207, 214-216, 223, 225, 241; *see also* Important Deeds/Persons/Places
Important Deeds, 77-79, 107, 120-122, 130-131; liturgy, 5, 9-10, 63-64, 123, 136

259

Important Persons, 68-73, 79, 106, 107, 108, 114-117, 119, 122; heroes, 110-111, 120-121, 128, 138, 142-145, 162, 171-172, 235

Important Places, 5, 7-9, 73-77, 79; Agincourt, 115-117, 119; church/grave-yard, 5, 6-7, 73, 77, 82-83, 122-123, 235; sacred grove [Dodona], 74-76, 119-120, 121; sacred trees, 76, 123, 139-141

Inference, 25-26, 29-39, 33-35, 40, 54, 58-59, 64, 146

Intensification, 99-117; see also, Elimination, Subordination, Simplification, Typification

Irony, 218-219, 222

Irrationalism, 29-30, 37

Jacobins, 88-89

James, William, 31, 62

Kairos, 106, 110

Kant, Immanuek, 30-31, 39, 40, 48, 53-55, 56

Kierkegaard, Søren (Johannes the Seducer), 108-111

Kuhn, Thomas, 31

Larkin, Philip, 231-241

Leibniz, G.W., 203

Locke, John, 33

Luther, Martin, 90-91

Malory: Arthur's birth, 174-175; Arthur's kingship, 175-177; Arthur's incest, 177-178; Arthur's death, 179-183, 188; Excaliber, 178-179, 187

Marx, Karl, 31

Massiveness; spatial, 1-5, 57, 98, 107-108, 164; temporal, 5-10, 58, 71, 79, 98, 107, 165, 229

Mimesis, 84-85, 86, 89, 93, 194, 196, 204-205, 207, 208, 209, 217, 234

Monmouth, Geoffrey of, 144-145, 159-172, 185; Arthur's birth, 163, 170; Arthur's kindship, 163-165, 165-166; Arthur's death, 166, 185; prophecy, 167-171

Myth, 117-118, 122, 125-129, 132-134, 154-156, 193, 210-211; cosmogonic, 217; narrative, 135-138, 146, 152

Necessity, 61-62, 65, 133-134, 137, 145-152, 154, 176; manifest destiny, 121, 148, 152, 155

Newton, Isaac, 36, 38, 223

Nietzsche, Friedrich, 56

Oak trees, 2-4, 44, 50-51, 52, 57-60, 233, 237; Dodona, 74-76, 87, 119-120, 139,

140, 141; Druidic, 141; Nemi, 139-140

Pasxcal, Blaise, 30

Peirce, C.S., 44-45, 118

Pentimento, 111

Plato, vii, 13, 75, 218

Present moment, 14, 27-28, 32, 34, 38-39, 40-41, 42, 49, 54, 56, 98, 105, 117, 199, 214

Puritans, 87-88, 121, 148

Racism, 72

Reformation, 86, 90-92, 122

Relativism: see Deconstructionism

Religion, 129-131

Restoration, 81, 86-90, 122

Rorty, Richard, 31, 208, 212-213

Russell, Bertrand, 15, 37, 39

Santayana, George, 15, 28, 30, 193

Sartre, Jean-Paul, 150-151

Selection: seeElimination

Shakespeare, William, 116-117, 207, 208

Simplification, 104-106

Sophocles, 75

Spengler, Oswald, 209-210

Spinoza, Baruch, 71, 149-150, 151

Subjectivism, 21, 32

Subordination, 102-104

Sunyata/tathata, 111, 122

Symbols, linguistic, 69-70, 81-84, 131, 132-134, 195, 201, 205

Taoism, 216, 220, 222

Telos, 203, 205, 206, 213, 214, 225

Theoria, 218

Tolkien, J.R.R., 136, 154

Toynbee, Arnold, 84-85, 194-196, 199, 202

Transmission thesis, 34-36, 39, 40

Typification, 108-117, 118-119, 122

Value, social, viii, ix

Wesley, Charles, 113

Whitehead, A.N., 37-38, 39, 41, 45-46, 50, 118, 203

Whitman, Walt, 148-149

Wicker, Brian, 136-137

Winthrop, John, 87-88, 148

Zen Buddhism, 111